PUNISHMENT IN AMERICA

A Reference Handbook

Other Titles in ABC-CLIO's
CONTEMPORARY WORLD ISSUES
Series

Consumer Culture, Douglas J. Goodman and Mirelle Cohen
Courts and Trials, Christopher E. Smith
Dating and Sexuality, Jeffrey Scott Turner
Environmental Activism, Jacqueline Vaughn Switzer
Families in America, Jeffrey Scott Turner
Forest Conservation Policy, V. Alaric Sample and Antony S. Cheng
Gay and Lesbian Issues, Chuck Stewart
Media and American Courts, S. L. Alexander
Media and Politics in America, Guido H. Stempel III
Nuclear Weapons and Nonproliferation, Sarah J. Diehl and James Clay Moltz
Police Misconduct in America, Dean J. Champion
Racial and Ethnic Diversity in America, Adalberto Aguirre Jr.
Racial Justice in America, David B. Mustard
Religion and Politics, Glenn H. Utter and John W. Storey
The Religious Right, Second Edition, Glenn Utter and John W. Storey
Reproductive Issues in America, Janna C. Merrick and Robert H. Blank
U.S. Immigration, Michael C. LeMay
Voting in America, Robert E. DiClerico
Women and Equality in the Workplace, Janet Z. Giele and Leslie F. Stebbins
Women in Prison, Cyndi Banks
Work and Family in America, Leslie Stebbins

Books in the Contemporary World Issues series address vital issues in today's society such as genetic engineering, pollution, and biodiversity. Written by professional writers, scholars, and nonacademic experts, these books are authoritative, clearly written, up-to-date, and objective. They provide a good starting point for research by high-school and college students, scholars, and general readers as well as by legislators, businesspeople, activists, and others.

Each book, carefully organized and easy to use, contains an overview of the subject, a detailed chronology, biographical sketches, facts and data and/or documents and other primary-source material, a directory of organizations and agencies, annotated lists of print and nonprint resources, and an index.

Readers of books in the Contemporary World Issues series will find the information they need in order to have a better understanding of the social, political, environmental, and economic issues facing the world today.

PUNISHMENT IN AMERICA

A Reference Handbook

Cyndi Banks

CONTEMPORARY WORLD ISSUES

ABC CLIO

Santa Barbara, California • Denver, Colorado • Oxford, England

Library of Congress Cataloging-in-Publication Data

Banks, Cyndi.
Punishment in America : a reference handbook / Cyndi Banks.
p. cm. — (Contemporary world issues)
Includes bibliographical references and index.
ISBN 1-85109-676-0 (hardback : alk. paper); 1-85109-681-7 (eBook)
1. Punishment—United States—History—Handbooks, manuals, etc. 2. Criminal justice, Administration—United States—History—Handbooks, manuals, etc. I. Title. II. Series.

HV9466.B35 2005

364.6'0973—dc22

2005000659

08 07 06 10 9 8 7 6 5 4 3 2

This book is also available on the World Wide Web as an eBook. Visit abc-clio.com for details.

ABC-CLIO, Inc.
130 Cremona Drive, P.O. Box 1911
Santa Barbara, California 93116-1911
This book is printed on acid-free paper ∞.
Manufactured in the United States of America

For James and our intellectual journey together

Contents

Preface

Punishing offenders is something we take for granted. We expect that those who break the law will be punished by the criminal justice system, and we naturally link crime with punishment. One of the aims of this book is to provoke a different way of thinking about punishment.

Why should offenders be punished at all? How did punishment originate, and what should be its purpose? How does society decide what are the most appropriate ways to punish, and how have these methods of punishment changed over time and why? Do we punish because we believe in retribution, or do we just think it is better to lock up all criminals and incapacitate them so they cannot reoffend?

These and other questions will come to mind when using this book as a reference tool on the topic of punishment in America. There are many fascinating and thought-provoking themes arising out of the history of punishment worldwide as well as in the United States.

They demonstrate that punishment is not something well understood and that it operates in a haphazard and arbitrary way, which often causes unfairness and injustice. Punishment is not just about a court sentence following a crime—it is also about intolerance or tolerance, compassion and human dignity; it is about disciplining people by placing them in solitary confinement and arguably also about using prisons to control those who have no work or who are poor or who are minorities.

The history of punishment offers a number of themes, which illustrate just how problematic something we take so much for granted, like punishment, can be. For example, in the past, almost all punishments were carried out in public—whether placing someone in the pillory or hanging them in the public square in view of many thousands of spectators. Yet by the end of the eighteenth century the public seemed to have developed a distaste for the public nature of punishment. Punishments began to be carried out in private. The whippings and tortures that had been practiced in public were now performed behind prison walls. Some argue that this was a result of the "civilizing process" and that the public became more sensitive to watching others' pain, whereas others suggest that the state had by this time already consolidated its power and no longer needed to stage public spectacles of punishment to ensure obedience or to intimidate its citizens with the power of the king. Others contend that the great crowds assembled for the public hangings constituted a danger that might get out of control and spark a revolution, such as those which occurred in France, the United States, and England.

Punishment seems always to have been imposed most on the poor and jobless. This is true today when looking at the number of African-Americans in prison compared with their representation in the population as a whole. Why is this so, and how did it come about? It is a reality that as the feudal period came to an end in Europe vagrants and beggars began to appear on the roads and to move toward the cities. Some suggest that those in authority decided this new shifting population represented a threat to their power and that they therefore declared a connection between joblessness, idleness, and crime. Thus, a criminal class came to be created that was composed of those without work. The idle poor constituted a threat, and what better way to control them than to incarcerate them and make them work so they would no longer represent a menace. Thus developed the idea of the workhouse, and later, the penitentiary and the modern prison. Why are prisoners and work always linked together? Why do so many countries link prison with hard labor, and why do many people become incensed if prisoners are given a basic level of amenities? These questions have no single answer but are fascinating in and of themselves and are bound up with the overall conception and role of punishment in society.

When we think of penitentiaries we think of discipline and confinement. We can still see the forbidding walls of the older prisons standing as a testament to the power of the state to punish us. Punishment may have moved inside the walls, but we are still awed by its visible representation in the form of the prison. We also associate prisons with solitary confinement and lockdowns, when prisoners are isolated from other inmates and staff. In the past it was thought that solitary confinement would prevent moral contamination among inmates and accelerate their moral regeneration. In effect, it was felt that prison would operate like a church, as inmates would be able to reflect on their transgressions in the privacy and quiet offered by solitary living in a small dark cell. With the development of maximum-security prisons, where inmates are permanently locked down and isolated for twenty-three hours each day, we see a reinvention and return to the old practices of the penitentiary. Some argue that solitary confinement is necessary to discipline prisoners, but others also call attention to the mental and physical effects of solitary confinement on the inmates. Historically, even after a court-imposed punishment of incarceration, prisoners continued to suffer punishment behind the walls of the prison through whippings and even sustained physical torture. Have things changed much over time, and why?

Nowadays we leave most of the decisions about punishment to the specialists and the experts. Historically, many more citizens were involved in the process of formulating punishment than is the case today. Where are the reformers of today? In the United States, politics captured crime control as an issue from about the 1960s and has never looked back. Now crime is the number one issue for politicians, even though it is declining. The media and the politicians ensure that it is always in the front of our minds. Punishment is linked to the threat of crime, and thus our ideas about punishment become clouded by our fears about crime. We cease to raise the questions about punishment we ought to be asking. What role ought punishment to play in U.S. society today, and where will current policies on punishment lead us? It is hoped that this book will lead readers to ponder these core and crucial questions.

1

The History of Punishment in America

This exploration of punishment in America is not concerned with the kinds of punishment that a parent might inflict on a child or a school on a student. Rather, it is concerned with the forms of punishment administered and enforced through the courts of the United States and with certain kinds of extralegal punishment. This kind of punishment is usually intended to be burdensome or to cause a degree of pain, is imposed on a convicted offender for an offense by someone with the authority to do so, and is not the natural consequence of an action (Flew 1954 in Bean 1981: 5; Duff 2001: xiv–xv). In terms of the history of punishment, this chapter discusses the classical forms of punishment, shows how forms of punishment were brought to America during the colonial period and how they were developed, especially in the form of the penitentiary, and brings the story of punishment into the modern period. One way of tracing and exploring the history of punishment is to present changes in punishment according to a series of specific events and topics as follows:

- Early forms of determining guilt and administering punishment
- Forms of corporal punishment
- Transportation
- Punishment in the colonial period
- The reform of the criminal law from 1776 to 1825
- The birth and growth of the penitentiary
- Chain gangs and convict leasing

- Reformatories, parole, and probation
- Eugenics and punishment
- The rehabilitative ideal
- Punishment in the community
- Vigilantism
- Lynching
- "Getting tough on crime"

This chapter employs the history of punishment as a framework within which to examine why particular punishments were used, how the nature and form of punishment changed over time, why those changes took place, and how punishment can be viewed in different ways from a societal viewpoint. Generally speaking, the history of punishment is characterized by modifications and changes to previous practices through devising new strategies, but often these new approaches acted to supplement existing strategies rather than to replace them. It is possible to see punishment as simply society imposing a sanction on a person for breach of its rules and norms. On the other hand, it is also possible to see punishment as an attempt by those in power to control individuals' activities as part of an overall strategy to impose social control. Further, punishment can be seen as an aspect of a "disciplinary society" where individuals are thought to be in need of direction and control through punishment and discipline so as to render them compliant and unresisting to the actions of those in power. These theoretical perspectives, derived to a large extent from the history of punishment, help to cast light on how punishment was shaped by certain factors, how it operates within society, and why punishment has changed and evolved into different forms. Providing explanations about how punishment has worked within society and how it now operates is just as important as describing the specifics of actual punishments. Similarly, extralegal punishments, like vigilantism and lynching, help clarify the dynamics of punishment at work within society.

Early Forms of Determining Guilt and Administering Punishment

In early times there was no formal or fixed process for determining guilt and administering punishment. Guilt and punishment were usually determined directly and on the basis that some person's act had injured another in some way, perhaps through physical or property damage, and that punishment or recompense was justified. The state or the government was not involved in determining guilt or in applying punishment. Thus early forms of punishment involved acts of private vengeance, and during the pre-A.D. 700 period, disputes between tribal societies were usually settled through processes such as *blood feuds* (Blomberg and Lucken 2000: 12). From about A.D. 700, private dispute settlement using violence came to be replaced by demands for compensation for injuries, and during this period codes of law evolved, such as the Justinian Code of A.D. 529, which laid down a scale of punishment and compensation for specified acts (Blomberg and Lucken 2000: 18). In this early period there was more emphasis given to controlling disorder and on keeping the peace; less attention was given to achieving "justice." This meant there was a tendency to believe the accused person was guilty, and the notion of giving him the chance to try to demonstrate his innocence was regarded as a privilege and not a right.

Over time, three basic methods were developed for settling the issue of guilt or innocence and settling, therefore, the question of whether punishment ought to be imposed. These were used in the greater part of the Middle Ages and comprised: *trial by battle,* the *ordeal,* and *compurgation* (Barnes 1972: 7). In the case of trial by battle, battle took place between the offender and the wronged person or one of their relatives, and the outcome of the conflict was considered the "just" decision in the dispute, because it was believed that the gods granted victory to the innocent party (Barnes 1972: 7). Naturally, any fighter who enjoyed a high degree of competence would have an advantage under this form of justice and punishment. Trial by battle ceased as a practice in France in 1260 and died out in England around the same time, because it could be avoided by an appeal to the court.

Again, the notion underlying the ordeal as a form of trial and punishment was that the gods would favor the innocent party, and this would be made manifest by the accused undergoing torture or some similar feat and surviving that ordeal. Modes of ordeal included carrying a piece of hot iron, walking through fire, plunging an arm into boiling water, and running the gauntlet (Barnes 1972: 8). Ordeals died out following their condemnation by the Lateran Council in 1215, leading gradually to the emergence of trial by jury, which had first appeared in

England at the end of the first quarter of the thirteenth century (Barnes 1972: 26).

In the remedy of compurgation an accused person collected together a group of relatives or neighbors known as compurgators. The accused would swear his innocence to the group of compurgators, and they themselves would then take an oath attesting to their belief that the accused was telling the truth in making his declaration of innocence. Usually there were twelve compurgators, reflecting the religious significance of this number in the Christian gospels. In this procedure it did not matter whether the relatives or neighbors knew the accused was guilty; the oath giving really constituted only a formal process not to be equated with giving testimony under oath as is found in modern day trials. The decision about guilt rested on the conclusiveness of the oaths, and if no decision could be reached through trial by battle or an ordeal, compurgation would decide the issue or a demand for compensation would be made (Barnes 1972: 9). Over time, compurgation was transformed into a form of testimony concerning the good character of an accused. Compurgation was usually reserved for the elite or higher-class members of a society (Blomberg and Lucken 2000: 14).

As these forms of assessing guilt and punishment died out, they were replaced by the notion of *justice in the king's court* and the ancient notion of *vengeance* divided into concepts of civil and criminal law, and trial by jury became the accepted mode of ascertaining guilt (Barnes 1972: 9). Thus during the period of the early Middle Ages from about A.D. 700 to A.D. 1000, local systems of law and punishment became more centralized. Alongside the king's law, there existed canon, or church-made, law, and the church enjoyed great power by maintaining its own laws of punishment and protecting its own clergy through doctrines like *benefit of clergy,* which granted members of the clergy immunity from the ordinary civil courts (Blomberg and Lucken 2000: 15). This doctrine was not confined to clergy; the benefit came to be extended to anyone who could read or recite a verse from the Bible.

In terms of criminal process and procedure, *torture* was widely employed in Europe to gain evidence and elicit confessions, and even where torture was not used, the defendant was often not permitted to call witnesses on his own behalf or have a lawyer represent him. The use of torture in forcing a confession should not be confused with the application of torture as a punishment after a determination of guilt (Barnes 1972: 10). Where torture was employed to extract a confession, its infliction was generally preceded by a period of imprisonment, usually in a cell so small that the accused was forced to stand. He was also likely to be half starved and was not provided with any means of warding off the cold or combating the heat (Barnes 1972: 11). The accused would be taken out of his cell and brought into the torture room, which was often lighted with red fire and designed to terrify the accused. Those conducting the torture would be seated or standing around a long table, which would be covered with a red cloth. Again, the purpose of this environment was to intimidate the accused, and this stage of the process was sometimes called the *territion* stage, amounting to a form of psychological torture (Barnes 1972: 11). The accused would be able to see the instruments of torture arrayed on the table before him, and this in itself would be an intimidating factor.

Tying the hands of the accused behind his back and then drawing him up by a rope and pulley was often the beginning point of his torture. This was called the *strappado* (Barnes 1972: 12), and the result of being hoisted by the wrists in this manner was to wrench the accused's shoulders from their sockets. In the next stage of the torture, the accused was usually stretched on a ladder with his hands fastened to the top of the ladder and his feet tied to a pulley. In this way he was stretched, and during this process, it was common practice to drop hot pitch or sulfur on the body of the accused and to burn off the hair under his armpits (Barnes 1972: 12). In addition to stretching and other preliminary processes, the accused might also be subjected to thumbscrews. Here, pieces of wood were locked down on the thumb so as to crush the flesh and bones. Another device called *Spanish boots* operated in a similar fashion, but these were placed on the lower leg rather than the thumb and resulted in crushing the shinbones. It was common to intensify the pain by lining the inside of the Spanish boots with sharp iron spikes that pierced the skin before crushing the bones. Other means of torture at this stage included allowing drops of water to fall on the bare stomach or back in a steady rhythm and applying salt water to the soles of the feet and allowing goats to lick them (Barnes 1972: 12). Although these practices appear mild when compared with more physically intense forms of torture, they did in fact produce great agony over a lengthy period. Yet another method of torture was to place heavy leather boots on the accused and pour hot water onto the leather. This would cause the flesh of the lower leg and foot to burn and slough off. Sometimes molten lead was used in the boots instead of boiling water (Barnes 1972: 13)

A multitude of devices for torture were used and included, for example, in later stages of the process, *the schnure*. Here, a rope was tied around the wrists and then drawn back and forth with a sawing motion gradually cutting through the flesh to the bone. In a similar technique a rope was wound so tightly around the arm that the flesh was forced to press between the coils of the rope. Another common method was to combine water torture with strangulation. In this process a damp cloth would be placed on the tongue and a stream of water allowed to fall upon it. As the accused breathed and swallowed, the cloth would be drawn into the throat, causing partial strangulation. At that point the cloth would be removed and the process repeated. During the torture known as the *scavenger's daughter,* the knees of the accused were pulled up against the chest and the feet against the hips. The victim was held in this position by iron bars, eventually causing heavy bleeding from the nose and mouth. The ribs and breastbone were often crushed in the process. Other forms of torture included having to wear spiked collars and the removal of strips of flesh with iron pincers, tearing out of the tongue, poking the body with white-hot irons, and flogging. In this fourth stage of torture the *rack* was used as was the process known as *squassation,* where weights were tied to the feet and the accused was pulled high into the air and then allowed to drop suddenly with the aim of tearing his tendons and dislocating his joints (Barnes 1972: 14).

Women were subjected to all of the tortures used on men, but they were also subject to sex-specific tortures, such as having the breast cut off with shears.

If, after the first four stages of torture no confession was forthcoming, the torturers proceeded to the fifth stage, which often led to death. In this stage, the *spiked barrel* and *spiked cradle* were used (Barnes 1972: 14). In the cradle version, the accused was rocked backward and forward in a *V*-shaped receptacle, and his body was penetrated by sharp nails that had been embedded in the cradle. The rack and the *iron maiden* were also used in this final stage, as were breaking on the wheel, sawing or hacking the accused into pieces, and the torture known as *peine forte et dure,* in which the accused was stretched on the rack so thoroughly that death resulted as the body gave way under the strain. The iron maiden was a shallow statue constructed of iron or wood with iron strips and long spikes so that when the accused was placed within it and the entrance closed, the spikes would pierce his body. In the process known as breaking on the wheel, the accused would be placed on a heavy platform with his elbows and knees fastened in the form of a cross to spokes. The torturer would then use an iron bar to break the limbs of the accused. Sometimes a person would be sawed into pieces while still alive; for example, he might be hung upside down by his feet and then sawed into two pieces lengthwise. In practice, the first four, not to mention the fifth, stages of the process of torture were seldom used, because the accused's resistance usually broke down early in the process. The forms of torture that resulted in death were usually inflicted as punishment or penalty and not for the purpose of extracting a confession (Barnes 1972: 15).

The advent of *trial by jury* put an end to these other forms of determining guilt. This mode of determination has a relatively recent origin and did not appear in the highly developed legal systems of Greece or Rome. Its origin can be traced to the late medieval period when the king used the procedure known as an inquisition, during which he sought to establish his rights, especially to land. The inquisition was an enquiry into a specific issue and usually resolved the issue. In time the king came to use the inquisition to secure a statement from a group of leading citizens concerning the taxable wealth of their community or the state of peace and good order, especially in relation to offenses against the king's peace (Barnes 1972: 25). This group of citizens was known as a *jurata* and their report to the king was a *veredictum.* When the Normans conquered England in 1066 they took this process with them, and in time, the royal form of inquisition came to be called an *assize.*

By 1166 the grand jury had taken form. During this process, a number of country gentlemen were summoned before the king's agents to report about any offenses that had occurred against the king's peace in their community. At least twelve of those summoned had to agree about the accuracy of any report. The need to summon a relatively large number of gentlemen was a result of the fear of retaliation a single person would experience if he were obliged to make a solo report, especially if there had been significant breaches of the peace by powerful persons in his community. Those accused of a crime by this grand jury were usually subjected first to an ordeal or trial by battle in order to determine their guilt. The church's pronouncement against the ordeal in 1215 hastened the use of the jury trial, and in England the grand jury gradually gave way to a specific trial jury. Even so, for at least a century it was possible for an accused person to decline a jury trial and opt instead for trial by battle or to accept torture. One concern for an accused was that conviction by jury also resulted in the seizure of his property and the likely resulting destitution of his relatives. Although trial by battle was later outlawed, torture continued to be a lawful process in many countries right up to the close of the eighteenth century (Barnes 1972: 27).

In its initial phase the jury served both as the judge of the case against an accused and as a body of witnesses who usually knew the facts of the case and who based their judgment on their own prior knowledge. However, by the beginning of the fifteenth century, the jury had become a body that made its decisions based on evidence put forward by witnesses. Initially only the prosecution was allowed to call witnesses, but gradually this right was given to the accused as well, and with this right came the development of rules of evidence, the right to challenge jurors for cause, and procedures for empaneling juries (Barnes 1972: 28). During the period following the Middle Ages, between 1400 and 1700, feudalism declined and the new nation-state consolidated its role as the authority in the land. As capitalism developed and economic transformation took place, vagrants and beggars became a concern to those in power, and their concerns led to attempts to legislate control of the poor and those who wanted to sell their labor for the highest price (Blomberg and Lucken 2000: 17). In this period, the poor began to be seen as constituting a criminal class by the very fact that they did not work, and idleness began to be equated with immorality.

By the second half of the sixteenth century the *workhouse* had evolved as a means of confining the poor and vagrants, with the first workhouse beginning operation in England in 1557. The workhouse aimed to transform those whose character was considered immoral through the use of labor and discipline. Here we see the beginnings of the notion that criminal characters could be reformed and rehabilitated through confinement and work under a regime of strict discipline. The monastic orders with their disciplined mode of life also contributed to the emergence of the workhouse, providing a model to draw upon. By the end of the eighteenth century, people had developed a distaste for the public spectacle of punishment. The "civilizing process" worked to increase the level of human sensitivity to such events. Some have suggested that such public spectacles were no longer needed to enforce and reinforce the authority of those in power, which by that time had been consolidated (Blomberg and Lucken 2000: 20), and that in fact allowing them to continue was a potential threat to that authority and a possible breeding ground for criminality. There was fear that the great crowds that assembled at these events might sympathize with the victims and turn against their rulers. Whatever the actual cause, the public displays retreated into the background and punishments began to move behind closed doors away from public view.

Corporal Punishment

From the earliest days of society right up until the close of the eighteenth century, corporal punishment was the commonest method of punishing crime (Barnes 1972: 56). The most commonly used methods of corporal punishment have been flogging, mutilation, branding, the stocks, and the pillory. Other less common forms of corporal punishment will also be discussed.

Flogging

Flogging has been used over the ages not only to punish criminals but also within the home, the military, and academic institutions. Until about 1800, when punishment by imprisonment increasingly began to be substituted for flogging, flogging was the primary method used in the punishment of offenders. It is still used today in some countries, for example, Singapore (see Chapter 2). Even after flogging was prohibited as a punishment for crime, it continued to be used within prisons as a means of enforcing discipline.

Instruments and methods employed in administering a flogging have varied over time, but in punishing criminals the lash in the form of the *cat-o'-nine-tails* has enjoyed preeminence. The name is derived from the construction of this instrument, which consists of nine knotted cords or thongs of rawhide attached to a handle (Barnes 1972: 58). In its heyday flogging was executed with great vigor and brutality, and the backs of criminals were cut to ribbons with salt often being rubbed into the wounds to increase the pain.

Mutilation

Mutilation as punishment accords with the *lex talionis,* which directed that punishment be inflicted by using the same method employed in the original injury. Thus, under the *lex talionis,* punishment demanded an eye for an eye, a tooth for a tooth. Apart from retaliation in the form of *lex talionis,* mutilation as punishment was also justified on deterrent grounds, that is, it was believed to prevent the repetition of a particular crime. According to this reasoning, thieves and counterfeiters had their hands cut off, liars their tongues torn out, and spies their eyes gouged out, and those guilty of rape were castrated. As well, women guilty of adultery had their noses removed or suffered other forms of disfigurement so as to render them unattractive to men (Barnes 1972: 60). In England, King Canute issued a law requiring that corporal punishment take the form of mutilation: "Let the offender's hands be cut off, or his feet, or both, according as the deed may be. And if he have wrought yet greater wrong, then let his eyes be put out and his nose and his ears and his upper lip be cut off, or let him be scalped, whichever of these shall counsel those whose duty it is to counsel thereupon, so that punishment may be inflicted and also the soul preserved" (Barnes 1972: 61).

In similar terms, William the Conqueror ordered the use of mutilation as a deterrent, stating in his decree, instead of killing or hanging, the punishment would be plucking out the eyes and cutting off the hands, feet, and testicles so that whatever remained of the body would be a living sign of the criminal's crime (Barnes 1972: 61). In England, mutilation as a form of punishment continued until after the beginning of the sixteenth century, and the practice of cutting off ears and hands did not end until the eighteenth century.

Branding

Classical societies like the Romans often branded criminals with a mark on the forehead, and in late medieval France, the criminal suffered branding on the shoulder with the royal emblem. This was later replaced by branding the accused with the first letter of the crime committed. In England, branding was extensively used, and as late as 1699 the law required that criminals be branded on the face with a letter designating the crime committed. Thus a murderer would be branded with the letter *M,* thieves with the letter *T,* and fighters and brawlers with the letter *F.* Branding was also commonly in use as a form of punishment in colonial America. For example, the laws of colonial New Jersey stipulated that a first offense of burglary would be punished by branding the letter *T* on the hand of the accused, and a second offense by branding an *R* on the accused's forehead (Barnes 1972: 62). Branding was abolished as a punishment in England in the second half of the eighteenth century.

Stocks and Pillory

The pillory was in use in England until 1837, and when used alone was really a form of psychological punishment designed to humiliate and shame a criminal by exposing him or her to the contempt of members of the citizenry. However, the pillory was seldom used alone and was often combined with other punishments, such as making the pilloried person a target at which members of the public threw rotten vegetables and even stones. Sometimes those locked in the stocks were pelted to death. It was also possible to whip or brand a person in the stocks or pillory or to nail his or her ears to its beams. Similar to the *stocks and pillory,* was the *Spanish mantle,* comprising a barrel with a hole for the head and arms. The criminal was required to wear this structure while being marched through the streets and derided by members of the public passing by. A similar device comprised an iron frame fastened about the body.

Other Forms of Corporal Punishment

Other forms of corporal punishment included confinement in a cell in irons, whereby the prisoner was fastened by chains attached to his hands and feet to the sides, ceiling, or floor of the cell and left in that position for days or weeks at a time (Barnes 1972: 64). As late as 1830, an investigating committee in the state of New Jersey revealed that convicts were being strapped on their backs to a plank and left there for up to twenty days. Chains were commonly used to harness convicts together, especially in the southern United States where prisoners were used to perform labor. Prisoners used in this way were referred to as *chain gangs* (see later). The *ducking stool* was used for minor crimes, especially for village scolds and gossips. Having been placed in the stool or chair fixed to the end of a long pole, the victim would be submerged in the water while being jeered at by onlookers.

Transportation

The punishment of transportation exiles a criminal from his own country and was used in most ancient societies. Two factors influenced the use of transportation as a criminal punishment in England in the early modern period: the end of the practice of making criminals serve as galley slaves and the great increase in the number of convicted criminals. In relation to galley slaves, it had been common practice during the Middle Ages, and continuing into the time of Elizabeth I, for criminals who had been sentenced to death to be sent to work as galley slaves. However, by the end of the sixteenth century, with the coming of the sailing ship, the galley was no longer seen as an effective warship, thus putting an end to the practice of sending prisoners to the galleys. During this same period, a great increase in crime occurred in England during the transition from the medieval to the early modern period. The problem of what to do with an increasingly large number of prisoners might have resulted in a more extensive application of the death penalty, but those in authority preferred to look for alternatives. The newly discovered colonies offered a solution. Shipping convicted persons overseas was considered an appropriate means of ridding England of its criminals (Barnes 1972: 69). The first law that authorized deportation was enacted in 1597 and provided for banishment "out of this Realm and all the dominions thereof." Returning after banishment without license or warrant was considered a capital offense (Barnes 1972: 69). The final legislative framework for transportation passed in 1717 noted that present laws were not effective in deterring crime and that there was a need for servants in the colonies and plantations in America. Its operative part read that a person convicted of an offense for which he was liable to be whipped or branded on the hand or delivered to the workhouse might be sent to the colonies and plantations in America (Barnes 1972: 70).

By 1775 England was transporting about 2,000 convicts each year to America, usually as indentured servants. It is estimated that during the colonial period in America, as many as between 50,000 and 100,000 criminals were transported to America. The American Revolution of 1776 put an end to transportation, forcing the authorities in England to warehouse convicts in prison hulks consisting of old rotting ships. This practice continued until 1787, when it was decided to transport prisoners to the colonies in Australia, this time as convicts rather than as indentured servants. This practice ended in 1857 by which time it is estimated that about 135,000 convicts had been transported to Australia (Barnes 1972: 76). In contrast to those prisoners transported to Australia, convicts deported as indentured servants to America possessed value, and their masters therefore had good reason to keep them healthy. In 1838 an English Parliamentary Committee compared the transportation of convicts to America with that of those to Australia, noting that convicts sent to America were sent to communities composed of men of "thrift and probity," whereas in the Australian colony of New South Wales the community was made up of "the very dregs of society" (Barnes 1972: 77).

Punishment in the Colonial Period

During the colonial period, beginning with the establishment of the colony of Virginia in 1607 and ending in 1775 with the rebellion against the English, many punishments had their source in English practice simply because the majority of colonists were of English descent. The so-called Bloody Code of England, imported into America, appeared to be rigid in prescribing the death penalty for numerous offenses ranging from murder to the forgery of a minor document. In practice, however, penalties were applied very flexibly, and judicial discretion in sentencing and the power to grant mercy, as well as the doctrine of benefit of clergy and the jury system, provided numerous means to avoid the death penalty (Ignatieff 1978: 17). In fact the practice of pardoning capital offenders led to the development of the previously discussed punishment of transportation (Ignatieff 1978: 19).

The colonists were at liberty to discard those English laws and practices they no longer favored, and generally criminal codes were more lenient than those applied in England (Blomberg and Lucken 2000: 23). In Virginia, however, during the early colonial period, starvation and hostile relations with Indians featured significantly in daily life, and it was therefore deemed appropriate to govern the colony according to its true status as a military outpost. From the time that it gained a new charter in 1619, Virginia was a colony that most closely followed

English practice in punishment, and English common law and statutes formed the basis of local law (Preyer 1982: 329). The fact that each colony could choose its own approach to crime and punishment gave rise to divergent practices based on the pace of change in each colony, the rate of economic growth, and the extent to which the population increased over this period (Preyer 1982: 326). For example, as late as 1760 only seven sites within the colonies had populations of more than 3,000 people, with Philadelphia, the largest, having a population of a little more than 23,000 in 1775. This compares to London's population at the same time of around 900,000 (Preyer 1982: 327). Colonies did, however, share common features that shaped their ideas about how to deal with criminals and crime. The family, the community, and the church shaped colonial life, and these institutions formed the nature of the society and were considered important assets in the fight against crime and sin (Rothman 1990: 16).

At that time, communities were close-knit and fearful and wary of strangers, with each member having his or her defined role. In such societies conforming to local norms and rules was imperative in order to maintain cohesion (Blomberg and Lucken 2000: 24), and two central values of the time were maintenance of community order and obedience to God. Religion permeated all aspects of life, including beliefs about crime and punishment. Thus, crime was regarded as sin, and because a crime was an act against society it constituted a crime against God. Like sin, crime was thought to be the result of a depraved human condition. Its causes were of no concern and, like sin, crime had to be punished (Blomberg and Lucken 2000: 26), but it was generally understood that crime was also endemic and would never be eliminated. People believed that all men were born to corruption (Rothman 1990: 15, 17).

A wide range of behaviors perceived as abnormal could be sanctioned, including acts such as profanity, drunkenness, flirting, gossiping, blaspheming, and practicing witchcraft. For example, in Boston in 1656 a Captain Kemble was placed in the stocks for two hours for "lewd and unseemly behavior" on the Sabbath. In fact his offense was to have kissed his wife after having returned from three years at sea (Friedman 1993: 33). Prosecutions for morality offenses dominated the period (Preyer 1982: 334). Traditional Puritan conceptions of crime regarded punishment as a process that should be tailored to the individual offender and should have as its aim, the integration of the offender back into the community. Punishment, according to Puritan notions, would cleanse the offender, and in order to give effect to this objective of community reintegration, magistrates were often willing to retract punishment or remit a fine provided that an offender admitted wrongdoing and showed contrition (Cahn 1989: 127). These Puritan notions did not fit well with English conceptions of punishment, because the Puritan emphasis on individual punishment conflicted with the capriciousness and unpredictability of English modes of punishment (Preyer 1982: 333).

Methods of punishment employed in colonial America were derived from English practice and included levying fines (by far the most common punishment), whippings of up to forty lashes, banishment, various shaming techniques, and forms of slavery or bondage. Shaming punishments were unusual, but could include wearing emblems on clothing or placards on one's head or being placed on the gallows with a rope around the neck (Preyer 1982: 335). Whippings of a more severe nature seem to have been applied in cases of mutiny by slaves or in cases involving false accusations. For example, a servant woman who falsely accused her mistress of being unchaste received a punishment of one hundred lashes on her bare back (Preyer 1982: 331).

Public punishments were common in the seventeenth century and paralleled the custom of public confession in church. Both situations involved the community in the delinquencies of members of the community (Kealey 1986: 164). Rothman notes that, at least in theory, the purpose of a public spectacle was to emphasize the king's majesty, because a crime was an affront to the peace the king guaranteed to his subjects. Public punishment also served as a deterrent to others who might consider offending against the king's laws (Rothman 1990: xxiii). In Virginia it was common for justices to customize punishments for individual cases, such as requiring an offender to build a ferryboat for an act of fornication, or repair a church for illegally possessing arms (Preyer 1982: 331). Banishment was usually reserved for those considered a danger to the community, for those who would not change their ways, and for those not originally of the community. Methods of shaming included the stocks, the pillory, branding, mild mutilation, and the public cage (Blomberg and Lucken 2000: 31). The death sentence could be imposed for murder, arson, for stealing horses, for those who would not give up their criminal ways, and for incorrigible youths. However, the death penalty was not overused, and in fact, executions were relatively infrequent during this period (Colvin 1997: 33). Capital sentences could also be mitigated through the device of benefit of clergy, and by 1600 this doctrine protected anyone who could read, not just clergy, from the death sentence (Colvin 1997: 37). In Virginia the privilege was extended by statute to women, slaves, and Indians. Under this practice, a person convicted of an offense who was granted the privilege, would "plead his clergy" and instead of receiving the usual sentence would be burned on the thumb and then released. This burning showed that the offender had been punished and that he or she had used the clergy privilege, which could not be used more than once (Preyer 1982: 331). Capital punishment was employed more often in the South than the North, and the greatest incidence fell on slaves.

The point of punishment was not to act severely as much as to ensure repentance and to administer a swift lesson (Friedman 1993: 37). One alternative for punishment employed in Philadelphia in the late 1780s involved sentencing offenders to public hard labor in supervised work gangs. These prisoners were known as *wheelbarrow men,* and they were often harassed and abused by the public (Colvin 1997: 38). It was not, however, considered appropriate for women convicts to labor in public, and instead, female convicts were forced to sew clothing in the city workhouse (Millender 1998: 168). The public did not always excoriate the wheelbarrow men, in fact some ordinary people provided them with alcohol, tobacco, and food. The wheelbarrow men often fought their guards and conspired to escape. Thomas Jefferson commented that this group of prisoners, "exhibited as a public spectacle with shaved heads and mean clothing, working on the high roads, produced in the criminals such a prostration of character, such an abandonment of self respect as, instead of reforming, plunged them into the most desperate and hardened depravity of morals and character" (in Masur 1989: 78). In 1788 more than thirty wheelbarrow men escaped from custody, and by 1790 the state had determined that the process was a failure and instead placed these convicts in the Walnut Street Jail (Millender 1998: 169; Masur 1989: 80).

Servitude or slavery was enacted as a punishment in the Body of Liberties of Massachusetts of 1641, but before that time, it was already used in New England as a form of punishment for crimes such as failing to pay a fine or theft and could be applied to whites, blacks, Native Americans, either male or female. However, after 1665 the punishment of slavery was mainly imposed on nonwhites (Hunter 2000: 73). In Massachusetts, before 1785, if an offender could not pay a fine, he or she would be sold into servitude (Kealey 1986: 171).

It was not only methods of punishment that were of concern during the colonial period. The power of magistrates to impose a wide range of punishments also caused apprehension in some people. For some two decades prior to 1648 the people of Massachusetts Bay Colony had negotiated and debated about the powers invested in magistrates. Until 1648 when the Laws and Liberties was enacted, magistrates were free to impose whatever penalties they thought appropriate for offenses because penalties were not prescribed by law. The freemen of the colony viewed this situation with some concern because they did not believe that magistrates always exercised their sentencing powers with fairness and justice. The magistrates, on the other hand, took the view that they had few limitations on their powers. Their justification was that the Charter of the Massachusetts Bay Company drafted in 1629 imposed few restrictions on magistrates' powers and even fewer restrictions on the punishments they might impose (Cahn 1989: 112). The charter reflected the roots of the colony in English law and practice, where English courts had wide latitude in defining offenses and determining punishments.

Along with this wide power to punish came a right to mitigate punishment by applying "latitude in mercy" (Cahn 1989: 111). In the early years of the colony, punishments were quite severe with the sanction of banishment often being imposed together with severe corporal punishment. In one case, for example in 1631, Phillip Ratliffe, a servant who had been convicted of uttering "most foul, scandalous invectives against our churches and government," it was ordered that he be whipped, have his ears cut off, and be fined and banished (Cahn 1989: 114). It was punishments like this that led the freemen of the colony to press for legislation that would curb magisterial powers. In response to this pressure, magistrates argued that, once elected, they were to apply God's law, and this law could only be interpreted by the chosen few. They also argued that magistrates had to answer only to God for their actions, not the community. They took the position that it was preferable for magistrates to have discretionary power to punish rather than allow a legislative body to set penalties. They contended that God had provided a pattern of punishments through Scripture and that justice was best served through a magistrate who employed a discretionary approach. Only magistrates possessed the faculty to interpret and enforce the principles set out in Scripture, and they would apply the Rule of God. Magistrates defended their position by asking by what right a legislature could decide upon punishments for offenses. According to their view, fixed punishments, which would be set by a legislative body, subverted God's prerogative to punish, as would be expressed through His magistrates.

Freemen were not troubled about magistrates imposing lenient penalties, but they did have concerns about the apparent arbitrary nature of some punishments, for example, in cases of crimes committed against magistrates that were punished particularly severely (Cahn 1989: 122–123). When they were finally enacted, the Laws and Liberties regulated the work of magistrates by prohibiting certain punishments, such as the use of torture to exact a confession, and limiting the number of strikes that could be used in whippings. Magistrates' powers were severely curtailed when it came to punishments for offenses such as drunkenness, for which a formula was outlined in the Laws and Liberties: ten shillings for a first offense and twenty for a second offense. Similar rules applied to offenses like burglary. In all, penalties were prescribed for more than twenty-five offenses, but magistrates still retained the power to admonish, and punishment for offenses against magistrates was left up to the magistrates to determine (Cahn 1989: 136).

In Massachusetts no one could be put to death without supporting testimony from two or three witnesses, and corporal punishments considered barbarous or inhumane were not permitted. For example, whippings were limited to forty strokes, and there was no provision for benefit of clergy (Preyer 1982: 333). Another contrast to English penalties was in the punishments assessed for crimes such as robbery, larceny, and burglary, which could not be punished with death as in England, but instead with penalties of fines, whipping, or payment of damages in restitution to the victim (Preyer 1982: 333). In the early period of the colony of Massachusetts fining was the penalty most often chosen for petty offenses like drunkenness, but once levied, a fine could be remitted if the magistrate thought it appropriate to do so (Hirsch 1992: 4). New York was in a special position among the colonies, being the only one not originally settled by the English. Here, offenders were usually fined and whippings were imposed rather than brandings. Magistrates often lectured offenders privately to secure repentance and reform, and later the offender would appear in court and receive a formal admonition from the magistrate. In Massachusetts, public punishments were the standard response to most property and moral offenses, and capital punishment was not enforced very stringently, for one reason, the small population militated against any extensive use of this penalty (Hirsch 1992: 6).

Two institutions of confinement were established to punish offenders. These were *jails* and workhouses, and they were the forerunners of the modern prison. Jails were used mainly to confine those awaiting trial and to lock up debtors and religious and political offenders (Barnes 1972: 114). They were not generally used to confine convicted criminals, and when this did happen the sentence did not usually exceed ninety days and more often lasted for only twenty-four hours (Colvin 1997: 47). In Massachusetts, the Boston jail, opened in 1635, was the only place of confinement for eighteen years, but by 1776 Massachusetts had been split into twelve counties, and each was legally mandated to have its own jail (Hirsch 1992: 7). Jail was generally a second choice over some other penalty, or it supplemented another penalty. As was generally the case, jail terms in Massachusetts rarely exceeded three months and sometimes were as short as only twenty-four hours (Hirsch 1992: 8).

At each session of the local court an event called *gaol delivery* occurred, where a jail was effectively emptied of all its inmates, leaving only debtors and political and religious offenders. As places of confinement, jails were not constructed in any particular form, and in fact resembled any house within the local community, with offenders confined to rooms in groups. Jails therefore reflected the values the community believed would influence offenders to change their criminal ways, especially the concept that the family was the best model to follow. For example, the jail keeper and his wife lived in the jail, and prisoners wore no special clothing (Rothman 1990: 55). In the county jails inmates had to provide for themselves, and it was not uncommon for those without resources to starve to death (Barnes 1972: 192). Generally, jails were overcrowded and unsanitary, and women were not separated from men or children from adults. Moreover, they lacked proper security. In many colonies persons imprisoned for debt were able to come and go as they pleased as long as they stayed within the bounds of the jail (Friedman 1993: 49).

Workhouses, or houses of correction, began to appear about

the middle of the sixteenth century in Europe and were used to confine vagrants and paupers but not to house convicted felons. Colonial America reproduced this example combining the functions of the poorhouse with the jail (Blomberg and Lucken 2000: 33). Often the workhouse was an adjunct to the local jail and little real work was provided by those confined there (Colvin 1997: 47). A few more densely populated colonial communities erected separate workhouses or almshouses (Rothman 1990: 25) with the aim of discouraging needy strangers from remaining in the community, using the threat of confinement with hard labor (Rothman 1990: 25). For example, legislation in Connecticut of 1713 calling for the establishment of a house of correction declared that its concern was "persons who wander about" with the rogue vagabond placed first on the list of those who might be confined in the workhouse (Rothman 1990: 27).

The Jersey and Pennsylvania Quakers foreshadowed modern penology by substituting imprisonment for corporal punishment and by combining the jail and the workhouse to create the prison where they believed the offender could be rehabilitated. They favored incarceration as a punishment for criminality but also promoted the notion that an incarcerated criminal should not be kept in prison in idleness but should be employed at hard labor. In 1682 Pennsylvania maintained a mild criminal code as compared with other colonies, with murder alone carrying the death sentence. This reflected both the Quaker belief in the ability to reform even the worst offenders and their conviction that the causes of crime could be found in social and economic conditions such as poverty. Restitution was mandated for property crime, and rape was punished with a combination of whipping and imprisonment for the first offense, and for a second offense, life imprisonment. Adulterers were required to wear the letter *A* on their clothing after being whipped (Preyer 1982: 336). However, by 1700 penalties had become more severe, with a first offense of theft and a third conviction for adultery both being punished by branding. Those offenders not able to pay restitution for arson could be sold as servants to benefit the victim (Preyer 1982: 337).

Kathryn Preyer (1982: 347) argues that the death penalty did not figure greatly in colonial punishments and that this reflected the existence of small populations and recognition that labor was needed in the community to sustain life. Whipping was the penalty most often imposed because it was the simplest, cheapest, and most immediate form of punishment available. Like the death penalty, shaming punishments do not figure greatly in the punishment records of Virginia, Massachusetts, Pennsylvania, or New York during the colonial period. The fine was overwhelmingly the punishment of choice.

Reform of the Criminal Law (1776–1825)

The writings of Montesquieu, Voltaire, and their English sympathizers like Adam Smith, Jeremy Bentham, and Tom Paine stimulated a process of reform in Europe, and their assault on the old order precipitated the French Revolution of 1789. New ideas were also being expressed on the subject of punishment. Montesquieu, for example, in *The Spirit of Laws* (1748), argued against severe punishments, contending that extreme violence violated the rights of citizens, showed that a government was unfit, and declared that excessive punishments were quite inappropriate for republics (Masur 1989: 51).

This period of the Enlightenment in Europe coincided with the explosion of the population in the United States. For example, in the period between 1790 and 1830 the population of Massachusetts doubled, that of Pennsylvania tripled, and the population of New York increased fivefold (Blomberg and Lucken 2000: 36). Towns began to develop, followed by cities. There was a high degree of labor mobility, and then the expansion West began. The former communal lifestyle broadened out into an individualistic perspective. In Europe, the Enlightenment elevated the status of man and emphasized rational thought and perspectives and the ability of science to define the universe for man. God was seen in less terrifying terms, becoming a benevolent power interested in promoting the good and happiness of man. Notions of utilitarianism, equality, and liberalism transformed earlier beliefs about man, society, and God. As Adam Hirsch (1992) notes for Massachusetts, the initial range of penalties held crime in check during the seventeenth century, but during the eighteenth century crime was distorted by radical social change, especially in the form of population growth and labor mobility, and the state became exposed to a floating population of men and women at the lower end of society. Thus not unexpectedly, property crime began to increase and was perceived to be the fault of this shifting population described by Justice Nathaniel Sargeant as "vicious persons . . . roving about the country disturbing peoples' rest and preying upon their property" (in Hirsch 1992: 36). By the late eighteenth century, this in turn led to the view that offenders should be considered as a separate and distinct criminal class. Population movement was also a factor in shaping punishment patterns after the Revolution. As in all wars, the end of the Revolution released large numbers of troops into the community looking for employment and a return to stability. Thus, the Revolution may have played a part in creating the social and economic conditions that prompted the search for better modes of crime control in the later eighteenth century.

It followed from these developments that traditional sanctions, designed to work in a small community where everyone knew everyone else, were no longer regarded as effective. For example, in Massachusetts the sale into servitude collapsed as a sanction because the practice depended on being able to find a willing buyer. Although this had never been especially easy, it now became almost impossible because employers were not willing to take on wandering vagrants (Hirsch 1992: 37). The notion that punishment should be rehabilitative also suffered because it was one thing to show compassion to offenders in a small, tight-knit community but quite another to forgive criminality in complete strangers (Hirsch 1992: 39). The fine also suffered as a form of punishment, because social change resulted in more offenders having no means to pay fines. Similarly, banishment no longer seemed effective as urban communities expanded and it became more difficult to identify those who had been punished with this penalty (Hirsch 1992: 39). In Massachusetts, the legislators' response to these issues was to establish wider recourse to capital punishment for major offenses relating to property, but juries frustrated the effect of such legislation by refusing to indict for capital crimes or downgrading indictments to noncapital crimes (Hirsch 1992: 41).

The *Federalist Papers* contended that the administration of justice in both its criminal and civil forms was the paramount purpose of government, and the authors perceived punishment to be an important and necessary function of government, arguing, "every government ought to contain in itself the means of its own preservation," and warning that without punishment there might be sedition (Christianson 1998: 89). They saw punishment as a deterrent to sedition. With republicanism came the notion that physical punishments were appropriate to a monarchical system of government and that a new republic like the United States should regard them as unsuitable and follow its own course. Unlike a monarchy, a republic was to rely on the virtue of its citizens to survive. There was a general postrevolutionary desire to innovate in public policy areas, including areas of punishment, and this meant many of the new free assemblies were ready to wipe the slate of inherited laws clean and make new ones that they thought would better reflect changes in society (Hirsch 1992: 49). David Rothman argues that following the Revolution, Americans believed that they could locate the causes for deviance in the imported criminal codes that reflected British notions of severe and cruel punishments (Rothman 1990: 59). A central axiom of the new republicanism was that government should function to serve the common good. This meant that, although liberty was to be guaranteed, it was to become restrained liberty, because if the good of the whole was not kept constantly in mind the viability of the entire social contract might be affected (Hirsch 1992: 50). Thus, there might have been a connection between republican thinking and notions of how crime should be dealt with. For example, republicans stressed the idea of liberty, and this might have drawn attention, as a contrast, to imprisonment as the most suitable deterrent for crime. Another tenet of republicanism in the United States was the idea of individual merit and opportunity, and this, too, might have prompted thinking about crime in terms of rehabilitation linked with incarceration (Hirsch 1992: 53).

Following the Revolution, the conceptions held were not that crime was an inherent feature of man, but rather a product of the environment and that constructing a special setting for the offender would remove him or her from the family and provide an opportunity for reform (Rothman 1990: 71). Essentially, republicanism called for the sacrifice of private interests for the common good, and only by that means would public virtue become established. Accordingly, those who would not follow this precept deserved severe punishment. Virtue was at the core of republicanism, and as John Adams declared "Public virtue is the only foundation of Republics," and this meant that all should work to fight vice by adopting the virtues of "justice, moderation, temperance, industry and frugality" (Masur 1989: 61).

In any event, by the second decade of the nineteenth century most states had amended their criminal codes, replacing the death penalty with incarceration (Rothman 1990: 61). This suggests that in the minds of decision makers and legislators, republicanism meant milder and more benevolent punishment, whereas monarchism signified severe and cruel punishments. However, at the same time, Christian thinking required that republicanism be joined with Christian notions of virtue, linking the religious and the secular (Masur 1989: 61).

The United States was influenced by these new ideas from Europe, and the large number of Frenchmen who had been in the United States during the Revolutionary War brought new ideas with them and stimulated U.S. interest in reform. Also, many Americans had traveled to and lived in France and Europe during the period of the American Revolution, and Philadelphia in particular, in the years immediately following the Revolution, was greatly affected by the progressive developments taking place in Europe. Benjamin Franklin had himself resided in France, and all the political leaders of Philadelphia in that period were familiar with the advanced thinking current in France and England. Colonial ways were regarded as crude, backward, and irrational, and "reason" was to supply a new way forward. Crime began to be seen not as sin but as an act of free will, and a distaste developed for public forms of punishment and also for the penalty of death, which was beginning to be seen as arbitrary and irrational.

Contacts between Europe and the United States made Pennsylvania and Philadelphia well suited to executing reforms in criminal law and practice. In Pennsylvania it was thought that the Criminal Code of 1718 was not a native product but rather a colonial work forced upon the colony. This was especially the belief of the important Quaker element in the now independent Pennsylvania. In fact, this reaction against the criminal law was a natural outcome of the struggle for independence. William Bradford, justice of the Supreme Court of Pennsylvania and attorney general of the United States, designed the reformed Pennsylvania Criminal Codes of 1790 to 1794. In 1793 he explained his mission as:

> . . .the severity of our criminal law is an exotic plant and not the native growth of Pennsylvania. It has been endured, but, I believe, has never been a favorite. The religious opinions of many of our citizens were in opposition to it; and as soon as the principles of Beccaria were disseminated, they found a soil that was prepared to receive them. During our connection with

> Great Britain no reform was attempted; but, as soon as we separated from her, the public sentiment disclosed itself and this benevolent undertaking was enjoined by the constitution. This was one of the first fruits of liberty and confirms the remark of Montesquieu, "That, as freedom advances, the severity of the penal law decreases" (Barnes 1972: 105).

Bradford believed that imprisonment in solitary confinement or with hard labor would act as a deterrent to crime. He contended that the objective of punishment was to prevent crime and that penalties ought to be proportionate to the crime committed (Kealey 1986: 183).

In 1776 the new constitution of the state of Pennsylvania directed a speedy reform of the criminal law with the aim of replacing the various types of corporal punishment with imprisonment. The constitution specifically recognized the perceived deterrent effect of imprisonment as its chief virtue and called for prisoners to perform labor for the benefit of the public or as reparations for injuries caused. It called for "punishments [to be] made in some cases less sanguinary, and in general more proportionate to the crimes" (Masur 1989: 72). Similarly Maryland's Declaration of Rights stated, "sanguinary laws ought to be avoided" (Masur 1989: 72).

It was not until 1786 that a law was passed in Pennsylvania to give effect to the aims of the constitution, and this law expressed the underlying justice and rationale of punishment as "the wish of every good government to reclaim rather than to destroy" (Barnes 1972: 106). This clearly expressed liberal theological, and particularly Quaker, beliefs opposed to strict Calvinism, about the ability of man to reform and the presence of a benevolent God (Masur 1989: 76). At the same time the law recognized that social change had brought problems in crime control. The law cited the fact that experience had shown that "the punishments directed by the laws now in force as well for capital as other inferior offenses do not answer the . . . ends of reform (and) deter[rence] . . . which is conceived may be better effected by continued hard labor" (Hirsch 1992: 42). The law provided that in place of the death penalty for offenses such as robbery, burglary, and sodomy, all property of a convicted person should be forfeited to the state and a sentence of imprisonment not exceeding ten years be imposed (Masur 1989: 73). In the case of horse stealing there was to be full restoration to the owner and the forfeiture of the value of the animal to the state and imprisonment with hard labor, not to exceed a term of seven years. Simple larceny attracted a penalty of imprisonment not exceeding three years, and petty larceny, a maximum of one year. Also, penalties previously provided for, namely, "burning in the hand, cutting off the ears, nailing the ear or ears to the pillory, placing in or upon the pillory, whipping, or imprisonment for life" were replaced by imprisonment for a maximum of two years, with hard labor (Barnes 1972: 106). In 1794 the reforms continued with an act being passed that abolished the death penalty for all crimes other than murder in the first degree and substituted imprisonment or fines for all other crimes in place of corporal punishment. This code led the way for reform in other states that used it as a model.

In 1785 in New York, a bill was passed that applied only to the city and permitted officials to substitute up to six months hard labor in the workhouse for corporal punishment. Again the laws referred to pressure on society by vagrants and "idle persons" (Hirsch 1992: 42). In Massachusetts it took time for new forms of punishment to appear on the statute books. In 1785 twenty-four categories of crime were made punishable with hard labor, but generally incarceration was an alternative and not a replacement for older forms of punishment. By 1797 the sanction of hard labor was well established (Hirsch 1992: 58). After 1805 all crimes in Massachusetts were punishable only by fine, incarceration, or the death penalty, thus reflecting the modern system of penalties (Hirsch 1992: 58).

Cesare Beccaria (1738–1794) produced the most influential work in the reform of criminal jurisprudence and was an enormous influence in the development of thinking about crime and punishment both in Europe and America. He came from a noble family and enjoyed a comfortable lifestyle. From 1768 to 1770 he was professor of political economy in Milan, and in his later life he served on occasion as a magistrate and as a member of various investigating commissions. His famous *Essay on Crimes and Punishments* was published in 1764. Beccaria was not a professional lawyer, jurist, or criminologist, but wrote as an intelligent outsider. At the time he wrote his *Essay,* criminal procedure was extremely adverse to an accused. The use of torture, the extensive number of crimes that were punishable by capital punishment, and the inability of an accused to call witnesses on his behalf characterized a criminal justice system that penalized an accused from the outset. Beccaria recommended changes to the criminal justice system and to its social framework that would alleviate many of its adverse effects. These proposals included:

- The basis for all social action ought to be achieving the greatest happiness for the greatest number of persons (the utilitarian philosophy).
- Crime ought to be seen as an injury to society, and the extent of the injury would be the measure of the crime committed. In other words, he promoted the notion of proportionality in punishment.
- Crime prevention was more important than the punishment of crime, and in fact punishment could only be justified if it helped to deter criminal conduct (the theory of deterrence). Measures that would prevent crime included improving and publishing laws so that everyone would be aware of their content, of the rewards for virtuous acts, and of the improvement of education concerned with law and life.
- Secret accusations and torture should be abolished; trials should be speedy, and the accused should receive humane treatment prior to trial and must be allowed to call evidence on his own behalf.
- The purpose of punishment was to deter future crime and not to provide a measure of revenge. Certainty and expedition in the process of imposing punishment would best ensure that deterrence operated effectively. Before Beccaria, most had thought that deterrence was linked only to the severity of punishment.
- Punishment ought to be sure and swift, and the penalties imposed must be in proportion to the social damage that the crime had caused.
- Only fines or imprisonment should punish crimes against property. If a fine could not be paid, banishment provided an excellent punishment if a crime was committed against the state itself.
- There should be no capital punishment because this penalty did not eliminate crime, and life imprisonment would provide a more effective deterrent. Furthermore, capital punishment was irreversible and did not therefore allow for mistakes and the need for further rectification.

- Imprisonment as a punishment should be employed much more widely, but better facilities should be provided for prisoners, and they should be separated and classified according to age, sex, and nature of offense.

Beccaria's philosophy of punishment is summarized in the following statement: "In order that every punishment may not be an act of violence committed by one man or by many against a single individual, it ought to be above all things public, speedy, necessary, the least possible in the given circumstances, proportioned to its crime, dictated by the laws" (Barnes 1972: 97–98).

Beccaria's work represented the most important advance in the history of criminology and set the scene for the advances that were to take place during the next century and a half. For the first time intensive consideration had been given to the issue of punishment itself and to questions such as, what was the purpose of punishment? how should punishment be inflicted? and what were the most effective forms of punishment? The *Essay* had therefore an enormous influence on Beccaria's contemporaries and his successors in the field of criminology and was a great influence in the reform of the criminal law in the United States after 1776 (Barnes 1972: 98).

The reform of the brutal English criminal law, with its two hundred and twenty-two capital offenses, was influenced by the work of Sir Samuel Romilly, Sir James Mackintosh, Sir Robert Peel, and Sir Thomas Foxwell Buxton. Sir Samuel Romilly (1757–1818) was a lawyer who created awareness through education programs and legislative agitation of the need to reform the criminal code. His conception that improved social conditions would result in fewer crimes was especially important and expressed his view that prevention of crime was of far greater importance than punishment. Following the lead set by Romilly, Sir James Mackintosh (1765–1832) and Sir Thomas Foxwell Buxton (1786–1845) supported and advocated criminal law reform and the improvement of prison conditions, and it was largely owing to the legislative work of Sir Robert Peel (1788–1860) that the criminal code was revised and reformed (Barnes 1972: 102).

Between 1820 and 1861 complete reform of the English criminal code was achieved. In 1822, for example, the death penalty was removed as punishment for approximately one hundred offenses, including a law that made it a capital offense to steal five shillings worth of goods from a store. In 1823 the punishment of death for the offense of making false entries in a marriage license was replaced with the punishment of deportation, and in 1832 the death penalty was removed for the offenses of housebreaking, stealing horses and sheep, and counterfeiting. Finally, in 1861 the death penalty was removed for all offenses other than murder, treason, and piracy (Barnes 1972: 103). Although it was true that though mandated, the death penalty had seldom been imposed with any regularity or completeness, the reform of the criminal law did lead to an increased focus on imprisonment as punishment, and this gradually came to be seen as the predominant form of punishment for most offenses (Barnes 1972: 103).

The Birth and Growth of the Penitentiary

The prison system of today is of quite recent origin, and at the beginning of the eighteenth century imprisonment was unusual. However, by the middle of the nineteenth century it had become the conventional method of punishing crime in both Europe and the United States. How and why did this happen? What led citizens to believe that the penitentiary was certain to remedy deviance in society? Why did other punishments cease to be employed?

A number of theoretical approaches have attempted to answer these questions and to account for this radical change away from previous modes of punishment. David Rothman, author of one work considered authoritative on the history of the penitentiary, argues that U.S. reformers turned to the penitentiary hoping that it would instill the self-discipline in prisoners that they lacked, being products of dysfunctional families and as the products of a changing and increasingly mobile society. Rothman therefore sees the penitentiary as a political response to fears about social disorder in the new republic and not solely as the outcome of humanitarian concerns about the treatment afforded criminals. Rothman sees reformers as being influenced by the new thinking that arose in the United States after the Revolution as discussed previously.

Michael Ignatieff contends that the United States adopted the English capitalist model of the penitentiary and stresses its employment of factory-like routines and rules. He also notes that the penitentiary embodied the hierarchical social order that many felt was coming apart after the revolution (Ignatieff 1978: 84). The French philosopher and historian Michel Foucault, on the other hand, locates the emergence of the penitentiary in a modern technology of power that sought to punish and discipline those considered dangerous to society. Rothman, Ignatieff, and Foucault have very different approaches to the issue, but they all appear to agree that reform of the system of punishment was a more complex process than a simple revulsion at cruel punishment or administrative ineptitude. In particular, they all agree that the penitentiary itself should be seen as a new method of social control that, for the first time, was focused on reforming the individual character of a criminal. As Foucault (1977: 82) puts it, the aim was "not to punish less, but to punish better."

Hirsch (1992: xiv) argues that, on the basis of his study of events in Massachusetts and a survey of European and U.S. sources, the ideology that led to the development of the penitentiary came from England in the sixteenth century and the penitentiary in the United States was not the result of new ideas developed there but of a rebirth of old concepts that seemed appropriate in light of social and economic changes occurring in the late eighteenth and early nineteenth centuries. Rothman agrees about the importance of social change for ideas of social control, noting, "the social intellectual and economic changes that differentiated the states of the new republic from the several colonies prompted a critical reappraisal and revision of the ideas and techniques of social control" (1990: 57).

Michael Meranze (2000) believes that the emergence of the penitentiary in Philadelphia can be traced to the efforts of the elite of that city to understand the breakdown that occurred in traditional hierarchies following the revolution. He also proposes that the artisans of that city, newly politicized and able to influence the debate on punishment, favored the redemptive qualities of hard work and abhorred idleness, which they associated with vice. The Philadelphia elite of merchants, ministers, lawyers, and physicians doubted that other groups within society possessed their sensibility or knowledge and feared that criminals and others would subvert the republic by failing to participate in the common good. These groups of criminals and others needed to be disciplined and regulated, and the penitentiary would, in their view, fulfill that purpose. The humanitarians of Philadelphia were able to join with the elite and adopt the same viewpoint because their liberal understandings about the nature of the individual and the community could be linked to the wider republican objective of creating a virtuous society.

Writing in 1939, Georg Rusche and Otto Kirchheimer tried to establish a link between the birth of the prison and labor conditions, arguing that the penitentiary was a means of controlling surplus labor. They noted that although fines were frequently used to punish in the Middle Ages, in the later Middle Ages they were replaced by a system that relied heavily on capital punishment. They pointed out that deteriorating economic conditions were associated with these changes in penal policy and concluded that criminal punishment in any era must provide conditions that are worse than the lot of the poorest free people if such punishment is to be seen as a deterrent. This so-called amenity aspect of incarceration is discussed further in Chapter 2. In a similar argument, Dario Melossi and Massimo Pavarini see the development of the penitentiary as a response to economic dislocation in a society where being poor came to be equated with being a criminal (Melossi and Pavarini 1981: 119). These approaches have been criticized for focusing only on the economic aspects that might have played a part in the birth of the penitentiary and for effectively excluding all other explanations. Louis Masur (1989: 5) suggests that the changes that took place in the U.S. penal policy, including the development of the penitentiary, were not the product solely of Enlightenment thinking but resulted from ideas derived from republicanism, liberalism, and environmentalist psychology that combined with the experience of the American Revolution.

During the period of change itself, among prison reformers, John Howard, the English prison reformer, was influential in determining U.S. approaches to punishment. He wrote about the institutions for the confinement of offenders he had visited in Rome and Ghent that separated prisoners by placing them in cells and also classified them. Howard drew on his knowledge of workhouses and monasteries to design a regime of prison discipline that included a requirement for hard labor during the day and solitary confinement at night, and some local jails in England began to implement this idea in the 1780s. His notion was that solitary confinement would prevent moral contamination among inmates and accelerate their moral regeneration, and this focus on transforming morality was the major contribution by Howard and others who were inspired by their own religious beliefs to reform (Colvin 1997: 49).

Reformers like Benjamin Rush considered that in enforcing solitude the prison would operate like a church and that prison would, as he put it, "out-preach the preacher in conveying useful instruction to the heart" (Masur 1989: 82). On the other hand, some reformers emphasized the terrors of this practice. For example, William Paley, whose work *Principles of Moral and Political Philosophy* in 1785 was widely available in the United States, considered that solitary confinement possessed the great virtue that it "would augment the terror of the punishment," and Enoch Edwards, the president of the Philadelphia Court of Quarter Sessions, told a grand jury that solitary confinement was considered "a greater evil than certain death" (Masur 1989: 83). Here we can see how the concept of hard labor was joined to the notion of reforming the character of the offender. The practices and administrative arrangements adopted by jails in England seems to have indirectly affected penology in Pennsylvania, as English reformers adopted the principles and practices of these institutions and this later led to their further adoption by the Philadelphia prison reformers who were certainly aware of Howard's accounts of his travels inspecting jails.

However, the picture is not that clear. For example, in 1790, the members of the Philadelphia Society for Alleviating the Miseries of Public Prisons wanted to educate and inform the state legislature about prison reform in order to persuade it to adopt a reformed system of prison administration. Yet, their list of successful experiments in the new administration of prisons did not include the institutions at Rome and Ghent (Barnes 1972: 123). Instead, their emphasis was on reforms in English county prisons where the sexes were separated and criminals classified so that first and petty offenders were separated from more hardened criminals. In addition, at one prison there existed a well-equipped workshop for prisoners who could work. Nevertheless, the pamphlet of 1790 issued by the Philadelphia Society did contain lengthy extracts from Howard's work, and some two years earlier, the society had written to Howard inviting him to communicate with them about prison reform, explaining that they were certainly stimulated and influenced by Howard's work (Barnes 1972: 124).

As well as Howard's work, it appears that Bentham's *Panopticon*, published in 1787, might also have affected the course of reform in Pennsylvania, and in fact, the Western Penitentiary established by law in 1818 was one of the few institutions directly modeled on Bentham's conception of the Panopticon. In his work, Bentham designed a penitentiary that he called the Panopticon, modeled on a factory his brother had constructed in Russia. The structure was circular and allowed guards at the center to constantly keep under view all the prisoners located in cells around the circumference of the building. Bentham reasoned that constant observation of inmate conduct would instill a habit of obedience, good industry, and conformity (Colvin 1997: 49). Inmates would labor in their cells for as much as sixteen hours a day, and profits would go to the private contractor, Bentham, who would supervise the institution. He believed that the inspection principle he established in this design should also be applied to factories, asylums, schools, and workhouses. After some twenty years of negotiating to have his design constructed, Bentham finally abandoned the project (Ignatieff 1978: 111–112).

How did punishments change in light of this new thinking? In Massachusetts, population growth from the mid- to the end of the eighteenth century produced significant changes in the level of crime, and indictments handed down by the Superior Court also increased. Those issued in the period from 1790 to 1794 were almost six times the level of those issued between 1750 and 1754 (Kealey 1986: 164), and property crimes became more prominent. Punishments reflected this social change, because there was a trend toward a greater use of public punishments in property crime cases, a decrease in the use of fines, and the early employment of imprisonment at hard labor on Castle Island in Boston Harbor (Kealey 1986: 164–165). Castle Island was designated as a place of confinement for "thieves and other convicts to hard labor" in an act of 1785, and records indicate that here convicts lived a life under military-style discipline (Kealey 1986: 184). In the 1780s Stephen Burroughs, a preacher's son sentenced to three years imprisonment for counterfeiting, was sent to Castle Island, and in his memoirs written in 1798 he reflected on the fact that instead of being sent to a county jail he had been forced to endure three years in what he termed "close confinement" (Masur 1989: 87). The appearance and employment of Castle Island as a place of confinement marked a radical change in patterns of punishment in Massachusetts. In 1789 Castle Island was sold to the federal government, the prison shut down, and the prisoners dispersed (Hirsch 1992: 11).

By 1805 Massachusetts had opened a new state prison with a massive stone frame, which held three hundred inmates who began their sentences in isolation and then moved into shared cells where they worked from dawn to dusk (Hirsch 1992: 11). Within a year, a pilot prison project had started in New York and a statewide program had begun in Pennsylvania, and by the turn of the nineteenth century, eight of the sixteen states had programs for incarcerating criminals. In the South, Virginia opened its penitentiary in 1796, and Kentucky followed suit in 1798 (Hirsch 1992: 11–12).

According to Hirsch the notion of incarcerating criminals can be traced back to the reign of the Tudors in England. He points out the association that developed in England between idleness and crime, as laws were passed against vagabonds and vagrants who it was thought ought to be punished for their idleness. As long ago as 1557 the City of London had opened a place of confinement for vagrants at Bridewell where vagrants could be detained for up to several years. Similar sites were built in Europe, with the Amsterdam Rasp House established in the 1550s being the best known (Ignatieff 1978: 12). Bridewell did not resemble other prisons because they were disorderly places with little formal regulation or control. Subsequently houses of correction or workhouses came into being in other towns, again to hold vagabonds and the unemployed wanderers (Hirsch 1992: 14). The workhouse was not simply a place of confinement; it was intended that those placed there would learn the value of work so they would be rehabilitated. The aim was to replace the so-called "habit of idleness" with a "habit of industry" (Hirsch 1992: 14).

Writing in 1832, Alexis de Tocqueville noted the importance of work regardless of whether or not an inmate was reformed through the prison experience: "Perhaps, leaving the prison he is not an honest man, but he has contracted honest habits. He was an idler, now he knows how to work . . ." (in Duguid 2000: 71). Hard labor was seen as an especially appropriate sanction for property crime, and it had the virtue also of incapacitating criminals for a time (Hirsch 1992: 43–44). Also, the proponents of hard labor promoted the notion that the inmates' labor would pay for the actual cost of incarcerating them. Significantly, in order to have workhouses function effectively, administrators developed rules and regulations for their internal management and orderly operation, and workhouse keepers were to be fully qualified unlike jail keepers who lacked any real attributes for the work. It is easy to see how the conception that hard labor would benefit and reform vagrants could be applied to criminals whose idleness was thought to have manifested itself in delinquent behavior. From about 1625 on, a growing body of legislation authorized detention in the workhouse for petty offenses, and this trend continued into the eighteenth century (Hirsch 1992: 17).

Just as in England, on the Continent, the Netherlands and German states also began to send convicts to perform hard labor in work gangs or in a special institution called the Zuchthaus (Hirsch 1992: 17). By the eighteenth century English law permitted persons to be confined in workhouses for up to two years with hard labor, and in 1779 the Penitentiary Act mandated hard labor in place of transportation. Thus, from this perspective, the penitentiary in the United States did not spring from William Penn or from the practices of the continental reformers but had its origin in English practices brought to the United States by the colonists and drawn upon when social and economic changes were believed to necessitate a different measure of punishment. Associated with these rather ancient punishments were the new ideas about the individual that came with the Enlightenment and notions of reforming the individual consistent with Quaker notions of rehabilitation and overcoming sin. Hirsch (1992: 31) suggests there may have been an unwillingness on the part of U.S. commentators to credit England for the change in punishment patterns out of revolutionary Anglophobia.

This move toward adopting incarceration as the principal punishment for criminals was also seen as a kinder solution to crime than capital punishment. Thus imprisonment appeared more humane as well as more effective because of its incapacitating effect (Hirsch 1992: 44). It should also be remembered that in terms of deterrence the older forms of punishment had relied on the spectacle of public punishment to deter others from criminality. Incarcerating persons did not satisfy the desire for a public display, and it is for this reason that many favored hard labor in public compared with labor carried out within prison walls. But the advocates of penitentiaries had an answer to this point: If the labor was not visible the prison was, and that structure would strike terror into the hearts of would-be criminals. This explains the architecture of looming walls and the starkness that characterized many penitentiaries. Now what had been forms of public punishment would live on inside the prison in the form of whipping for disciplinary offenses and shaming techniques imposed on inmates. Nevertheless, as Ignatieff points out (1978: 90) compared with the rituals of public punishment, incarceration gave the state complete control over the level of suffering an inmate had to endure with no risk that the public would empathize with the offender or engage in disruptive or subversive undermining of the public rituals of punishment.

The origin of prison reform in Pennsylvania is associated with the name of Richard Wistar, a Quaker who, as a visitor to the provincial jail in Philadelphia had seen the misery of the inmates, some who had recently starved to death through administrative neglect (Barnes 1972: 126). Wistar acted to relieve the situation by having soup prepared at his own house and then distributed to the inmates. He and others formed the Philadelphia Society for Assisting Distressed Prisoners in 1776. In 1783 prominent citizens of Philadelphia, including Benjamin Franklin, Benjamin Rush, William Bradford, and Caleb Lownes, organized a movement advocating the reform of the Criminal Code of 1718, stressing the need to reduce the large number of crimes that carried the death penalty. In 1786 as a result of their efforts the death penalty was removed from a series of lesser felonies and replaced with the penalty of continuous hard labor that was to be "publicly and disgracefully imposed" (Barnes 1972: 126). However, the effect of exposing prisoners to the public gaze while undergoing hard labor was to engender public sympathy for their plight, a situation that would not have occurred had they been confined in jails.

The Philadelphia Society for Alleviating the Miseries of Public Prisons was formed on May 8, 1787, and its aims included extending compassion to inmates, preventing their suffering illegal punishments, and devising punishments that would restore inmates to the path of virtue and happiness (Barnes 1972: 127). The Quaker members of the society were the most active, including Robert Vaux and his son Richard, who were the leading proponents of the *Pennsylvania system* of prison reform. Important work was also carried out by non-Quakers such as Bishop White of the Episcopal Church. Generally, their reform agenda can be stated as (Barnes 1972: 128):

- Relieving prisoner's physical suffering
- Reforming the criminal law by reducing the number of capital crimes
- Replacing corporal punishment with imprisonment
- Developing a system of prison discipline, namely, the Pennsylvania system of confinement and discipline

In 1790, a Pennsylvania act established a system of imprisonment, a vital element of which was *solitary confinement* (Barnes 1972: 107). By further legislation culminating in 1794 the *Walnut Street Jail*, built in 1773 as a county jail, was converted into a state prison and adapted to give effect to what came to be known as the Pennsylvania system of prison discipline. Under this system those convicted of the most serious crimes were kept in separate cells in solitary confinement. The Walnut Street Jail had sixteen separate cells for solitary confinement (Friedman 1993: 78), each standing eight feet by six feet by nine feet and each having a small window and a mattress (Masur 1989: 83). Inmates were segregated by gender and age and provided with food and clothing at the state's expense. Corporal punishment was prohibited (Colvin 1997: 55). However, the principle that all inmates should be placed in solitary confinement was not followed at Walnut Street Jail or at Newgate Prison in New York. At Walnut Street only hardened criminals were regularly placed in solitary confinement at night, and the punishment of solitary confinement was otherwise reserved for use as a disciplinary measure for serious breaches of prison rules such as refusing to work. When placed in solitary, the inmate was not permitted to work and was denied light. Where a minor violation of prison discipline occurred, an inmate would be punished by losing one or two meals (Colvin 1997: 58). Most offenders at Walnut Street and Newgate had been convicted of property offenses, and at Walnut Street most inmates were not convicted felons. Many were there for the offense of vagrancy or for "due course of law," that is, for breach of a master and servant relationship or a labor contract (Colvin 1997: 59).

The experiment at Walnut Street Jail proved unsuccessful because the cells in the jail were never sufficient in number to accommodate all the convicts. By 1815 the jail was overcrowded because commitments to prison had increased substantially. This contributed to an increase in the number of escapes, and assaults on guards also multiplied (Colvin 1997: 67–68). There were serious riots, and some inmates were killed. At Newgate, inmates gained possession of weapons, and in 1881 a severe riot threatened to close the institution altogether. Generally, local politicians began to question the effectiveness of these penitentiaries and thought that a return to the gallows and to corporal punishment might be called for (Colvin 1997: 69). In 1817, in New York, in response to these issues, the death penalty was mandated for inmates who committed arson or who assaulted a guard with intent to kill, and in 1819 flogging inmates was authorized. These approaches assumed that these penitentiaries could not operate safely unless severe punishments were permitted.

At Walnut Street Jail corporal punishment remained illegal, but prison inspectors there did consider the use of the treadmill that compelled a prisoner to operate a milling machine with leg power for many hours (Colvin 1997: 70). Further, a board of inspectors of the Walnut Street Jail found discipline lax and revealed that prison staff and inmates were collaborating to smuggle contraband to inmates. Similarly, at Newgate, alcohol and other forms of contraband were being smuggled into the prison by contractors seeking to bribe inmates to produce work. Ultimately, unless the penitentiary in this form was to die out, it would be necessary to adapt and shape it to meet the issues identified through the experiments at Walnut Street and Newgate.

In 1818 and 1821 laws were enacted providing for the construction of the Western and Eastern State Penitentiaries (Barnes 1972: 129). These laws stipulated that both prisons should be constructed according to the principle of solitary confinement but there were no provisions about inmate employment. It was only in 1829 that the Pennsylvania system was finally established in its entirety with solitary confinement and hard labor.

The word *penitentiary* was first used in 1779 in the English Penitentiary Act (Colvin 1997: 47). This act provided for the construction of two penitentiaries in the area of London in which prisoners would be incarcerated for a maximum of two years. They were to house those convicted of offenses that would otherwise have led to the penalty of transportation. During the night they would be imprisoned in solitary confinement, and in the day would engage in congregate labor of "the hardest and most servile kind" (Ignatieff 1978: 93). Diet was also mandated and was to be bread and "coarse meat," and clothing would be provided but was to be "coarse and uniform apparel" (Ignatieff 1978: 93–94).

The Cherry Hill Prison (Eastern State Penitentiary) established in Philadelphia in 1823 was a massive stone construction with a 30-foot-high wall that looked like a medieval castle and with individual wings of cell blocks radiating out from a central core. Each cell was connected to a small walled courtyard. Inmates were completely alone at all times and wore hoods when they left their cells (Friedman 1993: 79). A new inmate was examined by the warden and then taken to a room where his own clothes were removed and taken away, his hair shorn, and his body cleaned. After receiving a physical examination the inmate was issued a gray uniform, hooded, and taken to his cell, which measured eleven feet nine inches long, seven feet six inches wide, and sixteen feet high (about twice the size of the cells at Sing Sing) (Christianson 1998: 134). A feeding drawer and peephole were built into each cell door, and a guard placed food or other objects in the drawer, which, when closed, projected into the cell forming a table. This device allowed food and other items to be passed to prisoners without any physical contact between the guard and the prisoner. An inmate would receive periodic visits from the warden and upstanding members of the community interested in prison work, which gave him an opportunity to confess his misdeeds. At Eastern State Penitentiary labor was seen as a privilege or reward. Convicts would come to fervently desire any kind of work to replace the alternative of continuous inactivity.

In many of the new prisons, inmates were not permitted to have any contact at all with their families because familial contact was considered a corrupting influence. However, over time, some prisons did relax this injunction, and by the 1840s Sing Sing was allowing convicts to send one letter every six months, so long as it was censored, and each inmate was allowed one visitor during his sentence. However, other than the Bible, no reading materials were permitted the prisoners (Christianson 1998: 145).

The perception that the Pennsylvania system was the epitome of penal excellence is reflected in a report of the inspectors of the Western Penitentiary of 1854 that referred to inmates having found "solace" in the penitentiary. Further, it was claimed that their "depraved tendencies" had been restrained through the teaching of Christ, that they had been taught to read, had been fed, taught work skills, had received the best of medical care, had books to read and writing materials, and each week were able to hear God's holy word preached. It was boldly claimed that the system had surpassed the confident expectations of its friends.

Following the Revolution, the situation in New York State mirrored that in Pennsylvania, with an extensive list of crimes carrying the death penalty and with corporal punishment as the normal mode of punishment for all noncapital offenses. Imprisonment as a sanction scarcely existed at all and there was no state prison (Barnes 1972: 131). A number of persons emerged as leaders in the *reform movement in New York State,* including Ambrose

Spencer (1765–1848), Philip John Schuyler (1733–1804), Thomas Eddy (1758–1827), De Witt Clinton (1769–1828), John Jay (1745–1829), and John Griscom (1774–1852). The New York reformers were helped by the fact that the Pennsylvania reformists were eager to show their reforms as an example to other states and actively promoted them. For example, as early as 1794 the Prison Society in Pennsylvania had resolved to maintain extensive correspondence with other states on the issue of prison reform. Governor John Jay recommended reform of the criminal code in New York early on, and Thomas Eddy, an active member of the New York group, remained in touch with members of the Pennsylvania society.

In 1794, on a visit to Pennsylvania, Thomas Eddy and John Schuyler met with members of the Philadelphia Society for Alleviating the Miseries of Public Prisons and were shown the new system in operation at the Walnut Street Jail. They were convinced that this was a model to emulate, and aided by Governor Jay, they promoted a bill in the state legislature to reduce the number of capital crimes to murder and treason only, to substitute imprisonment for corporal punishment for noncapital crimes, and to provide for the construction of two penitentiaries in the state at Albany and New York City (Barnes 1972: 133). In fact only one of the proposed prisons was constructed; Newgate Prison built in Greenwich Village was opened to receive inmates in November 1797.

Newgate Prison was unsuccessful because of its small size and its use of the aggregate confinement model that made classification and discipline very difficult. Owing to space limitations it proved necessary to pardon a number of criminals each year to keep the population within the physical capacity of the prison. Generally, the limitations of the Walnut Street model were perceived as the inmates being in close contact with one another and therefore reinforcing their criminality and the fact that those placed in solitary confinement were not given work but had been kept idle. The conclusion reached was that only complete isolation could succeed. In order to rectify the situation, in 1816 a law was passed authorizing the construction of a new prison at Auburn, which according to the legislation, was to be similar in construction to that now in use in the city with any variations deemed appropriate. The first warden of the prison, William Brittin, a carpenter by trade, was also in charge of its construction. However, the structure was built using the congregate method of confinement with double cells and rooms capable of accommodating ten or more inmates (Barnes 1972: 134).

In 1819, the Pennsylvania model of solitary confinement had become dominant in the state of New York. As a result, legislation was passed directing that certain classes of prisoners be confined in separate cells and the construction of a new wing to be built in accord with the principle of solitary confinement. By 1821 the prison reformers had instructed prison inspectors to select some of the oldest and most serious offenders and place them in solitary confinement. A further class of inmates was to be located in separate cells three days each week, and younger offenders were to be permitted to work in the prison workshops six days each week (Barnes 1972: 134).

The method of housing prisoners adopted at Auburn was not in line with that used in Pennsylvania. The latter comprised a system of silence and solitary confinement with hard labor in two large roomy cells, which included a workbench and a small outside yard. By contrast, the Auburn model initially opted for solitary confinement in a single small cell without labor and with no provision for exercise or communication. Predictably, this model proved to be a failure, resulting in sickness and insanity for the inmates in solitary confinement (Barnes 1972: 135). Consequently, this model of accommodating prisoners was discontinued, and in 1823 and 1824 the governor pardoned most of those still kept in solitary confinement. A legislative committee of inspection reported that the law providing for solitary confinement should be repealed and recommended against using such a system. While these events were taking place, the prison authorities at Auburn had begun experimenting themselves with a disciplinary and administrative model that was destined to become of historic significance (Barnes 1972: 135). This was the so-called *Auburn system* of confinement and discipline, comprising congregate work during the day and separation at night, accompanied at all times by enforced total inmate silence. With the death of Warden Brittin in 1821, the new warden, Captain Elam Lynds, worked on the new plan and was assisted by his deputy, John Cray, to whom credit should be given for originating and applying this new disciplinary system. In 1829 Captain Basil Hall, an English visitor to Auburn, described the system to his English readers:

> A narrow dark passage runs along the back of all the workshops from whence the convicts sitting at their tasks as well as their turnkeys can be distinctly seen through the narrow slits in the wall, half an inch wide

> and covered with glass, while the superintendent himself can neither be seen nor heard by the prisoners or by their keepers. The consciousness that a vigilant eye may at any given moment be fixed upon them, is described as being singularly efficacious in keeping the attention of all parties awake to an extent which no visible and permanent scrutiny, I am told, has the power of commanding (Ignatieff 1978: 194).

The new Auburn model allowed inmates to work during the day in groups in the prison yard and shops, and at night they were locked in individual cells. Silence was the rule at all times, and strict discipline was enforced through measures such as *the lockstep,* special regulations in the dining room, and whipping to enforce obedience to prison rules.

The lockstep was a special method of marching that required the prisoners to become interlocked in a human chain that kept them in strict formation and that prevented any communication between them. One prison officer reportedly said that it was intended "to give the spectator somewhat similar feelings to those excited by a military funeral; and to the convicts, impressions not entirely dissimilar to those of culprits when marching to the gallows" (Christianson 1998: 117).

Louis Dwight, one of its foremost advocates, described the Auburn system as, "a model worthy of the world's imitation." Dwight emphasized the fine construction of the prison and its neatness and "the entire subordination and subdued feeling of the convicts," which he believed had no parallel. He revealed that inmates were not permitted books in their cells other than the Bible, that they walked in lockstep at sunrise to their work and that "the silence is such that a whisper might be heard through the whole apartment" (Barnes 1972: 136–137). At Auburn the daily regime involved rising at 5:30 a.m. in the summer, after which the inmates emptied and washed their night-tubs and then worked until breakfast, which was eaten at 7:00 or 8:00 a.m. The breakfast tables were narrow, and prisoners sat on the same side so they could avoid any opportunity of seeing other faces (Friedman 1993: 80). After breakfast the prisoners would be marched in lockstep to the prison workshops, returning to eat at noon, and then marched back to the shops again where they would work until 6:00 p.m. At this time they were marched back to their cells and given containers of food and water, which they ate in their cells. They were not permitted to lie down until the appropriate signal had been given, and as they slept, guards in stocking feet patrolled the cell blocks, listening for the slightest sound. The next day the monotonous routine began again, with alteration only on Sunday when a day of rest was permitted and some religious instruction provided (Colvin 1997: 93).

The overall goal of the Auburn system of penalization was to break the prisoner's spirit and engender a state of complete submission to authority (Colvin 1997: 91). Whether an inmate could be reformed after being reduced to this state of submission was a matter of debate, and opinions differed on this issue among Auburn proponents. Some, like Louis Dwight, thought that religion and education could be introduced to the inmate after his spirit had been broken, but others like Lynds had no faith in the notion of reformation but rather, conceived the Auburn system as promoting deterrence from crime through terror as well as bringing about a healthy economic return in the form of prison labor (Colvin 1997: 91).

In 1825 the New York legislature authorized the erection of another prison to replace Newgate Prison in Greenwich Village, and this prison was ready for occupancy in 1828. It later became known as *Sing Sing Prison* and from the outset operated according to the Auburn system. Sing Sing (also known as Mount Pleasant Prison) occupied 130 acres, and the keeper's house was a three-story mansion commanding a good view of the Hudson River. The prison was 33 miles north of New York City and was located on the east bank of the Hudson River, allowing it to drain its sewage straight into the river. The cell block was 5 stories high and contained 1,000 individual cells measuring only 6′ 7″ high, seven feet long and three feet three inches wide. Other than blankets, each cell contained only a Bible, a cup, and a spoon.

There was no reward or privilege granted for good behavior in the Auburn system, and punishment almost always involved the lash. However, at Sing Sing, the level of punishment gradually increased, and severe punishments were inflicted for minor violations of rules. Guards at Sing Sing were permitted to strike inmates with any object at hand. Lynds defended flogging at Sing Sing on the basis that it was a time-honored punishment that had been inflicted in the military and that its use was generally supported by the public (Colvin 1997: 94).

Among the punishments administered at Sing Sing were lashing with the cat-o'-nine-tails (sometimes up to four hundred lashes), sticking hot pokers into cells, beating prisoners for making even the slightest noise in their cells, and lacing wounds with salt or brine. One insane prisoner was allowed to eat his own excrement and died, and another was flogged for asking for clean trousers. Food was quite inadequate, and one inmate spoke of having to eat roots, weeds, grass, or clay to survive (Christianson 1998: 125).

Some argue that the Auburn system was really an adaptation and development of the Pennsylvania system (see, for example, Barnes 1972: 138). However, once the Auburn model with its particular type of disciplinary regime had gained the status of a separate model, a competition developed between the two systems over which one would be adopted in other states. In the northeast, the Pennsylvania system was adopted temporarily by some states but was quickly abandoned by all except for New Jersey, which continued to use it until 1858. The Auburn system was favored because of its economic advantages and owing to the tireless efforts of Louis Dwight who promoted it throughout the country (Barnes 1972: 139). Dwight was a member of the Prison Discipline Society of Boston, whose activities he organized and directed from 1825 until his death in 1854. He had planned to enter the ministry but because of an accident was prevented from doing so. His reform activity included traveling through the eastern part of the United States distributing Bibles to prisoners. He was appalled by the conditions he found in jails and was determined that he would devote his life to reforming their conditions. The reports he wrote for the Prison Discipline Society of Boston are among the best sources on penology in the United States during this period.

In contrast to the widespread adoption of the Auburn system in the United States, most of those who came from Europe and inspected the two models invariably recommended the adoption of the Pennsylvania system in their own countries. For example, in 1831 France sent Gustave Auguste de Beaumont and the Versailles judge Alexis de Tocqueville to the United States to inspect the two systems, and during this visit de Tocqueville collected the material for his work *Democracy in America.* In their report comparing the two systems, the Pennsylvania system was considered more expensive to construct and operate, whereas the Auburn system was seen as difficult to administer successfully by the often-mediocre officials employed in penal administration. The authors of the report argued that the Pennsylvania system produced "the deepest impressions on the soul of the convict," whereas the Auburn system, while being less intensive, also effected reform. The difference between the two systems was perceived to be that, whereas the Pennsylvania system produced more men of honesty, the Auburn system produced citizens who were more obedient. There was, however, no dispute about the severity of both models, and the authors remarked on the contrast between the "complete despotism" of the prisons to the "most extended liberty" of the rest of U.S. society. The Frenchmen favored the Auburn system largely because it was more cost effective.

In 1832 William Crawford (1788–1847) of the London Society for the Improvement of Prison Discipline was sent to the United States to report on the two systems and in contrast to the Frenchmen, favored the Pennsylvania system. This was later adopted by England with some modifications (Barnes 1972: 103) principally in the form of the great Pentonville Prison modeled on the Eastern Penitentiary (Barnes 1972: 143). Other overseas visitors followed as the fame of the two systems spread throughout Europe. For example, Prussia sent their representative who remained two years and became a convert to the Pennsylvania system. In 1836 France, dissatisfied with the report of de Tocqueville and de Beaumont, sent two further commissioners to prepare a report that favored the Pennsylvania system. These studies and reports from outside the country had their effect in various penal administrations in Europe, and the Pennsylvania system was adopted in England, Belgium, Sweden, Denmark, Norway, and Holland (Barnes 1972: 144).

The proponents of the two systems at times waged a bitter battle over which should be adopted (Barnes 1972: 139). In fact, as early as 1826, the commissioners appointed to recommend a system of prison administration for the new penitentiaries in Pennsylvania were lobbied by the proponents of the Auburn system and converted to its merits. The conflict was waged between two rival organizations, namely, the Prison Discipline Society of Boston advocating the Auburn system and the Philadelphia Society for Alleviating the Miseries of Public Prisons urging adoption of the Pennsylvania system. In 1845, after its formation, the Prison Society of New York became a proponent of the Auburn system. As a proponent of the Auburn system Louis Dwight was often accused of unfairness and dishonesty by the rival society in Philadelphia, but it seems that both societies were partisan in their views and were willing to use whatever material was available to support their case, even manipulating statistical data in their cause (Barnes 1972: 140).

In the end, fewer states accepted the Philadelphia system largely because it originated first and was discredited early, whereas the Auburn system did not engender the same level of criticism until later. In economic terms the Auburn system scored well because it required less expenditure to introduce, and it also had the advantage of being supported by the Boston Society, which was well organized and widespread throughout the country. The difference in ideology between the two systems lay in the fact that the Pennsylvania model was committed to redeeming the offender's soul through silent and solitary meditation so that he would recognize the need for reform and achieve it through labor, whereas the Auburn model considered reform a lost cause (Colvin 1997: 83).

The prison industry in the models also differed. In the Pennsylvania system the emphasis was on small-scale production of craft goods by individual inmates, but in the Auburn system labor was aggregate in nature and organized around high-production factories. This revealed the relative economic merits of the Auburn scheme (Colvin 1997: 84). After 1860 the controversy between the Pennsylvania system and the Auburn system died away with the introduction into the United States of the *Irish model*. This model, as later developed by Frank Sanborn in 1865 and by others in the form of the *Elmira Reformatory* system, by 1875 came to be seen as far more sophisticated in contrast to the crude and elementary systems evolved at an earlier period (Barnes 1972: 141).

Overcrowding was a major factor in the demise of the penitentiary model. For example, in Philadelphia in 1861, 801 prisoners occupied 489 cells, and total admissions amounted to almost 21,000 (Blomberg and Lucken 2000: 58). In 1867 the New York legislature estimated that one-third of all prisoners were housed two to a cell. At the same time in New Jersey, prisoners were living as many as four to a cell measuring only seven feet by twelve feet or less (Blomberg and Lucken 2000: 58). The certainty that prisoners could be reformed by the penitentiary had faded by now. Other drawbacks included the difficulties faced by those who had work contracts with the penitentiaries in getting their instructions through to the prisoners via the guards. Increasingly, guards began to allow direct contact between contractors and inmates, breaking the rule against human contact. Contractors began to offer inducements and rewards to inmates to spur production levels such as smuggling in food and liquor (Colvin 1997: 99).

Discipline

As well, the rule of silence itself began to break down. Inmates resisted the rule in various ways, including devising systems of hand signals and sign languages and codes allowing for communication (Colvin 1997: 99). Prisoner mistreatment also became an issue, and serious charges of brutality were leveled against penitentiaries in Pennsylvania and New York. In one instance at Eastern Penitentiary during midwinter, an inmate was tied by the wrists to a wall and buckets of very cold water were thrown at him from on high, a form of torture known as the "shower bath." In another case an iron bar was fastened so tightly around an inmate's head that blood flooded into his brain and he was killed immediately (Colvin 1997: 102). The Massachusetts State Prison suffered from violence, escapes, and overcrowding from the outset, and in 1813 the inmates attempted to burn down their workshops. Three years later the inmates rioted (Hirsch 1992: 62). By 1826 the state voted to renovate its prison according to the Auburn model. In 1842, Charles Dickens visited Eastern Penitentiary (also known as Cherry Hill) and was shocked by what he considered the inhumanity of the system and its psychological tortures. By the late 1830s flogging had become so widespread at Sing Sing that even Louis Dwight condemned it. It seemed that methods of cruel punishment previously deployed in public were now being repeated and reinvented in private within penitentiary walls.

While the criminal law reforms replaced corporal punishment as a sanction with imprisonment, corporal punishment continued to be widely and cruelly employed to discipline prisoners. Methods of corporal punishment employed to reinforce prison discipline included flogging and tying prisoners up by the hands, allowing them to hang suspended with their toes barely reaching the ground. The stretcher, similar in design and effect to the medieval rack, was employed in U.S. prisons in the nineteenth century. It required that a prisoner's feet be fastened to the floor while his hands were attached to a rope running through a pulley fastened to the ceiling. Guards would pull on the rope to achieve the stretching process (Barnes 1972: 151). As late as 1878 an inmate in the penitentiary at Trenton, New Jersey, died by this method of discipline (Barnes 1972: 151). Also the practice of strapping prisoners on wooden benches and beds made of bars was in wide use in the nineteenth century, and one investigating commission in New Jersey in its report of 1829 noted that in the state penitentiary men had been strapped to planks in unheated cells for up to twenty days at a time, and a number had died from this treatment (Barnes 1972: 151).

Another mode of prison discipline employed at this time was the sweatbox, comprising unventilated cells located on either side of a fireplace. Sometimes prisoners suffocated while being punished in this manner. In 1878, another investigating body in New Jersey revealed that guards in the state prison had a practice of pouring alcohol on epileptics and setting fire to the alcohol in order to test for false or faked epileptic convulsions. Other common methods of prison discipline included forcing prisoners to take cold baths and pouring cold water on inmates. If carried out in winter, this punishment might cause a prisoner to freeze to death. Forcing inmates to wear iron yokes around their heads or to wear straitjackets were also popular methods of control and discipline as were the use of thumb screws and the gag (Barnes 1972: 152).

As late as 1929 Pat Crowe a prisoner at the Missouri State Penitentiary gave an account of the brutality of the prison discipline system there, revealing that men were whipped to death because they were unable to fulfill their labor contracts in the prison workshop (Barnes 1972: 153–154). In 1920 a prison investigator reported after a transcontinental tour of U.S. prisons that prisoners were flogged, routinely placed in solitary confinement for periods ranging from a few months to a few years, and that it was common for men to be confined in dark cells and given only bread and water to eat. The report went on to state that prisoners were handcuffed to the walls or cell bars or placed within an iron cage that enclosed their entire body and prevented them from bending their knees, leaning against the cell bars, or turning, while forcing them to stand straight like a post continuously (Barnes 1972: 158). Some older prisons had underground cells that were pitch black, unventilated, and dirty, and they were so cramped that a man could not stand up in them. The investigator found that men were kept in such conditions up to thirty days at a time.

In his annual message in 1850, Governor William Freame Johnston of Pennsylvania drew attention to the number of pardons issued to prisoners who had become victim to what he termed "ill health and imbecility," owing to the living conditions in the prisons (Barnes 1972: 168). The report of the Board of Inspectors of the Pennsylvania Western Penitentiary of 1866 explained that prisoners in solitary confinement and kept in silent conditions had expressed feelings of despair and hopelessness and had suffered acute loneliness and depression as a result of not having seen any faces other than those of the guards. It was the inspectors' view that "man is formed for society. He cannot live well without it. Ostracise him from the world and his fellow men, and he soon loses his own self-respect, because he feels that he has forfeited that of others" (Barnes 1972: 169).

Social Context

The emergence and development of the penitentiary took place in the context of changes to the way crime and criminals were perceived. Crime was no longer thought of as a matter of free will but rather was now regarded as a social disease, often considered to be an attribute of the lower classes and immigrants, and regarded to be the result of the social chaos and strains and tensions that were by-products of the emergent U.S. society. It was believed that morally weakened environments would breed morally weakened individuals who would turn to a life of crime. Perceiving crime as a kind of disease, or medicalizing it, opened the way for medical doctors of the day to proclaim their ability to cure criminals. For example, Dr. Benjamin Rush taught that disease resulted from taking wrong actions and all habits that could induce injurious tendencies were diseases (Blomberg and Lucken 2000: 52). He claimed that alcoholism could be cured through bodily labor and designed an immobilizing chair for the insane and the disobedient. Rush argued that a spell of two days in solitary confinement would allow a person to learn self-control (Blomberg and Lucken 2000: 52). In his publication *An Enquiry into the Effects of Public Punishments upon Criminals and upon Society* Rush argued that public punishments did not rehabilitate offenders but simply caused them to feel animosity toward the entire community that had inflicted the punishment upon them. He also thought that public punishments corrupted the spectators because some would always empathize with the offender and thereby lose respect for the law, and others would be incited to commit criminal acts. Thus, in Rush's view, confining offenders in penitentiaries would enable their characters to be refashioned through what he termed a regime that comprised "bodily pain, labor, watchfulness, solitude, and silence" (Millender 1998: 170).

The penitentiary reflected this notion of crime as disease in its physical design, its rules of separation, in the way it quarantined offenders from society, and in its emphasis on discipline and surveillance. Purifying the body of its disease came to be seen as the objective of this form of punishment while allowing the prisoner a period within which to reflect on his spiritual downfall. At the same time some have seen the penitentiary as a mechanism of class control (Dumm 1987: 26), and it is true that most inmates came from the bottom rungs of society. A good example is the Auburn penitentiary that drew many of its prisoners from youths who each summer came to the Erie Canal, looking for employment. The Erie Canal was only ten miles from the penitentiary. By winter these youths were without employment and turned to property crimes to survive (Colvin 1997: 81). Among the northern penitentiaries in general many inmates were immigrants from other states, and high proportions were black. In contrast, those who gave most support to the idea of penitentiaries came from the middle and upper classes, who knew how to manipulate and lobby the political system. Their conservative orientation favored social control and the maintenance of order in the broad sense, and to an extent the penitentiary provided both an example of absolute social control in a "total institution" and also set a standard and model against which other forms of control could be measured. In other words, the draconian nature of the penitentiary system sent a message to the dangerous and the lower classes.

As the penitentiary declined, the silent system began to dissolve as well, because silence could only be enforced if one man occupied one cell, and solitary confinement had proven to be an expensive proposition. Men were sentenced to prison faster than prisons could be built to accommodate them in the penitentiary model of separate and individual cells (Friedman 1993: 156). Corruption was common, and at Sing Sing in the 1870s, for example, a prisoner could buy prohibited items from guards (Friedman 1993: 158). Another issue arose out of the practice of putting prisoners to work at hard labor, which made inmates direct competitors with organized labor, provoking political struggles in many states. Ignatieff points out that support for the penitentiary could not be said to have rested on its capacity to control crime, because it failed to accomplish that goal. He argues that it fulfilled a wider social need and that reformers presented it not simply as a solution to the problem of crime "but to the whole social crisis of a period, and as part of a larger strategy of political, social and legal reform designed to reestablish order on a new foundation" (1978: 210). Prison reformers were therefore able to demonstrate the seriousness with which crime should be viewed, by drawing parallels between crime and the economic and social changes of the period, and pointing out the risk that those changes might bring chaos and disorder.

Organizations that had been devoted to prison reform began to disband or fall into oblivion in the 1850s, and the Prison Discipline Society ceased to operate following Louis Dwight's death in 1854. By the 1850s penitentiaries had reached the point of failure, stagnation, debt, and corruption and an almost total failure of the integrity of the two competing systems had occurred. As Hirsch (1992: 115) points out, one of the main differences between the pre- and post-penitentiary situation was that previously the community had played a role in the punishment and rehabilitation of offenders, but with the advent of the prison and the use of incarceration as the only mode of punishment for serious offenses, the focus of rehabilitation was now on the offender alone. As we shall see later, restorative justice approaches to punishment advocate a return to the time when the community played a part in sanctioning offenders.

Penitentiaries would nevertheless return in a more modern form in the so-called *supermax prison,* where penal conditions have returned to those prevailing during the golden age of the penitentiary. In these "new" prisons inmates live under conditions of lockdown, which permits them almost no time out of their cells and severely limits their exercise. Their conditions also constitute solitary confinement, since inmates have little or no contact with guards (see Chapter 2).

The Development of the Penitentiary in the South

In the South, the story of the penitentiary took a rather different course. There was little contact between the South and the zealous northern prison reformers, and slavery kept the majority of the southern poor under tight control. The slave owner punished his slaves himself or paid someone else to do it, and in the early period, the South seemed to have no real need for penitentiaries. Nevertheless, the southern states did build penitentiaries in the early 1790s and again in the 1820s.

In 1829 Maryland opened a penitentiary, as did Tennessee in 1831 and Georgia in 1832. Other southern states constructed penitentiaries after 1832, and only the Carolinas and Florida resisted the idea. The issue of whether or not to have a penitentiary was earnestly debated in the Carolinas for many years (Ayers 1984: 35). In fact, the penitentiary itself became a major subject of debate among southerners. In 1879 Virginia became the first state after Pennsylvania to build a penitentiary modeled on Bentham's Panopticon. When convicts arrived at the institution they underwent a period of solitary confinement from one-twelfth to one-half of their sentence (Ayers 1984: 38). The Virginia penitentiary was unsuccessful because in addition to the severe conditions for prisoners, the workshops failed to make a profit. Also, several successful escapes were effected, and few prisoners showed any signs of being reformed. Despite this failed experiment in Virginia, Kentucky, Maryland, and Georgia all built prisons before 1820. However, overcrowding rendered them useless after only a short period, and wardens acted brutally to keep order. It was at this point that the Auburn system was developed in the North.

To southerners, republicanism meant, among other things, the idea of freedom and the penitentiary represented a denial of that freedom and could therefore be seen from their perspective as the ultimate punishment. As well, republican notions of making the law fairer and less arbitrary meshed with the idea of the penitentiary as a place where an exact measure of punishment could be imposed. Although physical punishment could ruin a man, placing a criminal in solitary confinement to reflect on his crime represented a quality of punishment that had not previously existed (Ayers 1984: 44–45). The coercive power of the penitentiary offended southern notions of freedom, and the idea that placing a man in solitary confinement would reform him seemed to many in the South a much harsher punishment than the physical punishments it would replace. The core issue was denial of freedom, and questions were raised in the South, with its strong republicanism, about the right of the state morally or legally to inflict this kind of punishment.

Southern republicanism took the position that punishment should not simply mimic that used in the North and that republican southerners would make their own decisions about which punishments were appropriate in the South. These arguments and other similar ones seemed to be generally accepted in the South because on the only two occasions that southerners were asked to vote on a penitentiary system, the movement toward the penitentiary was overwhelmingly defeated (Ayers 1984: 49). One segment of the South, the ministers of evangelical churches, were especially hostile to the penitentiary and especially opposed abolishing the death penalty. For these ministers, death was an authorized biblical punishment, and even though the penitentiary relied on religion as an agent of moral reform, for the ministers, it constituted a threat to the authority of God's law, which made no mention of the institution of the penitentiary. Instead the Bible advocated swift, severe, and bloody punishments (Ayers 1984: 57).

For some states, racial issues were at the forefront of any debate about the viability of a penitentiary. Housing free blacks in penitentiaries with white prisoners was problematic for some. In the antebellum period most convicts were white and many southern states had only tiny populations of freed blacks. However, this was not the case in the upper part of the South, where more than a third of Virginia's and half of Maryland's inmates were freed blacks. Even though incarcerated whites were from the lowest strata of society, freed blacks were considered to rank beneath them, and putting the two groups together could not be contemplated. It was felt that putting blacks in with whites would destroy any chance of reformation for either blacks or whites, because, while white pride would be injured by mixing the two races, black pride would be inflated by it. As the governor of Virginia put it in 1849, putting the two races together in the penitentiary "can be productive of nothing else but mischief: it necessarily makes the Negro insolent, and debases the white man; it is offensive to our habits and prejudices as well as to our feelings and policy, and ought to be discontinued" (Ayers 1984: 62). The solution eventually arrived at was to lease free blacks to work outside the penitentiary.

At the same time as these debates argued the notion of the penitentiary there was general recognition in the South of the efficacy of regular labor, which was considered to be of benefit to and in fact a crucial influence on criminals (Ayers 1984: 65). For southerners, it was work and not religion or education that lay at the heart of the idea of the penitentiary. This general feeling was reflected by Georgia governor George Rockingham Gilmer who commented, "The habit of idleness and improper associations produce most of the offenses against society. It is therefore, that constant compulsory labor and entire seclusion from intercourse with others is the most dreadful as well as the most effectual punishment" (Ayers 1984: 65). Experiments with prison industries in the South produced little or no return for most states and, dismayed at having to spend money on convicts, Virginia, Georgia, and Tennessee considered the idea of leasing their penitentiaries to businessmen in the late 1850s.

Overall, prior to the Civil War the basic difference between the South and the North concerning penitentiaries was the importance northern reformers placed on solitary contemplation of one's sins. Both the North and South wanted to abolish physical punishments and public punishments. Both wanted to segregate and confine criminals, and both believed in the power of labor to reform at least a few prisoners, generally those who were younger.

Chain Gangs and Convict Leasing

In the southern states, factors such as slavery and a firm belief in the efficacy of labor resulted in the development of discrete southern forms of punishment such as chain gangs and convict leasing. Chain gangs mirrored slavery in their brutality; convict leasing offered a mechanism for channeling millions of freed black slaves into forced labor for the economic benefit of the plantation owners.

Chain Gangs

In southern chain gangs a dozen or more men were shackled to each other with chains affixed to their ankles, even when they were in their beds at night, thus severely limiting their freedom of movement. Moreover, prisoners were required to sleep in steel cages similar to those used to house circus animals, in very confined conditions, in all kinds of weather, and without any exercise at all. Twenty-two men would sleep in one eight by eight by twenty foot cage that contained only eighteen bunks, so that eight of the men were forced to sleep double in bunks only two feet wide.

Prisons in the South were unique in adopting a slavery model and in emphasizing the economic potential of free prison labor. This emphasis on the revenue possibilities of incarceration was prompted by the need to rebuild and reconstruct the South after the end of the Civil War (Blomberg and Lucken 2000: 59). Chain gangs were a direct evolution from slavery itself and were developed to satisfy the need for a docile and controlled agricultural labor force after the abolition of slavery (Colvin 1997: 199).

Neither North Carolina nor South Carolina constructed a penitentiary before 1865; instead they continued to use whipping, shaming, and the gallows as punishment. Crime in South Carolina was believed to be exclusively committed by blacks, the majority of whom were slaves, and consequently private justice through vigilantism and punishment on plantations took the place of a formal criminal justice system (Colvin 1997: 206). However, some forms of incarceration did exist. The workhouse in Charleston, for example, resembled a prison but was actually a form of private justice. Plantation owners who were reluctant to punish their own slaves could pay the master of the workhouse to punish them. In the workhouse in Charleston, slaves were whipped and forced to run on the treadmill as punishment. In contrast to South Carolina, other southern states relied less on these informal means of justice, because they were less under the control of plantation owners. The focus on black crime in South Carolina reflects the large black population there at the time: eight black people to every white. The other southern states did not suffer from the same fixation on black crime that South Carolina had, and, as had happened in the North, citizens created new penal codes substituting imprisonment for corporal punishment and the death penalty. This shift was encouraged by urban elites who wanted to see a growth in government institutions (Colvin 1997: 207).

In 1800, Virginia established a penitentiary in Richmond that resembled Bentham's Panopticon in design. It was located near the city's sewer, the cells were unheated, and prisoners were not allowed to work and were kept in solitary confinement. Escapes and other incidents were common, and the prison was not economically viable because it received little funding from the state. In 1858 Virginia decided to take its convicts out of the prison and lease them out to railroad and canal companies. This decision was the forerunner of other *convict leasing* systems that were found throughout the South after the Civil War.

In Frankfort, Kentucky, a state prison that had one hundred cells was opened in 1800, and it, too, was neglected by its state government. Finally, in 1825 a merchant offered to pay an annual fee to the state to lease all its prisoners, and Kentucky turned over the institution to him. A penitentiary was built in Baltimore, Maryland, in the first part of the nineteenth century in the form of a 320-cell prison employing solitary confinement and congregate work practices. Maryland adopted the Auburn plan in the 1820s and came to resemble northern states in its penal policies (Colvin 1997: 209). In 1817, Georgia built a small state prison that followed the Walnut Jail practice of congregate work, but its workshops failed to make money and the state government complained about the expense of its operation. It was destroyed during the Civil War (Colvin 1997: 209). Tennessee and Louisiana also opened state prisons, both following the Auburn plan, and each having only about a one hundred-cell capacity. In 1844 Louisiana imitated the Kentucky example and leased out its penitentiary to a private firm initially for five years (Carleton 1971: 9). Later in the 1840s, Texas and Mississippi built prisons which they leased to private businessmen and which maintained profitable enterprises. By contrast, in North Carolina and Alabama the idea of having a penitentiary was voted down. Even in those states that maintained prisons, there were very few prisoners, and informal types of justice continued unabated (Colvin 1997: 212).

Comparing the North and the South, there was a significant divergence in the religious aspects associated with incarceration. The South rejected the North's notion that the penitentiary served as a means to a convict's salvation through the inculcation of self-discipline, because southern ministers argued there was no mention of penitentiaries in the Bible, and therefore they had little use for them. They did not believe penitentiaries were an adequate alternative to corporal punishment or the death penalty (Colvin 1997: 212). The concept of benevolence, so prominent among the northern prison reformers did not figure at all in the southern view, and southern white males still relied on a code of honor that perceived family units as having responsibility for their own security and protection. Thus, justice in the South was achieved through personally avenging family members and not through lawfully constituted authorities. Upholding family honor was a major influence in vigilantism and lynching, which, compounded by a belief in white supremacy, created a situation most unfavorable to the black population.

The first chain gangs appeared in Georgia in 1866 when the legislature devolved the punishment of those convicted of offenses from the state penitentiary to the local counties, which were empowered to use convicts to build roads or lease them to private interests. As a result, those convicted of vagrancy offenses and work-related crimes as well as theft were sentenced to periods on the chain gangs where they could be whipped by guards if their work efforts slacked or they attempted to escape (Colvin 1997: 220). Planters and others who wanted labor went to county courthouses to purchase black convicts who would otherwise serve on county chain gangs. Conditions for the prisoners were slightly better with the planters, and in fact, county chain gangs maintained harsher conditions to encourage prisoners to see plantation work as preferable (Colvin 1997: 220).

In North Carolina, the legislature authorized judges to punish offenders by sending them to work on county roads or railroads in chain gangs for a maximum term of one year, and those who escaped would have to serve twice that sentence (Christianson 1998: 172). In Alabama, under the penal code of 1866, those sentenced to hard labor could be shackled if sentenced to imprisonment for two or more months, if they had attempted to escape from confinement, or if they refused or failed to work (Anderson et al. 2000: 6). By 1919 the brutality associated with chain gangs was recognized at the political level. In that year, Governor Kilby of Alabama declared that the state's chain gangs were "a relic of barbarism. . . . A form of human slavery" (Gorman 1997: 451).

Convict Leasing

Following the Civil War, convict leasing developed in an uneven pattern for about twenty years, and as Edward Ayers points out, the term convict leasing eventually became associated specifically with the South (Ayers 1984: 185). According to Ayers, the convict leasing system came about when southern state governments suddenly found themselves responsible for millions of blacks, who had previously, in the antebellum period, been divorced from the state and state control, having been housed on plantations and totally under the control of slave owners (Ayers 1984: 185). When slavery ended, the southern planters, faced with a limited labor pool, needed to secure a substitute labor force over which they had total control. Without such a labor force, planters faced grave economic challenges, because they had always relied on slave labor and could not pay enough to attract freed laborers. The dilapidated southern penitentiaries had been used in the antebellum period to house a few whites, some black men too sick to be worked, and a few women. Not only were the penitentiaries in no fit condition to house large numbers of convicts, but now there was a huge demand for labor from the planters, given that slavery had been abolished. Many states turned to leasing as a temporary expedient, as convict populations increased and there were no funds to refurbish the crumbling penitentiaries. Most of the inmates were African-American, and the skills they had displayed during slavery were now put to use in agriculture and especially on state penal farms (Carleton 1971: 14).

In 1867, the governor of Arkansas offered a temporary two-year lease of state convicts to help him buy time to plan a better system to deal with offenders (Ayers 1984: 189). Within fifteen years of the end of the Civil War all the former Confederate states had allowed contractors to bid for convict labor. Their options were extremely limited in light of demands that state expenditures be controlled, the need to avoid conflict between free and convict labor, and the general southern disinclination to support blacks in, as they saw it, "idleness." In the early period of leasing in the late 1860s and early 1870s, leases were granted for fairly short terms and convicts worked on farms and on railroads, but in later periods convict leasing was directed toward the mining industry. In Louisiana convicts were leased to private operators from 1844 until 1901 with hardly a break. Although profits from leasing would have been welcomed, leasing was seen mainly as a means of avoiding the expense of maintaining inmates in a penitentiary setting. After 1901 the state put prisoners to work on its own plantations (Carleton 1971: 7). With the first lease, the lessee company was not required to pay anything to the state. The arrangement was made merely to relieve Louisiana of the burden of supporting the state penitentiary. On a second lease, the lessee was required to pay the state of Louisiana one-quarter of its profits, and on subsequent arrangements, the state was to receive one-half of all profits (Carleton 1971: 10–12).

The enactment of black codes as a means of controlling the now freed black population was generally recognized as an attempt to reintroduce slavery under a different guise. By the end of 1866, because of the outcry against black codes in the North, most of them had been repealed. Nevertheless, the courts in the

South continued to enforce labor laws that were not racially specific. These laws mandated that freedmen found without lawful employment could be arrested and jailed as vagrants, and those who failed to pay their fines could also be jailed. If jail space was not available, they could be hired out to masters who paid their fines and deducted the amount of the fine from their wages. Thus many freedmen found themselves back in a situation akin to slavery (Christianson 1998: 171). However, the practice of leasing convicts was not a simple reinvention of slavery. For one reason, the slave owners were not the only group who wanted to use convict labor.

As Ayers describes it, the convict lease system operated to bridge the gap between the former agricultural slave economy of the South and a society now developing capitalism in the form of railroads and extractive industries. Contractors knew they had a dispensable labor force able to undertake the dangerous work of mining and railroad building. In fact, convict leasing was an ideal fit with the emerging capitalism of the South, because labor costs were fixed and kept to a minimum, there was no difficulty in securing enough workers, and convicts could be worked at a pace that free workers would not tolerate (Ayers 1984: 193).

Convicts on lease could and did resist the system. They would load their coal wagons with stones instead of coal to fill their quota or refuse to work at all and suffer the obligatory whipping, or would simply work less productively. Like slaves, they employed strategies of resistance, but overall they were seen as constituting a docile labor force that the South simply could not do without in that period of its development. Moreover, many contractors made huge profits from their labor (Ayers 1984: 194), as did the states themselves. Nine out of ten leased convicts were black, whereas before the war nearly all convicts had been white. Regarding life in the lease system, one convict said, "This place is nine kinds of hell. [I] [a]m suffering death every day here" (Ayers 1984: 200).

Southerners claimed that the convict lease system had one reforming effect—it taught blacks how to work. As well, according to some, the system had the effect of training and turning out good workers who were disciplined and skilled and who could command good wages and jobs after their release from incarceration.

During the period of Reconstruction, convict leasing enjoyed another innovation when in 1868 state authorities under federal reconstruction authorization agreed to a contract under which a businessman could work convicts in his agricultural camps. The convicts were placed totally under his control, and he was paid by the state for their maintenance and transportation. Ultimately, the businessman greatly benefited from this enterprise because he kept all the profits of the convicts' labor (Colvin 1997: 222).

In other states like Georgia and Tennessee similar schemes evolved as the state paid a private contractor to work and maintain prisoners. Later, arrangements for convict leasing would change as private contractors paid the state directly for the use of prison labor. A good supply of (usually black) convict labor was maintained by the enactment of laws in the South that had defined vagrancy broadly and allowed for the arrest of almost anyone who was without work (Colvin 1997: 233). In consequence there was an incentive to lease out convict labor to earn a good return, and in 1877, for example, the Florida legislature abolished its state penitentiary, replacing it with a system of hiring out convicts to private contractors. A similar move occurred in South Carolina, and other states also expanded leasing practices, therefore leaving their prisons to run down and house the remaining small number of white and infirm black convicts. Business competed for convict labor, and by 1880, except for Virginia, all the southern states had leased out all or a portion of their convicts to private enterprises (Colvin 1997: 234).

It was in the late 1880s and early 1890s, with crime rates rising in the South, that a further impetus was given to the use of chain gangs and convict leasing, because more blacks were arrested and therefore provided a greater pool of convict labor for leasing. Now private enterprises were eager to obtain this labor and paid fines and court fees to secure them from county sheriffs who also benefited personally from the deals struck (Colvin 1997: 243). Local sheriffs habitually arrested African Americans and falsely charged them with offenses in order to secure their labor as convicts (Fierce in Gorman 1997: 449). Sometimes blacks were charged with trivial offenses but awarded heavy sentences with alternate fines so that orders for labor placed by plantation owners with magistrate's courts could be filled. The plantation owners would pay the fines, and the convicted person would be released to their custody for labor (Fierce in Gorman 1997: 450).

Convicts suffered brutal conditions in both chain gangs and convict lease camps. They were required to sleep in iron cages, shackled together on narrow wooden slats, and had to relieve themselves in the same bucket in which they washed (Colvin 1997: 246). In Alabama leased convicts were punished by methods that included being hanged from makeshift crucifixes, being stretched on racks, and being placed in sweatboxes for lengthy periods. In the mining camps convicts often had no shoes during the winter. There was no incentive to treat convicts with any measure of a minimum standard, and unlike the situation with slavery, there was no investment to protect because contractors could rely on a continuous supply of convict labor.

A high death rate marked the years of convict leasing, for example, in 1868 and 1869, 17 and 18 percent, respectively, of leased Alabama convicts died (Colvin 1997: 247). The rate increased to 41 percent in 1870, and in 1883 one doctor reported that in Alabama most convicts died within three years. Similar death rates applied in other states, for example, in Arkansas the rate was 25 percent in 1881, and in Texas the average life expectancy of a convict was only seven years after being leased (Colvin 1997: 247). Describing the lack of incentive to treat leased convicts with human dignity, one Louisiana prison official said, "Before the Civil War we owned the Negroes. If a man had a good Negro, he could afford to take care of him; if he was sick, get him a doctor. He might even get gold plugs in his teeth. But these convicts, we don't own them. So, one dies, we get another" (Christianson 1998: 182).

In 1886 a state committee visited some of the work camps in Louisiana where leased prisoners were employed and observed a black convict, Theophile Chevalier, who had no feet. He had been forced to labor outside without shoes during the previous winter and had suffered frostbite, which soon developed into gangrene. One of his feet had been amputated with a penknife, and the other had simply rotted away. He was serving a five-year sentence for stealing five dollars (Carleton 1971: 37).

Convict leasing also took place in the North but under a different process. There, a company would contract with the state for the labor of a particular number of prisoners, but the state would continue to be responsible for feeding, guarding, and caring for the prisoners. The contractor would provide all the resources such as supervisors and trainers as well as the raw materials used in production necessary to produce the goods involved in the business. Northern administrators argued that this system could produce sufficient revenue for the state to defer up to two-thirds of prison costs (Christianson 1998: 184).

Incidents of brutal treatment under convict leasing occurred in the North, too. For example, in Trenton, New Jersey, in 1878, a prisoner died after being "stretched" for not working, and an investigating commission found that the prison authorities had poured alcohol on epileptics and set them on fire to detect possible shams to avoid working. In Ohio, "unproductive" convicts were made to sit naked in pools of water and receive electric shocks (Christianson 1998: 184).

Sometimes the North and the South had similar convict-leasing issues. For example, in 1906, northern penologist and reformer Frederick Wines inspected the penal farms in Louisiana and agreed that the emphasis on agricultural work for the inmates was appropriate. Addressing the Congress of the National Prison Association, Wines had this to say:

> The negro is not fitted for indoor life. He is not wanted as an industrial rival to the white man, and there is no possibility (and perhaps this is not desirable) of introducing into southern prisons those forms of carrying on industries by machinery common in our (Northern) prisons. . . . (Louisiana's prisons) are agricultural prisons such as we know nothing about, and I cannot imagine, except for the question of reformation (and they are not reformatory), anything more ideally suited to the conditions which exist down there than the large plantations on which the convict population is assembled, properly cared for, and governed. (Carleton 1971: 90)

During the 1890s and early part of the 1900s the convict leasing system began to decline because of changes in the labor market, subleasing, and the states' demands for high fees from contractors. These adverse factors reduced the comparative advantages of convict labor over free labor, but only Tennessee, North and South Carolina, and Louisiana actually abolished convict leasing before 1900 (Colvin 1997: 252). In Mississippi, leasing continued until 1916, but by the 1920s, only Florida and Alabama still maintained the practice. The decline in leasing did not spur prison-building programs because instead of being leased, prisoners were kept on state-owned prison farms and worked in state-owned fields and on public roads in chain gangs. Gradually, state farms began to replace convict leasing altogether (Colvin 1997: 252).

On state farms, prison walls were replaced with chains, dogs, and guns, and brutality was used to control the prisoners. In Louisiana, for example, in late 1944 Governor Jimmie H. Davis announced that flogging would no longer be practiced at the state prison farm at Angola, but evidence of floggings came to light in 1946, and the practice continued into the 1950s. At Angola, prison officers were provided with convicts to cook and clean for them as well as with accommodation and supplies and lived like "the passing plantation aristocracy" (Carleton 1971: 144). In 1967 it was revealed that in Georgia labor camps, inmates were chained together and required to break rocks. Working conditions became so bad that some inmates broke their own legs instead of the rocks, in order to escape the brutal conditions. These incidents came to national attention, and the labor camps were abolished (Anderson et al. 2000: 5).

By the 1960s chain gangs had disappeared from all the southern states. However, the actual conditions imposed during leasing and on chain gangs have left their legacy in the tough conditions that prevail in modern southern prisons. Chain gangs still retain their attraction to some; in 1995 Alabama announced that it would reintroduce chain gangs to their prison system (Colvin 1997: 253) (see later).

Reformatories, Parole, Probation, and Jails

Changes in penal thinking, resulting from the effects of massive population growth, the emergence of the city, and a general belief in the capacity of science and the scientific method to reform criminals, led to the development of the reformatory and probation and parole. Underpinning these new forms of punishment was the idea that a criminal could be provided individualized treatment under an indeterminate prison sentence. After release from incarceration on parole or being placed on probation, parole or probation officers would monitor the offender in the community and measure and assess the extent of his reformation based on a treatment plan. The reformatory, indeterminate sentencing, and systems of probation and parole brought new dimensions to the practice of punishment.

Reformatories

In the Progressive period between the 1880s to the 1930s there was a further change in penal thinking. Now there was a sense that government ought to be responsive to the needs of citizens and should adopt an activist strategy in dealing with the many problems confronting U.S. cities that had developed through a process of unchecked urbanization (Blomberg and Lucken 2000: 63). People had faith that government and science could solve problems, including those relating to crime, and that criminals themselves could be socially and economically reformed and rehabilitated. This shift in penal philosophy produced reformatories, indeterminate sentencing, and new types of punishment in the form of probation and parole that would permit reform to be continued even after a prisoner had left confinement. In effect, his confinement would be continued but in the community rather than in the prison. In this sense, as David Garland (1985: 23) recognizes, the prison was "decentered," that is, the position of the prison as the central institution for sanctioning crime was shifted, and it became only one of a range of institutions within a grid of penal sanctions.

This change occurred during the period of national population explosion as huge waves of immigrants entered the country. During the period between 1890 and 1917, nearly 18 million immigrants arrived in the United States (Blomberg and Lucken 2000: 66), and the cities saw tremendous growth with, for example, the population of Brooklyn growing from two and a half million to five and a half million between 1890 and 1920 (Blomberg and Lucken 2000: 67). The city provided immigrants with jobs, but it also bred loneliness and what early sociologists like Émile Durkheim called "anomie" in the form of unrealized expectations as compared to the promise and dream that was thought to define America.

In this era, scientific knowledge claimed to have an answer for all issues, including how to control crime and how best to punish criminals. The notion that crime had a biological basis and that criminals were "born that way" surfaced in the work of criminologists such as Cesare Lombroso. Biological theories argued that criminals were an inferior class and that criminality was inherited. This kind of thinking led logically to the *eugenics movement,* which argued that population studies could identify the good and the bad families and eliminate the bad ones through processes such as sterilization. In a broader sense, eugenics claims as its objective, the improvement in the "racial qualities" of generations to come, either physically or mentally, so that an improved "stock" will result, from which all traits of criminality have been eradicated (Garland 1985: 142).

This approach and other sociological explanations gained a following, and early sociologists and social observers began to study the cities and places where new immigrants worked and lived. There was general agreement that criminals could be "treated" individually, and that, given the appropriate information about an individual, a treatment regime could be designed to eradicate his or her criminal tendencies (Blomberg and Lucken 2000: 70). In 1870, in Cincinnati, at a meeting of the American Prison Society, these treatment notions were formalized in the form of a declaration of principles that explicitly accepted the premise that individualized care and the scientific treatment of criminals based on the medical model would reform the offenders. The recommendations from the meeting included establishing adult reformatories linked with indeterminate sentencing, classification systems, intensive academic and vocational training, labor, parole, and humane disciplinary regimes (Blomberg and Lucken 2000: 71).

The notion that a reformatory type of prison discipline ought to be introduced to replace an oppressive system was realized, and then only in imperfect form, in the Elmira Reformatory system introduced into New York State in 1876. Elmira housed first-time felons aged between sixteen and thirty who had received indeterminate sentences. Other reformatories were set up in Michigan in 1877, in Massachusetts in 1884, and in Pennsylvania in 1889, as well as in other parts of the country up to the end of the nineteenth century. One important element in the development of the reformatory model was the work of

Captain Alexander Maconochie, who came to Norfolk Island penal colony, off Australia, in 1840. He introduced a scheme involving the commutation of sentences for good behavior, under which every convict, according to the seriousness of his offense, was not sentenced to a fixed term of years but was allocated a certain number of points that he had to redeem before he could be released. An inmate could earn points for good behavior in the prison and through labor and study, and a speedy accumulation of points would be rewarded with a speedier release (Barnes 1972: 145). This scheme was later adopted into the Irish prison system developed by Walter Crofton in the middle of the twentieth century. Crofton added to the notion of the indeterminate sentence the practice of classifying inmates into groups of ascending grades through which each inmate had to pass in order to earn parole. The U.S. reformers who established the Elmira Reformatory in about 1875 followed the model set by the Irish prison system.

Parole

At about the same time the notion of an indeterminate sentence originated, Scottish reformer George Combe and English reformers Frederick and Matthew Davenport Hill were devising the *parole* system. The Irish model and English reforms attracted the attention of U.S. reformers, notably, Theodore W. Dwight and E. C. Wines of the New York Prison Association, Frank Sanborn of Massachusetts, Zebulon Brockway, the superintendent of the Detroit House of Correction, and Gaylord Hubbell, warden of Sing Sing Prison. This group prepared reports and recommendations urging the adoption of these new reforms into the United States, but were only able to secure acceptance in the treatment of younger first offenders. Zebulon Brockway was the first superintendent of Elmira Reformatory. There, the indeterminate sentence was employed and inmates were divided into classes through which they might ascend until eligible for parole as a result of their good conduct. This would enable them to leave the institution before the end of the maximum sentence imposed upon them.

In contrast to the Pennsylvania and Auburn systems, the Irish and Elmira models linked the term of a sentence of incarceration to progress made by an inmate on the path to ultimate reformation. Both systems, therefore, emphasized reformation as opposed to retaliation or deterrence. This represented an important landmark in the development of punishment in the United States, and by 1923 almost one-half of all offenders admitted to prisons received an indeterminate sentence (Blomberg and Lucken 2000: 73), with the typical minimum sentence being one year and a maximum sentence fixed. At the end of the minimum sentence, a prison board would decide upon a release date, and this would be determined by the number of credits the inmate had earned. Parole helped support the indeterminate sentence, because the decision to release an inmate could be made, with the knowledge that an offender would remain under the supervision of a parole agent. By 1900 every reformatory offered parole and twenty states had laws regulating parole for nonreformatory institutions like prisons and penitentiaries. By 1923 one-half of all releases from prison were under parole (Blomberg and Lucken 2000: 73).

Probation

Probation was not linked to the reformatory but did evolve during the same era. As a penal practice it was a good fit with the notion that offenders now had to be assessed and classified. As John Hagan (1983: 209) points out, the institution of probation put into operation the concept of individualized justice by means of the preparation and submission to the court of presentence reports describing the offender's social background and containing the individualized recommendations of a probation officer about sentencing. It also had the effect of including nonjudicial probation officers and parole officers in the penal system and inviting into the system information of a nonlegal nature in the form of probation reports (Garland 1985: 26).

The new penal practices of probation and community supervision constituted "normalizing practices," that is, their aim was the inculcation of definite norms and practices, and in this sense they sought (and continue to seek) to refashion an offender into a good citizen (Garland 1985: 238). Probation's origin seems to have been based on the efforts of John Augustus, a businessman in Boston who, between 1841 and 1859, personally posted bail and served as guardian to about two thousand offenders. Boston institutionalized Augustus's practice by implementing a professional probation service in 1878, and in 1891 a further law in the state of Massachusetts authorized a statewide system of probation (Blomberg and Lucken 2000: 74). Other states followed suit, and by 1930, the federal government and about thirty-six states had established probation systems.

Unlike parole, probation offered an alternative to incarceration and could be made available to those who did not require incarceration in order to achieve reform. Again, there was an emphasis on "knowledge" about the offender and on treatment provided. Here again, presentence reports provided courts with detailed information about the social and economic background of an offender as well as the probation officer's recommendations for the offender's treatment under probation. It was envisaged that a probation officer would supervise the daily life of an offender but would also befriend him and give good counsel. Caseloads would not be excessive so as to allow constant interchange between the probation officer and probationer, and a caseload of about fifty offenders was considered the optimum workload for each probation officer.

In a detailed study of the history and operation of the Elmira Reformatory, Alexander Pisciotta argues that the new penology practiced by Brockway set the stage for the U.S. correctional system for the next century. However, he maintains that despite benevolent reform aims, the Elmira Reformatory, along with other reformatories following that model, in fact practiced benevolent repression (Pisciotta 1994: 4). This took the form of a cruel and brutal regime that did not reform offenders or inculcate Christian values as was intended. Therefore, by the time the reformatory movement came to an end in 1920, no real changes had been effected in penal policy or practice.

At Elmira, Brockway employed a three-stage model to implement the process of transformation. The first stage was an initial interview at which Brockway explored the social, economic, and psychological reasons for the offender's deviance. The process was intended to identify the defect that needed correction. The inmate would then be assigned to an appropriate class and industry and sent to a cell. During the second stage, the inmate was awakened early, given a short time to dress, eat breakfast, and clean his cell, and then spent the hours between 7:30 a.m. and 4:30 p.m. laboring in the iron foundry, the shoe or broom factories, or at the farm. Here, the inmate was supposed to learn a trade and absorb the disciplined habits thought necessary to function successfully in the workplace, as well as learn to respect authority. There was a break for lunch at noon, and thirty minutes was allocated for the evening meal. From 5:00 p.m. to 6:00 p.m., Brockway conducted interviews and guest lecturers addressed inmates on a range of subjects from history to communications. At 7:00 p.m. all inmates attended school with seven levels of instruction offered.

Parole represented the third and final stage, and the five managers of the reformatory made up the parole board and considered various factors in deciding on release. Every inmate was required to secure employment before release would be granted, and the release criteria emphasized the Protestant work ethic and obedience (Pisciotta 1994: 20–21). The golden age at Elmira ran from 1883 to 1899, and it was during this period that Brockway actively promoted the Elmira model, so that by the turn of the century, it was regarded with awe and as the most important penal institution in the United States (Pisciotta 1994: 22). When inmate labor was prohibited because of labor union pressure, Brockway created a military model and system within Elmira, with inmates wearing uniforms, being assigned ranks, and divided into companies. They were required to march for up to eight hours each day. Visitors were welcome at Elmira, and Brockway himself gave guided tours of the establishment.

In examining the reality of the Elmira Reformatory, Pisciotta relies on the report of the New York State Board of Charities following its 1893–1894 investigation of Elmira. The investigation followed charges of brutal conduct made by some inmates against Brockway, and the inquiry revealed the difference between the promise and the reality of Elmira. The institution was judged by the investigators to be overcrowded, understaffed, and grossly mismanaged (Pisciotta 1994: 33). Specific charges brought against Brockway alleged that he had acted in a cruel, brutal, and inhumane manner in his treatment of the inmates, and these charges were proven.

In particular, the methods of punishment included "spanking" at interviews with a twenty-two-inch-long leather strap that was three inches wide and nearly one-quarter of an inch thick. In his defense to the charges, Brockway claimed that the severe forms of punishment employed at Elmira were an essential component of professional-scientific reform and justified their infliction as having therapeutic value (Pisciotta 1994: 38). Solitary confinement was also employed, and again Brockway justified this as a temporary inconvenience or deprivation, calling the cells used for this purpose as "rest-cure cells" (Pisciotta 1994: 40). The investigation found that Brockway used these and other forms of punishment to terrorize the inmates and maintain order within the institution. The State Board of Charities commented that, "the brutality practiced at the reformatory has no parallel in any modern penal institution in our country" (Pisciotta 1994: 42).

It was not only in the area of discipline that Elmira was found flawed. The parole board failed to properly consider applications for release on parole, spending an average of only one minute forty-eight seconds on each application (Pisciotta 1994: 48). Parole supervision was ineffective because the parole officer was grossly overworked and relied greatly on untrained amateur and volunteer assistants. So far as the inmates were concerned the reformatory was simply a prison in disguise, and many applied to be transferred out of the reformatory believing they would receive better treatment at a penitentiary or prison.

Overall, Brockway did not deny allegations made against him of whipping inmates, punching them in the face, striking them with his whip, and chaining them for months in so-called rest-cure cells on a diet of bread and water, as well as using corporal punishment to extract confessions. He argued that harsh methods were justified because of the mental and moral backwardness of the inmates, and he told his critics that his treatment methods were consistent with the new laws of scientific criminology (Pisciotta 1994: 54). Faced with the report's harsh criticisms of the state's premier institution and the supporters of Brockway, both in the United States and overseas, Governor Roswell Flower followed his political instincts and appointed a new committee to reconsider the findings. A majority of this new committee rejected the Board of Charities report, however, a minority report submitted by the judicial member of the committee supported the findings of the Charities Board. The governor accepted the majority report, and the final outcome of the investigation was minimal for Brockway. He and his staff kept their jobs, and Elmira's reputation was secured. Now Elmira is a maximum-security institution for felons regardless of age.

These punishment reforms, like the indeterminate sentence,

failed to provide much in the way of psychological tools to assist in the reformation of inmates. The system of discipline did not change but remained repressive and even despotic and cruel. No significant attempts were made to educate inmates or to introduce them to the idea of responsibility and accountability for their crimes. They continued to be locked away within a regime that was repressive and cruel and offered little hope for the future.

Although parole and indeterminate sentences offered prison administrations a way of dealing with overcrowded prisons and a means of controlling prisoner conduct, these powers could easily be abused. If an offender did not comply with the prison regime he could be detained for much greater periods so that disparities could easily develop between the amount of time prisoners served for similar offenses. Unfortunately, the scientific approach to treatment was not mirrored in the parole release decisions that were vested in prison boards and officials who failed to conduct proper inquiries and who lacked specific release criteria. As for parole as a form of rehabilitation, it had little to offer beyond an emphasis on work. For example, parolees had to remain employed, submit monthly reports about their conduct at work from their employers, could not change jobs without permission from their parole officers, and at all times had to conduct themselves in a sober manner and avoid associating with undesirables (Blomberg and Lucken 2000: 78–79).

Probation suffered from similar defects as parole in that probation officers were not adequately trained for the tasks they were required to perform, especially in providing a treatment regime, and many probation officers gained their jobs through political connections. Their salaries were low, and their work facilities inadequate. Personal contact with offenders soon became infrequent and because professionalism did not emerge as a guiding principle of probation work, many presentence reports were little more than collections of gossip (Blomberg and Lucken 2000: 79). Increased and finally overwhelming caseloads mitigated any possibility of affording appropriate treatment to offenders, and it was not uncommon for an individual probation officer to have a caseload of more than one hundred fifty probationers.

At Elmira, offenders were studied by the "experts," and

inmates were referred to as "students" or "patients." In fact, Elmira was often termed the "college on the hill" and the "reformatory hospital" (Blomberg and Lucken 2000: 71). The indeterminate sentence was intended to result in offenders developing self-discipline, because release dates were dependent on demonstrating reformation. The daily regime within the reformatory comprised paid work and job training, exercise, and a proper diet. In relation to grading at Elmira, if the offender followed the institutional rules for at least six months from the time he was committed, he could ascend to the first grade, which allowed privileges such as spring mattresses, a uniform, a daily writing allowance, and access to books and improved food. Conversely, demotion would result in an inferior class of uniform, lockstep marching, and denial of mail and visiting privileges (Blomberg and Lucken 2000: 72). Work in the reformatory contrasted with penitentiary work because reformatory work earned the inmate pay and had the aim of inculcating industriousness as a new social attribute and a means of transforming economic worthlessness to worthiness (Blomberg and Lucken 2000: 72).

Jails

In the county jails, conditions did not improve until in the nineteenth century, when changes were made in the composition of the jail population. By that time, jails had to house not only those awaiting trial but also those convicted of minor offenses, who were serving their sentences in the jail. The debtors who had made up a good proportion of the jail population in the colonial period had by now been removed, this practice having been abolished in the decade after 1828 through the efforts of the Boston Prison Discipline Society and the democratic government of Andrew Jackson.

Eugenics and Punishment

As noted previously, the early part of the twentieth century saw the birth of the eugenics movement and associated genetic theories of crime. The movement can be seen as part of the battle against immorality and vice, and it was associated with fears about the effects of large-scale immigration into the United States, which was seen by some as threatening the values of those already established in the country and polluting the nation with inferior peoples. The proponents of eugenics believed that "defectives" and "degenerates" would engulf "true Americans" and their values, and the only solution was to sterilize them. The rationale was that this would prevent them from breeding and overwhelming the nation.

One of the foremost proponents of this new approach to crime was Cesare Lombroso, whose focus was on the individual criminal as an animal. Using methods adopted from physical anthropology, he measured thousands of offenders and compiled a list of their physical abnormalities, which he associated with "the criminal type," and by 1887 he had catalogued many "suspicious" traits. For example, possessing an excessively large jaw or a receding forehead typified, in his view, physical characteristics of a criminal. Lombroso's theories were widely accepted in the United States (Christianson 1998: 192), especially in the new field of criminology, and researchers naturally turned to the prisons to test out his theories and conducted experiments in a number of penitentiaries. From about 1880, the field of physical anthropology gained a respectable following in academic and professional journals that focused on criminals and viewed the individual offender as both a victim of heredity and as someone who perpetuated that inherited criminality.

Overall, these efforts expressed and symbolized a search for the causes of crime. By the 1880s, physicians and social scientists had become the most vigorous proponents of the new scientific theories, and the physician at Elmira Reformatory, Dr. Hamilton Wey, was especially influential in urging that criminals be studied like guinea pigs in a laboratory setting (Christianson 1998: 195). Starting around 1910, Katherine Bement Davis began psychological testing at Bedford Hills State Reformatory for Women in New York and John D. Rockefeller created a Laboratory of Social Hygiene at Bedford Hills, where female inmates were measured and tested and probed for the causes of their criminality. Their intelligence was tested, their family history explored and tabulated, and their physical characteristics compared with those of noncriminal women.

The eugenics movement spread throughout the country developing into specialties like intelligence testing. Those engaged in this testing claimed that feeblemindedness was a major cause of criminality, and psychologists like Henry H. Goddard of Princeton explained "every feeble-minded person is a potential criminal" (Christianson 1998: 196). Typical of this thinking are the statements in a report of 1919 to the governor of Kansas, "All the feeble-minded lack self-control. . . . Their immoral tendencies and lack of self control make the birth rate among them unusually high. . . . We know that the social evil is fed from the ranks of feeble-minded women, and that feeble-minded men and women spread venereal disease. . . . their tendencies to pauperism and crime would seem to be sufficient grounds to justify the claim that the feeble-minded are a menace to society" (Christianson 1998: 198).

Indiana was the first state to legislate a policy of sterilization. In 1907 it passed legislation declaring sterilization to be official state policy and pronouncing heredity to be a major player in the transmission of crime. However, this law extended beyond criminal conduct into "idiocy and imbecility." It required every institution in Indiana that contained criminals, "idiots, rapists and imbeciles" to add two surgeons to its staff. Inmates could be recommended to the surgeons for assessment about whether, in light of their condition, they should be prevented from procreating. If procreation was considered inadvisable, the surgeon was empowered to operate to prevent it (Friedman 1993: 335–336).

Similarly, in 1909, California passed legislation that allowed for the "asexualization" of prisoners who had twice committed sexual offenses, had three convictions for any other crime, or were serving a life sentence, if there was evidence that the inmate was "a moral and sexual pervert" (Friedman 1993: 336). Ultimately about half the states passed eugenics laws, many of which did not discriminate between criminals and the mentally challenged. In 1927 the Supreme Court upheld eugenics legislation that endorsed the sterilization of a white woman in Virginia who was eighteen years old and "feeble minded." Justice Oliver Wendell Holmes Jr. in his judgment wrote that it was better for society not to delay "to execute degenerate offspring for crime" and that society should deny the ability to procreate to those who were "manifestly unfit" (Friedman 1993: 337).

Linked to the eugenics movement was the supposed science of criminal anthropology. It was contended by its advocates that analyzing the physical features of persons would reveal criminality, and as late as 1939, anthropologist E. A. Hooton argued, like

Lombroso, that there was such a person as "the born criminal" who could be identified from an analysis of physical attributes and defects. He especially believed that "low and sloping foreheads" were indicative of criminality and thought that a criminal's nose tended to be a particular shape. Along with the desire to control and purify the new waves of immigrants who overwhelmingly constituted the dangerous classes, it is clear that there was a substantial element of racism in eugenics policies. In 1942 the Supreme Court struck down an Oklahoma statute that permitted the forced sterilization of a person who had been convicted of three or more felonies involving moral turpitude. The court found that the statute violated the equal protection clause because it drew irrational and unjustifiable distinctions. The court also warned that marriage and procreation were basic civil rights (Friedman 1993: 339).

The Rehabilitative Ideal

From the 1900s until the 1960s, penal policymakers pursued the objective of rehabilitation and focused on a search for the causes of crime. In 1900 there emerged from the newly established University of Chicago the so-called Chicago School, comprising a group of sociologists who used social research techniques like interviewing and studies of city areas and types and frequency of crimes to try to formulate theories about the causes of crime. Many different theories emerged from this research, but the main focus was on the individual characteristics of offenders, their group and peer associations, and their areas of residence. In penal policies the maxim "more is better" prevailed as correctional and penal establishments expanded with the rationale that with more services there would be a greater capacity to provide individual treatment and rehabilitate offenders (Blomberg and Lucken 2000: 100). The overall framework established by theorists and by studies of crime during this period was to focus on the individual offender and on the rehabilitative ideal, which called for the identification of the causes of crime in order to fashion strategies of punishment and correction that would address these causes.

Along with theorizing about crime and punishment came a major growth in the criminal justice system as a whole, including those aspects concerned with the punishment of offenders. Clearly, the notion of individualized treatment carried with it an obligation to provide expertise and services within the prison and through probation and parole outside the prison to meet offender needs. The perception that "more is better" envisaged multiple responses to the multiple causes of crime as well as to offenders (Blomberg and Lucken 2000: 107). Accordingly, during this period of expansion, attempts were made to professionalize criminal justice services, including probation and parole as well as services provided in prisons in order to fulfill the promise of rehabilitation through treatment fashioned for each individual offender. The era of specialization began with a differentiation of prisons into minimum, medium, and maximum security thus further classifying the experience of incarceration according to individual offender needs while also taking account of risk factors.

A team of professionals was to address offender treatment needs, and sociologists, psychologists, caseworkers, and vocational counselors entered the prison to exhaustively examine and script each offender with the aim of planning the most appropriate therapeutic regime for them (Blomberg and Lucken 2000: 108). The same team would initially classify the inmate, review progress, and recommend a release on parole at the appropriate time. Generally, treatment programs provided therapy, attempted to strengthen the educational level of the inmate, and included vocational programs that would render the inmate capable of coping with the world outside the prison upon his release. Techniques like group and individual counseling as well as psychological testing were deployed in the cause of rehabilitation. In 1929 the Federal Bureau of Prisons declared rehabilitation to be the fundamental aim and purpose of incarceration, and, reflecting this emphasis and focus, in 1954 the American Prison Association changed its name to the American Correctional Association (Blomberg and Lucken 2000: 109).

Parole evolved from a community-based sanction in the first half of the twentieth century into a clinical model, beginning in the 1950s, that, like the treatment provided in prisons, emphasized the professional ability of parole agents to design treatment programs responsive to an offender's individual needs and concerns. By the 1970s parole was being criticized for administrative and professional shortcomings. Parole board members seldom had any professional qualifications and were criticized for meeting in secret and for exercising a wide discretion but still failing to provide any reasoned decisions. Thus, parole decisions became arbitrary and cases were routinely disposed of in three to six minutes (Holt 1998: 28).

Overall, some suggest that during this period, the ideal of rehabilitation through the prison process or the probation and parole process was not realized and that actual practice came to be characterized by a managerial approach that was concerned largely with control and punishment (Blomberg and Lucken 2000: 113). This widening of control and supervision was reflected in the expansion of these penal services and their increased cost. For example, between 1902 and the 1960s, expenditure on state-run penal systems increased from $14 million to $1.51 billion (Blomberg and Lucken 2000: 114).

Punishment in the Community

The reforms of the Progressive period described above established the basis for penal policy that would endure until quite recent times. Generally, it was agreed that a therapeutic approach toward individual offenders would work best in solving the problem of crime.

During a relatively brief period between 1960 and 1970 a movement advocating informal punishments supervised in the community gained favor in penal policymaking circles. The movement's call was "Less Is Best" (Blomberg and Lucken 2000: 153) meaning that the correctional system had failed to stem the tide of crime and it was time to go to the community for solutions. It was thought that informal solutions within the community could succeed where the coercion and force of the correctional system had failed. Advocates of correction in the community were supported by research studies that seemed to show that prisons did not prevent recidivism and that criminality had much to do with the way society labeled persons as criminals rather than psychological and environmental causes (Dean-Myrda and Cullen 1998: 11). It was thought that diverting offenders out of the criminal justice system and into the community would enable reintegration back into the community. The idea seemed attractive for other reasons also. Cost would be saved if offenders could work in the community at the same time as they underwent punishment, and programs would be able to apply intensive therapeutic techniques far more conveniently within the community than in prison. The halfway house would replace the prison, and offenders would come under the scrutiny of the community rather than the impersonal state.

Conservative thinkers attacked these notions about punishment in the community as being "soft on criminals," and liberals warned that these new ideas would "widen the net" of state control over citizens because offenders who might otherwise have been given only a short period of probation would instead be placed in these programs in the community.

During this same period, crime came to be viewed as an issue of national security when politicians seized upon it as a signature political issue. In 1968 The Omnibus Crime Control and Safe Streets Act was passed establishing the Law Enforcement Assistance Administration with a mandate to implement a national strategy to wage the "war on crime" in the United States. The federal government provided grants to assist with law enforcement, and in 1965 a President's Commission on Law Enforcement and the Administration of Justice was established. It produced nine reports specific to crime and criminal justice, and various recommendations were ultimately published in 1967.

Now there was a distinct turning away from professionalized managerial solutions to crime and punishment in favor of alternative dispositions using diversion in the community. Individual treatment was now regarded as unrealistic as well as overly optimistic, and great concern was expressed about labeling offenders, that is, classifying behavior as criminal behavior and widening the net of the criminal justice system. Juvenile justice was one area where informal sanctions were thought likely to be highly effective and a focus developed on diverting youth out of institutions and into programs that might be administered by criminal justice agencies or agencies located within the community. Unfortunately, one consequence of these programs was to widen the net still further because juveniles whose conduct might ordinarily have merited only an admonition were now channeled into diversion programs. In some cases diversion practices were applied to youth who would not previously have entered the juvenile justice system at all (Blomberg and Lucken 2000: 160).

In 1974, the enactment of the Juvenile Justice and Delinquency Prevention Act gave further impetus to the diversion approach. It advocated a much-reduced use of confinement for juveniles and replacing confinement with programs of community sanctions. The states were provided with funding for this purpose, and many made radical changes to their juvenile practice, including, for example, Massachusetts, which in 1972, simply shut down all juvenile institutions in the state. Of special importance was the promotion of the policy that so-called status offenders, that is, runaways and those youth who had committed acts judged delinquent but not criminal in nature, should not be subjected to the juvenile justice system at all, and these offenses should be decriminalized (Blomberg and Lucken 2000: 163). Unfortunately, studies of these initiatives conducted in the 1970s showed that diversion programs did not really affect offending rates and that there was little difference between those kept in institutions and those diverted out of them (Blomberg and Lucken 2000: 164).

For adult offenders, community-based programs for nonviolent and minor offenders were developed with mixed results. Michael Tonry (1999: 5–22) provides a useful overview of these community penalties and an assessment of their efficacy. Broadly it can be said that community penalties do not and never have attained the level of acceptance in the United States that they enjoy in Europe and Canada. The reason seems to be that Americans generally favor punitive punishments, and both the general public and the courts regard community penalties as inadequate forms of punishment.

Apart from probation what other forms of punishment are there in the community? Tonry (1999) identifies the following: boot camps (discussed more fully in Chapter 2); intensive supervision; house arrest and electronic monitoring; day-reporting centers; community service; and monetary penalties. Each will briefly be discussed.

Boot Camps

The concept of the *boot camp* as a form of punishment is taken from the military, and boot camps rely on structured forms of discipline to administer a short, sharp shock to offenders. Research has shown that most boot camp programs have no effect at all on recidivism. Many have drawn their populations from the front end, that is, from those who would not have been sent to prison anyway, and in many camps, up to half of all offenders fail to complete the program. Some camps save money that would otherwise have been spent on housing offenders in prisons, and these are the programs to which offenders are sentenced instead of undertaking a longer sentence in prison. There is a wide variation in the length of these programs, some running for ninety days and others for one hundred eight days. Many stress discipline and self-control, but others are broader in scope and offer drug abuse treatment and rehabilitation. Most admit only males 25 years old and younger (Tonry 1999: 10). Todd Clear and Anthony Braga (1998: 214) point out that shock incarceration programs like boot camps target first-time offenders and exclude those convicted of violent crimes or with prior records of imprisonment. Boot camps often specify minimum and maximum age limits for participation, and by designating very limited target groups, boot camps are not faced with the problems dealt with by correctional systems.

Intensive Supervision

Known as ISP and used for probationers and parolees, the practice of *intensive supervision* was adopted by most states in the 1980s and 1990s. During this period, penal conservatives wanted a way to be "tough on crime" that would also avoid any more prison overcrowding and thus increase prison expenditure while at the same time preserving the policy of punishment in the community. The answer was to develop the use of *"intermediate sanctions,"* that is, penalties lying somewhere between parole and probation that emphasize intensive supervision and compliance with conditions. Essentially, they provide a higher level of supervision and control of probationers and parolees. This form of punishment proved to be most effective in ensuring that offenders were punished further for technical violations of the conditions of their release into the community. The resulting issue faced by policymakers was whether or not to return violators to prison for technical violations, and thereby contribute to further overcrowding in prisons, or to ignore the technical violation and minimize the supposed effect of the intensive supervision (Dean-Myrda and Cullen 1998: 14). According to Petersilia (1998b: 68) the rationale for intermediate sanctions includes the following:

- They will save tax dollars by providing low-cost alternatives to incarceration for those going to prison or to jail.
- They have a deterrent value.

- They offer protection to the community because they incorporate more controls than traditional probation orders.
- They can be useful in rehabilitating offenders, especially those such as drug offenders who are undergoing treatment programs.

Issues associated with intermediate sanctions focus on the use made of these programs. As stated, they were originally designed for those who would be sentenced to prison or jail but ended up in practice being used mainly for high-risk probation offenders. The programs themselves have mainly focused on surveillance and monitoring as opposed to treatment, one of their supposed virtues. Essentially, these programs are punitive in nature and their viability in the future depends on a realistic assessment of what achievements are anticipated (Petersilia 1998b: 70). Interestingly, in a study conducted in Minnesota in 1994 by Joan Petersilia and Piper Deschenes (1998: 149), inmates were asked to rank various sentencing options, including intermediate sanctions. They ranked five years of intensive probation supervision as harsher than one year in prison but not as harsh as three years in prison. Five years in prison was judged to be more severe than any other sanction and had no equivalent among intermediate sanctions. This tends to suggest that inmates at least do not equate criminal punishment solely with incarceration and at some level intensive supervision probation is dreaded as much as a prison sentence.

House Arrest and Electronic Monitoring

House arrest, or house confinement, can be ordered on its own or as part of a sentence of probation or parole. In practice, most offenders sentenced to house arrest are permitted to leave their homes for employment purposes and to take part in treatment programs. Sometimes, but not always, house arrest is accompanied by *electronic monitoring* using bracelets. Originally, these programs were used primarily for cases of driving while intoxicated and for minor property offenses, and the programs are now quite large in some states. For example, in 1993 Florida had some 13,000 offenders on house arrest. Research suggests that these programs draw offenders who were otherwise bound for prison rather than for probation, but the situation is far from clear, and there is an absence of sophisticated evaluations of this sanction (Tonry 1999: 12). It has been noted that the use of electronic monitoring seems unrelated to crime itself and is directed toward program compliance only, so that when there is a failure it is usually not associated with reducing or preventing crime. In other words, monitoring and supervision become ends in themselves and are not associated with crime control at all (Clear and Braga 1998: 214).

Day-Reporting Centers

Day-reporting centers are locations where an offender spends the day under supervision and surveillance, taking part in treatment programs. Day-reporting centers date from the mid-1980s. Many of the centers are run by correctional departments, into which prisoners released early from jail or prison have been placed for treatment, and others are true sentencing options with programs lasting from forty days to nine months (Tonry 1999: 13).

Community Service

Community service is used mainly as a condition of probation or as a penalty for minor offenses such as traffic cases. As the name indicates, this is an unpaid service that benefits the community and is performed by offenders as part (or all) of their sentence.

Monetary Penalties

Although many offenses carry a fine as a penalty and millions of fines are imposed every year, the *monetary penalty* as a form of punishment does not have many advocates, primarily because judges do not regard it as a viable alternative to incarceration or probation (Tonry 1999: 14).

Restorative Justice

Restorative justice is another relatively new concept in community punishment, which has its advocates and opponents. Although not widely practiced as a sanction in the United States it has been used in some states and is well developed in Australia, New Zealand, and Canada, especially where offenses involve indigenous people of those countries. It is difficult to offer any precise definition of what constitutes restorative justice. Kathleen Daly (2002: 57) suggests that it includes a variety of practices at different stages of the court process that take the form of diversion away from court action, or actions taken at any stage of the court action such as meetings between the offender and victim. One definition is that restorative justice is "a process whereby all the parties with a stake in a particular offence come together to resolve collectively how to deal with the aftermath of the offence and its implications for the future" (Marshall in Daly 2002: 57–58). Generally, the following constitute the common elements of what is termed restorative justice: an emphasis on the victim in criminal cases; a process that involves all the relevant parties associated with the crime in discussing its effects and what should be done to repair the harm caused by the offense; and decision making by both the court and lay persons (Daly 2002: 58).

According to George Herbert Mead, there are two methods of responding to crime, one that shows hostility to the offender and calls for retribution, and the other that is more constructive and tries to comprehend why there has been a breakdown in this individual and seeks to repair that situation. Most restorative justice proponents favor the latter approach and do not regard the offender with hostility (Daly 2002: 59). The discussion of the effect of the crime that takes place between victim and offender, often with relatives and others present, is often termed "conferencing," which joins together forms of justice with elements of informal justice that may include elements of ethnic and traditional values from indigenous communities. A good example is the practice known as "peacemaking" in the Navajo system of justice, which blends traditional Navajo concepts of justice with Western forms of law.

In his overview of community penalties, Tonry (1999) points out that three major obstacles to the increased use of these penalties exist: the U.S. perception that only incarceration counts as punishment; the idea that the severity of a punishment should vary according to the seriousness of the crime, meaning in practice, that sentencing guidelines allow courts only to consider an offender's crime and criminal history and to disregard character and social and economic conditions relevant to the criminality that might suggest another penalty than incarceration; and net widening, that is, the tendency to use these penalties to punish those who would not otherwise have received any penalty at all.

The situation in the United States is markedly in contrast to that in Europe, where, for example, community penalties are widely employed to reduce the prison populations.

Andrew Von Hirsch (1998: 189) draws attention to some of the ethical and punishment issues surrounding intermediate sanctions, which operate as punishment in the community. The question of proportionality is one such issue, and the basic question is whether a particular community sanction is punishment that is proportionate to the offense committed. For example, intensive supervision often involves stringent conditions in supervision and reporting. Community service involves what is in effect forced labor, and the question is whether the offenses involved are sufficiently serious to make such sanctions an appropriate response. In many cases the answer will be negative because, for example, ISP tends to be applied to those convicted of the least serious offenses.

Another concern is that a particular punishment must be capable of being justified on its own merits. It is not enough to say that ISP is warranted because the alternative is imprisonment. Von Hirsch (1998: 192) also notes that issues of privacy can arise in ISP because offenders are obliged to accept home visits by enforcement agents.

Von Hirsch (1998: 193) has drawn attention to the fact that offenders ought to be treated with dignity. Philosopher Jeffrie Murphy asserts that a punishment will be unjust if it "is of such a nature as to be degrading or dehumanizing (inconsistent with human dignity)" (Von Hirsch 1998: 193). Despite their conviction, offenders are and remain members of the mortal community and do not surrender their right to be treated as such on being convicted of an offense. Thus as Von Hirsch (1998: 194) puts it "punishments. . . . Should be of the kind that can be endured with self possession by persons of reasonable fortitude." He suggests that the notion of an "acceptable penal content" would identify those deprivations that could be suffered by offenders according to the test of reasonable fortitude and provides examples of such punishments that include elements that humble or make an offender ridiculous in the eyes of others. Applying this principle to punishment in the community, Von Hirsch argues that punishments such as forcing a convicted drunken driver to carry a sticker on his or her car bumper indicating his or her drunken habits would offend against this test.

Probation and parole represent punishment in the community,

but both have run into major structural and policy problems. Thus, by 1979 the average caseload of a parole agent was seventy-nine, leaving only a few minutes each month for each parolee after having dealt with administrative duties (Holt 1998: 29). Between 1975 and 1985 indeterminate sentencing using parole was replaced in almost every state with determinate sentencing, and between 1976 and 1979 seven states abolished all or almost all of their parole boards' discretion. Many more states followed suit in later years and in other ways limited the powers of their parole boards, for example, by requiring that a minimum term be served before a prisoner could be considered for parole, or that life without parole be served for certain offenses (Holt 1998: 31).

By 1995 release on parole had been largely abolished in seventeen states as a result of these and other measures (Holt 1998: 32). With the advent of prison overcrowding, the role of the parole board has become more important as states look to parole boards to reduce overcrowding and minimize the proportion of state budgets spent on incarcerating offenders. Paradoxically, at the same time parole boards are trying to reduce prison populations they are also revoking parole and returning parolees to prison at a much greater rate, and between 1983 and 1993 the percentage of admissions to prison made up by parole violators increased from 19.6 to 30.2. In 1993 technical violations made up about 17 percent of all prison admissions.

The position of the parole board is no doubt difficult. The public views parole as a privilege, and one breach is considered sufficient for revocation of parole and return to prison. Regrettably parole boards add to their difficulties by imposing a large number of conditions on parolees, so that technical violations are more likely to occur. For example, in 1988 parole boards were surveyed and 78 percent indicated that among the conditions they routinely imposed were "gainful employment" and to support "family and all dependants." These are likely among the most difficult conditions for a released prisoner to fulfill, given the disadvantages of obtaining employment with a felony conviction on the parolee's record (Holt 1998: 36). At year-end 2002 some 753,141 persons were on parole in the United States, and in that year the nation's parole population expanded by 2.8 percent, a rate almost double the average annual growth since 1995. More than two out of every five persons placed on parole and discharged from supervision returned to incarceration because of a rule violation or a new offense (Glaze 2003).

Probation followed a similar path as parole, but probation officer caseloads expanded until they routinely exceeded one hundred cases, and with this came the need to routinize probation control, reducing a focus on the treatment ethic in favor of simply providing a basic surveillance service. Additionally, although probation was initially seen as suitable for misdemeanor offenses, nowadays almost half of all offenders placed on probation have felony convictions (Petersilia 1998a: 19). Currently, the gap between the role of parole agents and probation officers is closing as the more treatment-inclined traditions of probation are eroded in favor of a sterner parole-like approach to probationers. Police now work with probation officers in law enforcement operations, and in many states probation officers carry guns, something that at one time would have been thought quite inconsistent with their role and functions. At year-end 2002, 3,995,165 persons were on probation in the United States and 50 percent of those had been convicted of a felony. Twenty-four percent were on probation for a drug offense (Glaze 2003: 1).

Vigilantism

Forms of extralegal punishment such as vigilantism also figure in the history of punishment. Vigilantism has been explained or defined as "organized, extralegal movements, the members of which take the law into their own hands" (Friedman 1993: 179). Vigilante movements were to be found in the United States as early as the eighteenth century, for example, the South Carolina Regulator movement of the late 1760s. All the principal movements emanate from the South (Friedman 1993: 180). The absence of a strong formal legal system permits vigilantism to flourish, and this was certainly true of the South where organizations were set up to dispense their own form of law, such as the vigilante group called "Regulating Horn" operating in Montgomery, Alabama, in the 1820s. Its members tarred and feathered those adjudged guilty and ran them out of town.

The principal period of vigilantism began in the 1850s and continued into the turn of the twentieth century in the U.S. West. For example, in San Francisco in the 1850s there were two vigilante committees. At that time San Francisco was expanding because of the gold rush. According to local merchants the city was in the grip of crime, and when a merchant was robbed in

February 1851, beaten on the head, and rendered unconscious, a large angry crowd gathered when the police arrested two suspects, both from Australia. One merchant in the crowd demanded the crowd to convene a popular court immediately, and accordingly the crowd conducted a trial of sorts on the spot, appointing three of its members as judges and a jury and a prosecutor. The Australians were defended by some local lawyers and escaped with their lives, when the jury could not be satisfied that they had actually committed the robbery and assault. The prisoners were returned to the proper authorities and were later tried and convicted (Freidman 1993: 180–181). This incident was merely the beginning, and in June 1851, a so-called Committee of Vigilance was established and was active for a while, directing its attention to other Australians and succeeding in hanging four of them as criminals. One of them had been caught in the act of stealing a safe and was afforded a trial of sorts, given the death sentence, and hanged on the spot. The other criminals were simply expelled from town by the committee.

In 1856 a second vigilante committee was formed following an incident in which an Italian gambler shot and killed a U.S. marshal. He was arrested and tried but could not be convicted. This frustrated the local merchants who had no confidence in the local legal system. When yet another killing occurred, this time the culprit, a newspaper editor (who had been crusading against evil), and the Italian gambler were both seized and hanged from projecting beams on the roof of a building in Sacramento. The vigilante committee formed over this incident was much larger, comprising more than six thousand members. Two more men were hanged and thirty or so rowdy people forced out of the city. In the end the committee decided to stand for elective office and seek political power for itself (Friedman 1993: 182).

The concept of a vigilante committee involves an appropriation by that committee of the law for its own ends. Thus, such committees perceived themselves, not to be acting in vengeance, but as enforcers of the law in place of the state, which they usually considered too weak or ineffectual to protect the community. Thus, these committees did not see themselves as acting contrary to law or even as defying the law. A good example is the Vigilance Committee of Payette, Idaho, which operated according to a written constitution and bylaws, gave an accused the right to trial by jury, and imposed punishments including banishment, public horsewhipping, and capital punishment.

Vigilantes seemed to attract the approval of the public and were seen as putting an end to the reigns of terror by providing retribution to criminals and restoring law and order. In *Vigilantes of Montana,* published in 1864, Thomas Dimsdale gives accounts of various vigilante activities in Montana that he much admired. In one instance a person who caused public disruption and appeared out of control was warned by the vigilante committee to behave. However, he ignored these admonishments and even threatened a prominent vigilante. He was arrested by the committee and hanged. In another case a woman, Ella Watson, was lynched in Wyoming. She was a prostitute and also engaged in cattle rustling, yet it proved impossible to convict her of this offense. After repeated warnings she and her companion in crime were hanged in 1889.

Similar to the vigilante groups and movements was the terror that appeared in the South in the form of the Ku Klux Klan between 1868 and 1871. As Edward Ayers puts it, following the Civil War two groups in the south tried to "impose their vision of order upon the South." These groups were the Freedmen's Bureau and the Ku Klux Klan. Mississippi and South Carolina enacted their "Black Codes" in 1865 and widened the possible punishments for crimes that were considered crimes that only blacks would commit, namely, vagrancy, rape, arson, and burglary (Ayers 1984: 151). The Freedmen's Bureau allocated food and clothing to the poor and aided black schools, but its overall objective was to interpose the power of the federal government between the former slaves and the former masters. The bureau wanted the states to guarantee a status of legal equality to blacks but at the same time sent the message to blacks that they would have to survive in the South through their own efforts in the same way as northern workers did (Ayers 1984: 152).

The Ku Klux Klan intended to violently resist any attempts by blacks to gain political power in the aftermath of the Civil War. The Klansmen, unlike most vigilantes in other parts of the United States of that period, wore strange garb, comprising white sheets and cone-shaped hats, and rode at night on horses. The Klan used all methods to achieve its objectives, including whipping, burning, raping, and even killing their victims. In one case in Alabama in 1870 the Klan murdered a black legislator simply because he had been successful and had influence with his own people, and in Mississippi the Klan whipped another man who abused a white who owed him money. The Klan did not confine its activities to blacks and was ready to attack whites thought to be assisting blacks or opposing Klan activities (Friedman 1993: 188). The Klan played a vital part in bringing about the restoration of white control after the end of the Civil War, and although the Klan clearly had an agenda that called for the reinstatement and reinforcement of white control this was masked by its portrayal of itself as an organization concerned only with black crime and lawlessness. In 1868, one member of a Georgia Klan referred to the Klan as "a police, rather than a military force, an underground and nocturnal constabulary" (Ayers 1984: 163). In the North some were convinced that the Klan was indeed exercising a policing role, and one comment from a northerner drew a parallel between the terror of vigilantism and the terror of black theft and violence as if one were balancing out the other (Ayers 1984: 163). In 1924 the Klan claimed a membership of about two million (Emmanuel 1996: 220).

Black freedmen did not simply stand by and allow vigilante activities to dominate them and their lives. They resisted and struck back, and in one such incident, for example, in 1867, a white man who killed a black man during a fight in Greensboro, North Carolina, was seized by a large crowd of blacks who might have taken vengeance but for the efforts of the local marshal. The local newspaper reported that as the killer was being taken to jail in the custody of the marshal the blacks followed in large gangs asking for his life. At the courthouse some two hundred blacks armed with various weapons threatened to take the prisoner away from the marshal and lynch him but were persuaded to desist (Ayers 1984: 157). In another incident in 1867, after hearing of the murder of a black by his white employer in Greene County, Georgia, about forty neighboring blacks gathered together and marched on the white man's house, surrounded it, and opened fire on the premises, resulting in the white man being wounded severely. Apparently, the blacks made no attempt to hide their identity and were actually arrested (Ayers 1984: 157).

It was not until the 1870s that the Klan's activities began to die out and by that time the white man had consolidated his hold on power in the South as segregation and Jim Crow laws succeeded the violence of the Klan. Unlike other vigilante groups, the Klan did not claim to be upholding the law. Their movement was quite simply racist and aimed to terrorize and punish those blacks who dared to move into local positions of power or who otherwise offended against the racist beliefs of the Klan and its members.

Lynching

As Friedman (1993: 189) points out, the term *lynching* derives from the South and immortalizes the name of Colonel Charles Lynch of Bedford County, Virginia, a justice of the peace, who, in the 1780s organized an extralegal group to catch suspected Tory sympathizers in the period of the Revolutionary War, conduct trials, and inflict punishment, mainly in the form of whipping (Zimring 2003: 90). Essentially, lynching constituted a savage method of social control supported by large sections of society. The term lynching refers to groups of citizens killing one or more other citizens without the sanction of government (Zimring 2003: 90). As W. Fitzhugh Brundage (1993: 2–8) observes, in the South lynching was not an isolated event but a systematic, organized, and coherent expression of the social structure at that time.

One instance of lynching shows that as a practice it bears many similarities to vigilantism. In 1882, a white drifter in Tampa, Florida, broke into a businessman's home and assaulted his sister with intent to rape. The drifter was caught and placed in jail, but an angry crowd gathered, broke him out of the jail, and hanged him from the nearest tree (Friedman 1993: 189–190). In this case, instead of waiting for the law to take its course, the mob wanted to take direct action on the basis that the honor of the assaulted woman and her family demanded prompt and appropriate action to avenge what had occurred. As Friedman puts it, southerners distrusted the state and preferred an approach that demonstrated and effected personal justice. For them there existed state law and their own personal code of lynch law (Friedman 1993: 190). Between 1882 and 1927, 510 blacks were lynched in Georgia and 517 were lynched over the same period in Mississippi (Emmanuel 1996: 219).

Ayers (1984), in an in-depth discussion of the southern notion of honor, notes that various explanations have been suggested for southern violence, including that the unconstrained authority exercised by slaveholders tended to give rise to intemperate behavior and the upbringing whites experienced in the South where authoritarian patterns were stamped on children by their slave-owning parents. However, Ayers (1984: 11–12) also points out that these arguments do not fully explain why it is that non-slave-owning whites exercised the same level of violence or the fact that many slave owners actually possessed the virtues of patience and temperance they had learned from the experience of slave owning.

The notion of the frontier in U.S. history has also been advanced as an explanation, but Ayers (1984: 12) suggests that the frontier simply accentuated cultural traits that were already present in southerners. Other studies have proposed that the southern temperament and culture reflect a sense of grievance and frustration, an addiction to weapons, especially guns, and an expectation that violence is an inevitable outcome of certain situations. As Ayers (1984: 12) points out, however, these explanations might mistake the symptoms for the actual disease, and he locates the explanation for southern violence in the southern culture of honor, adopting their own justification for violent acts, that is, that they did it for honor's sake.

Ayers clarifies the concept of honor as, "a system of values within which you have exactly as much worth as others confer upon you. Women, children and slaves had no honor; only adult white males had the right to honor—and even they, if challenged, had to prove their worth through their courage" (Ayers 1984: 13).

Honor did not rest only with the planter and slave-owning class but existed within the entire white community, and failing to respond to an insult would mark a person as something less than a real man. As Ayers argues, gradually honor and public opinion merged so that men were compelled through the force of public opinion (which reflected cultural notions of honor) to enter into fights regardless of their actual willingness to do so.

Ayers also explains that liquor consumption was a major factor in southern violence because southerners drank large amounts of alcohol. Northerners also drank heavily during the nineteenth century but did not suffer the same levels of violence as in the South. Ayers believes that the notion of southern honor can be traced back to the values of the English upper classes, which were adopted by the planters and slave owners as worthy of emulation and replication in the South. Southern honor contrasted with the restraint called for by the Puritans (Ayers 1984: 23), and the two different approaches became reflected in attitudes toward the penitentiary. Thus southerners focused on the element of coercion inherent in incarceration that impinged on honor and dignity, whereas northerners, who supported the penitentiary, saw it as a means of recreating character so that a criminal mentality was replaced with a noncriminal one (Ayers 1984: 25).

However, lynching in the South is an issue associated with slavery and racism, and most of the victims of lynching have been blacks murdered by whites. Lynching was not employed during the period of slavery, because slave owners were able to inflict almost any punishment on their slaves without state interference. However, after the Civil War, lynching became an instrument of white supremacy and was employed by the Ku Klux Klan in its killing of some four hundred blacks between 1868 and 1872. Ayers (1984: 238) notes the various "causes" of lynching, namely, "racism, frustration, poverty, submerged political conflict, irrational white fears, a weak state," but suggests that explanations for outbreaks of lynching are centered around the alleged rape of white women by black men (1984: 240), arguing that fear of black rape was a deep-seated southern fear bound up with white conceptions about black sexuality.

In seeking to answer the question of why the wave of lynching occurred in the late 1880s and early 1890s, Ayers ascribes the cause to the existence of new generations of blacks and whites, who were polarized across race lines and lacked any real meeting point. He believes that most lynchers came from this new generation (Ayers 1984: 241). Issues of gender and fear about black sexuality meant that white women suffered a double standard. They were expected to remain virginal until married, while men were free to engage in sexual relations with black women. Moreover, any white woman who had sexual relations with a black man was stigmatized and treated as a social pariah. For white men, therefore, white women became a symbol of white male supremacy, which had to be protected at all costs (Ayers 1984: 243). It seems that lynching most often impacted those blacks who had come into a community as strangers and who were deemed to be a threat simply because of their strangeness and status as outsiders.

Claims about the validity of lynching were invariably connected to the alleged inefficiency and corruption of the legal system in the South, and local newspapers complained that punishment for crime was dilatory and the best remedy to counter lynching was to reform the legal system to accelerate the speed of punishment so that justice could be seen to be acting instantly. However, other proponents of lynching argued that the legal system was irrelevant because the law was too good for black rapists (Ayers 1984: 246–247). Yet again, some in the South thought that lynchings were too good for black criminals because blacks were said to enjoy the pomp and ceremony that a lynching engendered, and the attention and glory gained by the rapist outweighed the punishment itself. In Texas, lynchings were performed in response to imagined insults or lack of respect for conventions of behavior, and again the focus was often on relationships between black males and white females. An editorial in a northeastern Texas newspaper of 1905 explains this attitude: "Almost every day some negro brute assaults a white woman in this state, and often one to a half dozen murders are committed in an effort to hide the crime. . . . If rape and murder by brutish negroes are to become common, the negro must expect extermination" (*Times Clarion* cited in Marquart et al. 1994: 7)

Lynching did not, however, occur only in the South. For example, in Minnesota in 1857 three Native Americans were arrested for the murder of a peddler, and because of the public outcry, the county sheriff decided to take them to St. Paul, for safe custody. On the way, he was overtaken by a group who took the Native Americans away and forced them to confess to the murder. They were then hanged by the roadside (Bessler 1996: 586). Whites also suffered from lynching in that state, and in 1858 a mob of sixty entered the town of Lexington, Minnesota, to lynch a man charged with murder. The deputy sheriff refused to surrender the key to the jail but was eventually forced to do so. During the struggle over the key, the accused managed to rip off his handcuffs and held off the mob for more than an hour using the leg of a stove. He was eventually taken by the mob and dragged for about three-quarters of a mile and hanged from a tree branch.

Lynching as an extralegal practice for punishment was at its height after 1880 when any perceived resistance to white supremacy in the South made a man a target for the mob. In 1919 the NAACP reported on the toll of lynchings over the previous thirty-year period. On average more than one hundred blacks a year had been lynched by whites and 78 percent of all people lynched were black (Friedman 1993: 191). Reasons given for lynchings included insulting whites, living with a white woman, using inflammatory language, and throwing stones. Contrary to the usual image of lynching being linked to the rape of a white woman by a black man, the study found that rape was not alleged in 71 percent of the 3,224 recorded lynchings during the thirty-year period in question (Emmanuel 1996: 217). Lynch mobs did not always confine their activities to hanging a victim but sometimes used torture or mutilation, burned victims at the stake, or castrated them. In one case in 1899 in Atlanta, Georgia, the sheriff gave the jail keys to a mob so it could lynch a black man arrested for rape and murder (Emmanuel 1996: 218). The law enforcement authorities almost always turned a blind eye to lynch mobs, and almost no one was ever punished for this extralegal activity.

Lynching can be viewed as a symbolic ritual, a demonstration of white supremacy, and as a delineation of what conduct by blacks would be tolerated by white society. It is here that lynching can be distinguished from simple vigilantism that is concerned only with enforcing the law through extralegal means. There was little symbolic or ritual content in vigilantism. Ayers attributes the lynchings of the late 1880s and early 1900s to economic causes, that is, a deep economic depression that hit the South at that time, with dramatic swings in the business cycle causing failed businesses and crime to increase significantly. Once again, rapes of white women were attributed to vagrant blacks who wandered idle, without employment. W. E. B. DuBois referred to these vagrant blacks as a class of "bad niggers" who were a menace to both whites and blacks. A combination of economic depression, racism, sexual tensions, the code of southern honor, the rural and isolated nature of many southern communities, the gap between the new generations of white and black, and fears about "bad niggers" all contributed to the lynching epidemic of the period (Ayers 1984: 252). Lynching was most prevalent in rural areas especially those with low population densities and scattered isolated farms. In these parts of the South, weak or nonexistent law enforcement and poor communication with the outside made it comparatively easy to resort to extralegal measures to control the black population (Colvin 1997: 250).

Lynching continued to be undertaken well into the twentieth century, and its victims continued to be mostly black. Only with the enactment of civil rights legislation and an active campaign to promote equal rights for blacks has lynching come to an end. In the 1930s, Congress attempted to enact antilynching legislation, but it was not until 1942 that the federal government, citing the Fourteenth Amendment, intervened to prosecute members of a lynch mob (Colvin 1997: 251).

"Getting Tough on Crime"

At year-end 2002, the total estimated correctional population in the United States was 6.7 million (Glaze 2003: 1). Of this figure, 2.1

million persons were incarcerated by year-end 2002. During the period 1975 to 1990 the number of persons under correctional supervision increased by 203 percent (Blomberg and Lucken 2000: 180) and between 1980 and 1992 the number incarcerated in jails and federal and state prisons increased from 330,000 to 883,000, an increase of 168 percent (Blomberg and Lucken 2000: 180).

Many attribute the beginning of the present trend of mass imprisonment to an event in 1974 that seemed to sound the demise of the ideal of rehabilitation. In that year, after evaluating a number of rehabilitation programs, Robert Martinson and some colleagues at the City University of New York, published a study called "What Works? Questions and Answers about Prison Reforms," in which they concluded that "with few and isolated exceptions, the rehabilitative efforts that have been reported so far have had no appreciative impact on recidivism" (Christianson 1998: 277). The call that "nothing works" became a rallying cry for penal conservatives, and an increased political emphasis on crime control and punishment was taken up by the media. However, even before 1974 some politicians had seen the political value in claiming there was a need to get tough on crime.

Crime control first became a political issue during the 1964 presidential campaign of Barry Goldwater. He blatantly used fear of crime, especially by whites against blacks, in his political messages (Christianson 1998: 276). Succeeding campaigns at all levels of government have made similar use of the crime control issue. Getting tough on crime inevitably means also getting tough on offenders. For example, after Goldwater, both Lyndon Johnson and Richard Nixon declared "wars on crime." Giving crime control this high priority resonated with the public, and in 1968, for the first time since the start of polling on public issues in the United States, Americans rated crime as the top domestic issue in the country. In the same year following the assassination of Martin Luther King Jr. and Robert F. Kennedy, 81 percent of those surveyed thought that law enforcement had "broken down" (Christianson 1998: 276).

The slogan that "nothing works" was adopted and promoted by many opinion makers. It made no difference that Martinson (1979) later retracted his views and that other later studies showed that some rehabilitation efforts had in fact worked. The period from the 1980s to the present day has been marked by a crime control and penal philosophy that has maintained the need for a "tough on crime" platform. A conservative climate has promoted an approach to crime and punishment that stresses that crime is the result of individual choice and that economic and social factors are irrelevant. Associated with this thinking is a stress on the immorality of crime and a perspective that sees offenders as a distinct class of persons imbued with evil intent who should be kept apart from the remainder of law-abiding society.

Even though previous wars on crime had been initiated during the Reagan/Bush administrations, the current "tough-on-crime" approach has proved to be the longest-lasting and most notable and has been marked by policies that advocate the mass incarceration of criminals as a way of incapacitating them. Along with this emphasis on crime control has come a new approach to punishment. The previously prevailing philosophy of rehabilitation has been replaced with one of retribution, stressing the need for offenders to receive their "just deserts." The notion of just deserts advocates that all offenders committing similar crimes should receive proportionate sentences often determined by applying sentencing guidelines. In place of the wide sentencing discretion given to judges previously, and instead of indeterminate sentences, sentencing is now largely a programmed matter paying little or no regard to the social or economic circumstances of an offender.

The policy of incapacitating offenders, that is, effectively warehousing them in prisons for lengthy periods, has been seen as a solution to the problem of the habitual offender. The policy does not seek to understand the causes of crime or to rehabilitate offenders but aims simply at stopping the criminal in his or her tracks. Other crime control policies such as the war on drugs, truth in sentencing, and mandatory minimum penalties for violent (and in some cases nonviolent) offenders have generated an explosion in the prison population and in prison construction. In line with the abolition of indeterminate sentences, parole has also been abolished in many states and in the federal system or has been restricted in its use.

In light of prison overcrowding caused by the various wars on crime and the war on drugs, intermediate sanctions have been developed as a first line of defense against incarceration (see previous discussion of intermediate sanctions). By 1989, forty states and the District of Columbia operated intensive supervision programs, and intermediate punishments have now become an established feature of penal systems and penal practice in every state. However, in practice, these punishments have been imposed as supplements to incarceration rather than as alternatives to imprisonment and so have failed to alleviate overcrowding in prisons. As well, policing these punishments has become so strict that those undergoing them tend to commit numerous technical violations for which they are sent to prison, and thus are recycled back into the prison system. Strict enforcement of these sanctions is required, and such enforcement has meant undermining the goal of reducing the numbers of offenders in confinement (Blomberg and Lucken 2000: 184).

Other developments in penal practice have included the construction of "supermax prisons" designed to hold the most dangerous prisoners in maximum confinement (see Chapter 2). The conditions in these prisons are reminiscent of the early days of the penitentiary, because inmates are confined in their cells for up to twenty-three hours a day and in the most modern prisons have little or no contact with prison staff or other prisoners.

The privatization of the prison system (see Chapter 2) has been actively promoted in many states, and increasingly prisons have come to be seen as part of the economic fabric of society and as supplying valuable employment opportunities in rural areas. Questions have been raised about the morality of assigning the punishment of offenders to private companies, and some investigations have revealed staff inadequacies and poor work practices in private institutions. In many respects, present penal policies seem to reflect a return to the past, not only in terms of supermax prisons but also in terms of a diminishing state role in the punishment of offenders. The task of punishment is increasingly being handed over to private companies as business enterprises supply treatment programs and diversion schemes for various classes of offenders.

By 1991 the United States had more than a million people behind bars and an incarceration rate of 426 persons per 100,000, the highest rate of imprisonment of any nation, with South Africa ranking second with 333 and the Soviet Union third at 268. The European nations generally range from 35 to 120 per 100,000 (Christianson 1998: 283). In 2002 at year-end the U.S. rate was 476 per 100,000 (Harrison and Beck 2003).

Class inequalities grew rapidly in the period between 1979 and 1996 because during that period 98 percent of income increases accrued to the top fifth of American households. During the same period, the average family lived on less as the average wage rate declined (Colvin 1997: 270). The depression of the

1980s produced surplus labor that was increasingly absorbed by the correctional system. Public concern about the incarcerated seems to have reached its lowest point as politicians stress the need to be tough on crime and humanitarian considerations take second place to assuaging the public fear about crime and criminals often generated by moral panics spurred by the media such as the crusades against "sexual predators" and perceived youth violence.

The emphasis on individual responsibility and accountability has put social and economic causes of crime out of contention, and increasingly criminals are stigmatized and labeled as beyond redemption, as an "other" who does not even belong to the human race. As Colvin (1997: 273) notes, "the punishment system has increasingly become an avenue for channeling public anxieties and conveying a message that authorities are in control of an uncertain situation. The irony is that the more people we lock up, the greater the public expresses fear of crime and of the future."

Associated with the incarceration explosion has been the growth of prison construction by states and private contractors so that by the mid-1990s the penal system comprised more than five thousand correctional institutions, including local jails. By the late 1980s, privatization of prisons had become an economic lobbying point for many rural communities to such an extent, for example, that in the early 1990s the competition to have a new prison in one's locality grew so fierce that some communities offered free country club memberships and other benefits to prison administrators and guards as an incentive to site the prison in their community. From the 1980s the prison construction business began to represent a major benefit to many different companies with the average sized maximum-security prison generally costing from about $30 to $75 million (Christianson 1998: 287). During the period 1985 to 1995 the number of private prisons increased by 500 percent, and by 1996 at least thirty states had made arrangements to contract out prison labor to private companies (Christianson 1998: 291).

This history of punishment in the United States and elsewhere has mapped the changes in thinking about punishment in the past, with the overall aim of showing how changes in society and differing social movements, as well as cultural and economic factors, have been reflected in variations in penal practice. Most historians and theorists of punishment would agree that it is not possible to ascribe changes in punishment to any one particular cause, such as the work of the prison reformers, or the influence of the Enlightenment, or imported practices from England, because a multitude of dynamic social forces have affected the nature of punishment and brought about change at different times and for different reasons.

During the period under discussion the principal developments in punishment can be characterized by the following:

- The decline in public punishments that could be viewed by spectators and were designed to be a display of the power of the state over its delinquent citizens
- The advent of the sanction of incarceration as the paramount means of dealing with offenders
- The birth of the penitentiary and a range of institutions of similar character that emphasized control, supervision, and discipline, such as the asylum, the workhouse, and the factory, making up an interdependent and complementary regime of control by the state
- The development of the notion that a criminal's character could be changed through a process involving reform and rehabilitation
- The development of a depersonalized approach to inmates based on a regime that emphasized discipline and regulation
- The establishment of a greater social distance between the inmate and the world outside the prison, now seen at its most extreme in the supermax prison
- Almost all penal institutions incarcerated the lowest classes of society so that the prison and its associated institutions, such as the workhouse, concentrated criminality into the lower sectors of society, thus producing a pronounced social division between criminals and other citizens (Garland 1985: 38)

References

Anderson, James, Laronistine Dyson, and Willie Brooks Jr. 2000. "Alabama Prison Gangs: Reverting to Archaic Punishment to Reduce Crime and Discipline Offenders." *Western Journal of Black Studies* 24: 9–23.

Ayers, Edward L. 1984. *Vengeance and Justice: Crime and Punishment in the 19th Century American South.* New York: Oxford University Press.

Barnes, Harry E. 1972. *The Story of Punishment: A Record of Man's Inhumanity to Man.* Mont Clair, NJ: Patterson Smith.

Bean, Phillip. 1981. *Punishment: A Philosophical and Criminological Inquiry.* Oxford: Martin Robertson.

Bessler, John D. 1996. "The 'Midnight Assassination Law' and Minnesota's Anti-Death Penalty Movement 1849–1911." *William Mitchell Law Review* 22: 577–730.

Blomberg, Thomas, and Karol Lucken. 2000. *American Penology: A History of Control.* New York: Aldine De Gruyter.

Brundage, W. Fitzhugh. 1993. *Lynching in the New South: Georgia and Virginia, 1880–1930.* Urbana: University of Illinois Press.

Cahn, Mark. 1989. "Punishment, Discretion, and the Codification of Prescribed Penalties in Colonial Massachusetts." *American Journal of Legal History* 23/(April): 107–135.

Carleton, Mark. 1971. *Politics and Punishment: The History of the Louisiana State Penal System.* Baton Rouge: Louisiana State University Press.

Christianson, Scott. 1998. *With Liberty for Some: 500 Years of Imprisonment in America.* Boston, MA: Northeastern University Press.

Clear, Todd, and Anthony Braga. 1998. "Challenges for Corrections in the Community." In *Community Corrections: Probation, Parole, and Intermediate Sanctions,* edited by Joan Petersilia, 213–218. New York: Oxford University Press.

Colvin, Mark. 1997. *Penitentiaries, Reformatories, and Chain Gangs: Social Theory and the History of Punishment in Nineteenth-Century America.* New York: St. Martin's Press.

Daly, Kathleen. 2002. "Restorative Justice: The Real Story." *Punishment and Society* 4(1): 55–79.

Dean-Myrda, Mark C., and Francis Cullen. 1998. "The Panacea Pendulum: An Account of Community as a Response to Crime." In *Community Corrections: Probation, Parole, and Intermediate Sanctions,* edited by Joan Petersilia, 3–18. New York: Oxford University Press.

Dimsdale, Thomas. 1866. *Vigilantes of Montana.* Virginia City, MT: Post Press, D. W. Tilton and Co.

Duff, Antony. 2001. *Punishment, Communication, and Community.* Oxford: Oxford University Press.

Duguid, Stephen. 2000. *Can Prison Work? The Prisoner as Object and Subject in Modern Corrections.* Toronto: University of Toronto Press.

Dumm, Thomas L. 1987. *Democracy and Punishment: Disciplinary Origins of the United States.* Madison: University of Wisconsin Press.

Emmanuel, Anne. 1996. "Lynching and the Law in Georgia." *William and Mary Bill of Rights Journal* 5(1): 216–248.

Fierce, Milfred C. 1994. *Slavery Revisited: Blacks and the Convict Lease System 1865–1953.* New York: CUNY.

Foucault, Michel. 1977. *Discipline and Punish: The Birth of Prison.* London: Penguin Books.

Friedman, Lawrence. 1993. *Crime and Punishment in American History.* New York: Basic Books.

Garland, David. 1985. *Punishment and Welfare: A History of Penal Strategies.* Aldershot: Gower Publishing.

Glaze, Lauren. 2003. "Probation and Parole in the United States, 2001." *Bureau of Justice Statistics Bulletin* (August): 1–8. Washington, DC: U.S. Department of Justice.

Gorman, Tessa. 1997. "Back on the Chain Gang: Why the Eighth Amendment and the History of Slavery Proscribe the Resurgence of Chain Gangs." *California Law Review* 85: 441–478.

Hagan, John. 1983. "Pride and Punishment: On the Social History of Criminal Sanctions." *American Bar Foundation Research Journal* (Winter): 203–210.

Harrison, Paige, and Allen Beck. 2003. "Prisoners in 2002." *Bureau of Justice Statistics Bulletin* (July): 1–14. Washington, DC: U.S. Department of Justice.

Hirsch, Adam. 1992. *The Rise of the Penitentiary: Prisons and Punishment in Early America.* New Haven, CT: Yale University Press.

Holt, Norman. 1998. "The Current State of Parole in the United States." In *Community Corrections: Probation, Parole, and Intermediate Sanctions,* edited by Joan Petersilia, 28–41. New York: Oxford University Press.

Hunter, Donna. 2000. "Race, Law, and Innocence: Executing Black Men in the Eighteenth Century." *Studies in Law Politics and Society* 20: 71–97.

Ignatieff, Michael. 1978. *A Just Measure of Pain: The Penitentiary in the Industrial Revolution, 1750–1850.* New York: Pantheon Books.

Kealey, Linda. 1986. "Patterns of Punishment: Massachusetts in the Eighteenth Century." *American Journal of Legal History* 30: 163–189.

Marquart, James, Sheldon Ekland-Olson, and Jonathan Sorenson. 1994. *The Rope, the Chair, and the Needle: Capital Punishment in Texas, 1923–1990.* Austin: University of Texas Press.

Martinson, Robert. 1974. "What Works? Questions and Answers about Prison Reform." *The Public Interest* 35: 22–54.

Martinson, Robert. 1979. "New Findings, New Views: A Note of Caution Regarding Sentencing Reform." *Hofstra Law Review* 7: 242–258.

Masur, Louis. 1989. *Rites of Execution: Capital Punishment and the Transformation of American Culture, 1776–1865.* New York: Oxford University Press.

Melossi, Dario, and Massimo Pavarini. 1981. *The Prison and the Factory: Origins of the Penitentiary System.* Totowa, NJ: Barnes and Noble Books.

Meranze, Michael. 2000. "A Criminal Is Beaten: The Politics of Punishment and the History of the Body." In *Possible Pasts: Becoming Colonial in Early America,* edited by Robert Blair St. George, 302–323. Ithaca, NY: Cornell University Press.

Millender, Michael. 1998. "The Road to Eastern State: Liberalism, the Public Sphere, and the Origins of the American Penitentiary." *Yale Journal of Law and the Humanities* 10: 163–189.

Petersilia, Joan. 1998a. "The Current State of Probation, Parole, and Intermediate Sanctions." In *Community Corrections: Probation, Parole, and Intermediate Sanctions,* edited by Joan Petersilia, 19–20. New York: Oxford University Press.

Petersilia, Joan. 1998b. "Experience with Intermediate Sanctions: Rationale and Program Effectiveness." In *Community Corrections: Probation, Parole, and Intermediate Sanctions,* edited by Joan Petersilia, 68–70. New York: Oxford University Press.

Petersilia, Joan, and Elizabeth Piper Deschenes. 1998. "What Punishes? Inmates Rank the Severity of Prison Versus Intermediate Sanctions." In *Community Corrections: Probation, Parole, and Intermediate Sanctions,* edited by Joan Petersilia, 149–159. New York: Oxford University Press.

Pisciotta, Alexander. 1994. *Benevolent Repression: Social Control and the American Reformatory Movement.* New York: New York University Press.

Preyer, Kathryn. 1982. "Penal Measures in the American Colonies: An Overview." *American Journal of Legal History* 26: 326–353.

Rothman, David. 1990. *The Discovery of the Asylum: Social Order and Disorder in the New Republic,* revised esdition. Boston, MA: Little, Brown and Company.

Rusche, Georg, and Otto Kirchheimer. 1939 (reprinted 1968). *Punishment and Social Structure.* New York: Russsell and Russell.

Tonry, Michael H. 1999. "Community Penalties in the United States." *European Journal on Criminal Policy and Research* 7: 5–22.

von Hirsh, Andrew. 1998. "The Ethics of Community-Based Sanctions." In *Community Corrections: Probation, Parole, and Intermediate Sanctions,* edited by Joan Petersilia, 189–198. New York: Oxford University Press.

Zimring, Franklin E. 2003. *The Contradictions of American Capital Punishment*. Oxford: Oxford University Press.

2

Problems, Controversies, and Solutions

The Right to Punish

We have seen from the history of punishment in Chapter 1 that from an early period the state has assumed the right to administer punishment to individuals for breaches of the law. In 1764 Cesare Beccaria reminded Europeans that parties to the social contract consented to being punished for certain breaches of that social contract. In giving this consent, an individual was making a sacrifice to ensure that he or she enjoyed the benefits of the protection of the state against others who might interfere with their liberty (Dubber 1998: 4). As French philosopher Michel Foucault puts it, "the offense opposes an individual to the entire social body; in order to punish him society has the right to oppose him in its entirety . . . thus a formidable right to punish is established, since the offender becomes the common enemy" (Duguid 2000: 47).

A basic question about punishment concerns why offenders should be punished at all. In responding to this question we might note the following reasons for punishing an offender (Banks 2004: 104):

- The person deserves to be punished.
- Punishment ensures that all understand the need to obey laws.

- Punishment will discourage others from doing wrong acts.
- Punishment shows that society disapproves of the act that has occurred.
- Punishment will stop that person from committing other crimes.

These reasons and others relate both to the prevention of crime and to whether or not punishment is deserved, and most of them are recited in debates about punishment.

The philosophical approach to punishment asks questions like What is the purpose of punishment? What should the objectives of punishment be? What values should be advanced and promoted by criminal law? (Banks 2004). In answering these questions several theories about the philosophy of punishment have been advanced. Theories that have to do with *deterrence* are usually known as utilitarian because their source is utilitarian philosophy. Utilitarians argue that we punish citizens because we seek to deter crime and offenses and in this sense, therefore, punishment is justified because it is thought to have beneficial effects or consequences. Jeremy Bentham, an early proponent of punishment as deterrence explained deterrence as follows:

> Pain and pleasure are the great springs of human action. When a man perceives or supposes pain to be the consequence of an act he is acted on in such manner as tends with a certain force to withdraw him as it were from the commission of that act. If the apparent magnitude be greater than the magnitude of the pleasure expected he will be absolutely prevented from performing it (Bean 1981: 30).

Thus a utilitarian will argue that the right punishment is one that will produce the most beneficial effect on the general welfare of all those affected by the criminal act. Generally, studies have shown that there is no evidence that deterrence actually works to prevent crime from occurring (Hudson 1996: 23; Ten 1987: 9; Walker 1991: 16). A utilitarian would support a particular punishment as justified if it inflicts a level of suffering that is less than the harm caused by a criminal act that would occur if no punishment was applied (Banks 2004: 109). The theory supports the notion that if a range of punishments is believed to achieve the same result, the best punishment is that which is the most lenient and which minimizes potential suffering.

Retribution is the notion that punishment is justified because it is deserved. Retributionists argue that we should punish the guilty and that justice demands that we do so (Duff 2001: 19). This perspective does not pay any attention to the consequences of punishment; it is only concerned with responsibility and accountability. Retribution represents our often intuitive response to criminals, that is, that the guilty deserve to suffer, but as Duff points out, we must look further into this issue, because this intuition might be no more than a kind of envy (because they got away with something that we ourselves would not dare to do), hatred, or vengeance—emotions that are generally considered morally questionable (Duff 2001: 20). One example of a system of retribution is the *lex talionis* described in Chapter 1.

Retribution is based on the moral position that once a set of legal rules has been agreed upon by a society those rules must be adhered to, and when they are violated, the outcome should be an act of retribution. Retribution also advocates proportionality, that is, the punishment imposed should be proportionate to the wrongdoing that has taken place (Banks 2004). Thus, a retributionist would ask the question How do we calculate the just deserts of an offender? Justification from a retributive perspective usually rests on arguments such as: The offender should repay his debt to society (Walker 1991: 73); the offender should be "censured"; committing a crime is taking unfair advantage; and it is satisfying to see an offender punished. *Censure* relates to blameworthiness and holding someone accountable for his or her act as well as giving a message that society does not approve of that particular wrongful act (von Hirsch 1994: 120–121). Another aspect of censure is how punishment can communicate or express the censure of society. Duff (2001: xvii) argues that punishment for a crime should communicate or express to offenders the censure they deserve to receive for their crime and should attempt to make those who have offended repent their crimes, reform themselves, and to reconcile with those they have injured or wronged in some way. In this way punishment is seen as having a symbolic significance (Feinberg 1994: 74), that is, it is seen to represent society's condemnation of a wrongful act. Another way of justifying retribution is to see it as condemning an offender who, by his or her wrongful act, has taken an unfair advantage of others within society by committing that crime. Here, the effect of punishing that person is to restore fairness (Ten 1987: 5). Punishment, it is argued, is justified because it takes away that unfair advantage.

Those favoring a retributive approach to punishment may

argue simply that retribution is satisfying in terms of the wrong that has taken place. This very straightforward approach can be seen as endorsing the view that criminals should be hated and despised and that it is natural to want to express that hatred through imposing punishment. Those who do not support retribution often argue that retribution is really revenge or vengeance and that those perspectives are not morally justified. Against this view, it can be argued that "retribution is done for a wrong while revenge may be done for an injury or harm or slight and need not be a wrong" (Nozick 1981: 366).

The most important aspect of retribution in punishment today is the idea of *just deserts,* and this perspective is the one most often cited in justifying punishments today. We have seen in Chapter 1 how indeterminate sentences came about and how parole boards had the power to determine when an inmate would secure his or her freedom. This wide discretion in parole boards as well as the wide sentencing powers of judges led many states to pass legislation requiring that sentences be calculated by reference to a set of legal guidelines. This is often called *tariff sentencing* because there is a set amount of punishment for each offense calculated according to the nature of that offense (Banks 2004: 113). An example is the Minnesota Sentencing Guidelines. Just deserts approaches are criticized for excluding many factors in making the sentencing decision. For example, the social and economic conditions that might have impacted an offender are not taken into account.

We have also seen in Chapter 1 how the idea of *rehabilitation* developed over time, so that in the modern context it connotes a concern not only for the offense committed but also for the offender and his or her social and economic background. Those who support the notion of rehabilitation as an objective of punishment argue that punishment should fit the offender and that individual circumstances do matter in the task of reforming or rehabilitating an offender so that they will not offend again. Primarily, rehabilitation sees crime as the symptom of a social disease, and the aim of rehabilitation should be to produce a cure through treatment (Bean 1981: 54). Rehabilitation in consequentialist terms (the act is considered right or wrong depending on whether its outcome, or consequence, is good or bad) means looking at ways to modify criminal behaviors so offenders will refrain from further offenses or teaching them skills or providing them with training that will equip them for employment and keep them away from crime (Duff 2001: 5). As discussed in Chapter 1, the objective of rehabilitation enjoyed wide public support up until the 1970s, but since then it has, to a large extent, been abandoned in favor of a just deserts approach to punishment, at least in the United States. One reason for this is the perception that crime prevention using consequentialist approaches have not been successful.

Incapacitation is the notion that punishment can, through confining offenders, make it impossible for them to commit such acts again. Of course only capital punishment will permanently incapacitate a person, and incarceration is likely to come to an end for most offenders. Some claim that incapacitating offenders in a selective way will ensure that so-called career criminals will be unable to reoffend and society will be spared from the harm they cause through their criminal actions, thus assisting in the prevention of crime. The problem with this approach is that it assumes that a person will commit further crimes, and such predictions are problematic and often incorrect. There is also the question of the moral acceptability of punishing citizens based on a prediction of their future conduct, that is, for what they *might* do in the future. Another issue is that incapacitation only works if those we lock up are not immediately replaced with others who offend. The notion that we ought, as a society, to incapacitate offenders is seen in programs like "Three Strikes and You're Out," which imposes mandatory minimum sentences for certain offenses, and "Truth in Sentencing," which requires offenders to serve at least 85 percent of their sentence before they can even be considered for release on parole.

Explaining Punishment

Until quite recently, most questions about punishment reflected a philosophical or criminological perspective, that is, they were concerned with issues like ought we to punish and why does the state have the right to punish (philosophical issues), or with the policy, practice, and procedure of punishment through the criminal justice system (criminological issues), but did not examine issues such as why particular punishments were employed, why changes in punishment occurred, and why imprisonment came to be the principal form of punishment. With the publication of *Discipline and Punish* by Michel Foucault in 1977 and *Punishment and Modern Society* by David Garland in 1990, studies of the relationship between punishment and society have expanded significantly. In particular, researchers and commentators began to focus on social movements and social forces that prompted changes in punishment and how punishment represents our norms and values as well as the role we give to punishment in society. This has meant opening up a field of inquiry that had previously been neglected in favor of largely criminological approaches to punishment that concentrated on functional aspects such as sentencing practice, capital punishment, and the like. As Garland (1990: 3) puts it, "Punishment today is a deeply problematic and barely understood aspect of social life, the rationale for which is by no means clear." The contribution of Foucault, Garland, and others has been to reveal the cultural and social underpinnings of punishment, its history and currents in social thinking, and climates of tolerance and intolerance surrounding punishment itself. This in turn has broadened to a study of how order and authority are constituted and maintained in society. These are important issues because punishment, as Garland (1990) points out, is the product of social structure and cultural values.

Earlier commentators on the sociology of punishment included Émile Durkheim, Max Weber, and writers in the Marxist tradition like Georg Rusche and Otto Kirchheimer (1939; see Chapter 1). The French sociologist Durkheim explored social solidarity and tried to explain how society maintained social cohesion. His account of punishment relied heavily on material drawn from small-scale societies and he portrays punishment as being driven by intense emotional forces that express moral outrage. It is these outbursts, he argues, that produce social solidarity, as mutual beliefs and relationships are reaffirmed (Garland 1990: 33). Religious and moral factors figure largely in his account, which seems to a modern reader to be quite distanced from the modern professionalized systems of punishment. Durkheim concluded that less-developed societies imposed severe measures of punishment because of the intensity of emotion that was expressed when social solidarity was breached. In contrast, more advanced societies do not possess this same level of emotion, and therefore there is a more moderate reaction when violations occur. Thus for Durkheim, the role of punishment was to reinforce moral commands. He denied that punishment had any deterrent force or effect and stressed that we should think of punishment as an expressive form of action condemning breaches of the moral code (Garland 1990: 44). We can see this approach reflected in philosophical arguments about punishments expressing or communicating censure.

German sociologist Weber explained how the military and the factory both train citizens and how this process disciplines them into rationalized forms of action. Thus, within society natural rhythms are replaced by technical knowledge and rationalized forms of action, and calculation replaces belief (Garland 1990: 179). Weber formulated the notion of "bureaucratic rationality," which is seen today in the managerialism and bureaucracy associated with the punishment system and its focus on management and control. This rationality has displaced emotion and introduced "experts" who claim to have specialized knowledge into the penal system and whose task is seen as managing offenders in a neutral nonmoralistic manner. Thus the moral content of punishment has been de-emphasized, and this is seen in the way in which punishment has become a private affair and a matter for experts. Key decisions in the criminal justice field are now left to these experts, and what was once a moral and religious concern—punishing offenders—has become the province of expert penal administrators. This has developed a tension between the urge to punish and the rational forces that actually control the punishment process and reflects generally the ambivalence that we feel about punishment today.

Marxist studies of punishment have asked why imprisonment persists instead of other forms of punishment, especially since it is generally acknowledged in the modern period that imprisonment does not prevent or deter crime. Marxist theories about punishment center on the class struggle and ask how punishment functions in relation to class. Rusche and Kirchheimer (1939) focused on the forces that bring about the use of particular kinds of punishment, especially imprisonment, and explained that punishment must be understood as a social phenomenon beyond crime control. Generally, they argue that penal policy is another method of controlling the poor and ought therefore to be viewed as part of the class struggle. They contend that under the principle of less eligibility, diet and the general regime of the prison must be maintained at a level that will ensure the experience remains unpleasant enough to serve as a deterrent to the lower social classes who are committing crime. In their view, if conditions in prisons were less unpleasant this would cause the lower classes to commit crime in order to enjoy the better conditions found in prisons. The importance of these approaches lies in the fact that they point out that punishment is not simply a response to crime, but is caught up in other social structures and is affected by other social forces. The work of Rusche and Kirchheimer inspired a substantial series of studies on the relationship between crime and the labor market.

The publication of *Discipline and Punish* in 1977 revolutionized thinking about punishment and discipline in society. In a complex analysis of these topics, Foucault explains how inflicting pain on the body through early forms of punishment gave way to new forms of power through disciplining individuals in institutions like the factory or the prison, and how such practices created a class of "delinquents." For Foucault the prison should be seen not as an instrument of punishment alone but as an institution where modern techniques of control are seen in their fullest extent (Garland 1990: 134). He asks why the prison persists, observing that its defects have been recognized since the 1820s, and he suggests two reasons: First, prisons are part of the disciplinary practices that are deeply rooted in modern society, and second, prisons carry out functions that serve to create delinquency, and this works within the broader political framework of society to guarantee the authority of state agencies like the police. This new broader formulation of "penality" has created a vast literature that has followed Foucault's path in assessing the disciplinary techniques through which power is exercised in society. His emphasis on the role of punishment in creating the well-trained and disciplined individual has been enormously influential in prison and penal studies. David Garland's work also advocates a broad approach to understanding punishment so that all sociological and philosophical approaches are taken into account and that punishment is seen as a "complex social institution" and not simply as a means of crime control.

The "War on Drugs"

What is the appropriate punishment for drug offenders, and how should society deal with drugs and drug offenders generally? Is it appropriate to punish all drug offenders by incarcerating them, or is treatment in the community a better punishment option? These and other related issues find their focus in the so-called war on drugs, which has been conducted since 1972. How best to reduce illegal drug consumption in the United States has been evaluated within a criminal justice rather than a public health framework (Welch 1999: 52), and conviction and punishment have been emphasized at the expense of treatment. For example, in 1996 the Office of the National Drug control strategy revealed that 70 percent of federal funding on drug abuse was devoted to law enforcement and only 30 percent to treatment and prevention (Welch 1999: 52).

Drug control strategy has been conceptualized as having elements of supply reduction, treatment, prevention and education, and decriminalization, and three schools of thought have been identified on drug control policy: public health generalists, legalism, and cost benefit (Zimring and Hawkins 1991). The public health perspective emphasizes how drug abuse can lead to additional problems, such as impacts on employment, on the family, and ultimately on the quality and duration of life. Obviously the proponents of this approach favor treatment over incarceration or at least support more treatment programs in prisons. They tend also to support decriminalization because that would recognize the issue of drug abuse as a public health and not a criminal justice issue. The legalistic school of thought argues that drugs inflict social harm on society and drug abuse should therefore be sanctioned and punished. However, legalists endorse treatment programs and advocate forced treatment of drug abusers. Legalists also support the continuation of the war on drugs and resist the notion of designating the drug issue as a public health concern. They regard decriminalization as irrational and those who support it as naive (Zimring and Hawkins 1991: 113). The cost-benefit approach adopts a rational and calculating view that sees drug policy as balancing the costs of abuse against the costs of enforcement. This group approves of treatment so long as programs include the high-risk users who are the group most likely to commit offenses to support their drug habits. It also supports the policy of decriminalizing the less harmful drugs but wants to continue the prohibition of more harmful drugs (Zimring and Hawkins 1991: 109).

It was in 1972 that President Richard Nixon declared the first war on drugs and in 1973 created the Drug Enforcement Agency as the federal agency tasked with combating illegal drugs and drug dealing. Later, in 1982, President Reagan declared yet another war on drugs. The war had a number of objectives: to reduce individual drug use, to reduce drug-related crime, and to stop or at least minimize the flow of illegal drugs into the United States. In 1986 and 1988 legislation was enacted against drug abuse, but it focused on users and street-level dealers of drugs, with a special emphasis on crack cocaine (Bush-Baskette 1999: 212). The legislation was preceded by a media campaign concentrating on cocaine use in the state of California that portrayed the sale and use of crack cocaine as a national emergency and a national epidemic. According to all reports, the war on drugs was necessary to ensure the survival of the United States. By 1987, however, the media had lost interest in the war on drugs, but the issue was revived in 1988 when the presidential election raised again the profile of drugs and produced the 1988 legislation that contained funding for treatment and prevention but largely for enforcement and increased previous penalties for certain offenses.

The Anti-Drug Abuse Act of 1986 penalized drug trafficking and drew a line between the offense of possessing crack cocaine and the offense of possessing cocaine. A person found guilty of possessing five or more grams of crack cocaine was liable to a mandatory minimum sentence of five years imprisonment and a maximum of twenty years imprisonment. However, an offender found guilty of possessing powder cocaine was not liable for a mandatory minimum sentence unless he or she possessed 500 grams of that substance. This differentiation in treatment largely impacted the African-American population, who used the cheaper crack cocaine rather than powder cocaine. Mainly, members of the white middle class used the latter substance. Despite this effect, whether intended or not, no legislators have been willing to change the laws, apparently believing that any action to reduce or remove penalties for drug offenses will generate politically adverse consequences. This view prevails, despite the U.S. Sentencing Commission recommendation in 1995 to equalize the penalties for the possession of crack and powder cocaine (Welch 1999: 60).

By 1995 federal spending on waging the war on drugs had reached $13.2 billion, and the result of this enormous expenditure was a corresponding increase in the number of persons imprisoned for drug offenses. Between 1982 and 1988 convictions for drug offenses increased by more than 50 percent, and, while in 1985 drug offenders made up 34.3 percent of the federal prison population, by 1995 this had increased to 60.8 percent and to 72 percent by 1996 (Bush-Baskette 1999: 219). Owing to the issue concerning the penalization of crack cocaine, the war on drugs has had the effect of disproportionately incarcerating African-Americans, and at the state level there was an increase of more than 800 percent in the number of African-American women imprisoned for drug offenses between 1986 and 1991 as compared with an increase of 241 percent for white women (Bush-Baskette 1999: 22).

Would punishing drug abusers in the community be a more effective strategy than incarcerating them? At year-end 2002, 24 percent of all probationers had a drug law violation (Glaze 2003: 1), and probation, as we have already seen, is a sanction that operates in the community. According to Joan Petersilia (1998: 112) there is now a body of evidence showing that ordering offenders into treatment for drug abuse reduces recidivism. Although imprisoning drug offenders who commit crimes to maintain their drug supply will take them out of circulation, once they are released, their criminality might well resume. The cost of that incarceration also has to be considered. Treatment while under probation supervision within the community on the other hand, has been shown to be the least expensive method of reducing the use of cocaine (Petersilia 1998: 112). It might also be far more effective than treatment in prison, because length of treatment has been found to be an important factor in reducing drug use and criminality. Three months treatment is considered the minimum period, but twelve to twenty-four months are required for a positive outcome from treatment (Prendergast et al. 1998: 115). Researchers have shown that the supervision provided in prison is insufficient for offenders who have serious drug problems, because extended periods of treatment are essential for success. Thus, shock incarceration programs seldom work (Petersilia, Turner, and Deschenes 1992 in Petersilia 1998: 121).

In November 2000 voters in California overwhelmingly approved a proposition that would give drug treatment instead of prison to first- and second-time drug offenders who were not charged with any other crimes. This law was expected to divert up to 36,000 offenders out of the prison system in California (Spohn 2002: 250). Another indication that the approach to dealing with drug offenses was changing to treatment rather than incarceration was the February 2001 legislation that was brought to Congress calling for $2.7 billion to be spent over three years to improve drug treatment facilities and programs in prisons.

Capital Punishment

In 2002 thirteen states executed seventy-one inmates: sixty-nine men and two women (Bonczar and Snell 2003). At year-end 2002, 3,557 inmates were on death row, with California holding the largest number of 614, followed by Texas with 450.

Capital punishment refers to the termination of the life of a person in accordance with a sentence of a court, that person having been convicted of a crime. In the past capital punishment was enforced in a variety of ways, although in more recent times it has been limited to death by hanging, electrocution, or lethal injection. In Europe going back to the age of King Canute the method employed to inflict the punishment of death was flaying and impaling (Barnes 1972: 231). In this situation, the victim was first skinned alive and his body was then impaled upon a stake where he remained until death occurred. During the Middle Ages, death was frequently brought about by burning the accused at the stake. This method was especially popular for killing witches, and although victims were often left to be consumed by the flames, sometimes they were removed while partly burned only to be returned to the stake and the fire later to suffer the balance of their penalty (Barnes 1972: 233). Also popular in this period was drawing and quartering. This involved tying each leg and arm of the victim to a horse and then leading the four horses in different and opposite directions, pulling the victim to pieces in the process. For those of noble blood, beheading was considered a privileged form of death. This was often performed using a two-handled, broad-bladed sword, and in medieval and early modern times the block and broadax were usually employed. Of course, the most elaborate beheading device in history was the French guillotine, which was itself suggested by earlier English devices like the gibbet.

Of all the forms of bringing death to a criminal, hanging has been most widely employed. In some of its crudest forms hanging comprises simply throwing a noose around the neck and pulling the victim off the ground, bringing about death through slow strangulation. In more modern times hanging as a form of public execution has involved breaking the neck, in an attempt to speed up the process, instead of relying on the much slower process of strangulation. Breaking the neck uses "the drop" where the accused is taken up on a platform, the noose of the rope is adjusted about the neck, and then the floor of the platform upon which the accused stands is pulled away from beneath him allowing him to drop a distance believed sufficient to break the neck. Adjusting the drop distance can be a fine art, because sometimes where the drop is excessive the head can almost be pulled from the body (see for example Barnes 1972: 237).

Death by electrocution was first used in New York State on August 6, 1890 (Lumer and Tenney 1995: 3), and was defended as being a humane method of executing the death sentence. Under the legislation the condemned prisoner was to be transported to the state prison and kept there in solitary confinement until the time came for the death sentence to be executed. The prisoner was denied access to any person except officials of the prison, their lawyer, physician, or priest, and members of their family, unless a court ordered otherwise. A death warrant would be issued commanding the prison warden to carry out the sentence of death within four to six weeks after the sentence had been pronounced, and only persons invited by the warden could view the event. The law declared electrocution to be the new method of execution and also called for an immediate postmortem to be performed.

In 1921 the then-frontier state of Nevada, with a population of fewer than 80,000 passed a Humane Death Act, which provided that a condemned man should be approached in his cell while sleeping and executed by a dose of lethal gas. In February 1924 at the Carson City prison, Gee Jon became the first person to be legally executed by lethal gas in the form of cyanide crystals, but within the following two years Arizona, Colorado, Wyoming, North Carolina, and California had switched from electrocution to the gas chamber as a means of execution (Christianson 1998: 202). Death by lethal injection is now the favored method of execution perceived to be more humane than electrocution.

Even before challenges that they were cruel and unusual forms of punishments were made, gassing suffered from associations with the gas chambers of the Nazis and the electric chair conjured up images of burning and brutality. Moreover, the electric chair came to be seen as simply out of date and not consistent with modern scientific notions. It followed that a new method of dispensing death was needed that was both scientifically sound and seen as painless and humane, and the best candidate was clearly the lethal injection, with its connection to the impedimenta of medicine such as gurneys and syringes (Zimring 2003: 51). In 1977 Texas changed from electrocution to lethal injection, and its legislation provides a good example of how the law deals with this mode of execution. The statute requires that preparations for the sentence begin two weeks in advance. The means of disposing of the inmate's property are specified, and the categories of persons to be notified are also specified. The law specifies required practice sessions for the actual execution, security measures, and the actual procedure for administering the lethal injection is spelled out. By January 1981 three more states—Oklahoma, Idaho, and New Mexico—had followed Texas with their lethal injection laws (Marquart et al. 1994: 132–133). In 2002 the number of states authorizing lethal injection as the method of execution increased from twenty-two to thirty-seven, and in the year 2002, 99 percent of executions were performed using lethal injection.

Many states mandate in their laws that executions take place after midnight and before dawn, and in practice the regularly scheduled time for executions is one minute after midnight. Only rarely do executions occur during daylight hours. As discussed in Chapter 1, moving an execution behind prison walls reflects the move away from public punishments and toward a regime of private punishment where inmates and the inside of prisons are kept out of public view. Arranging executions late at night or very early in the following day continues this trend of avoiding any connection between punishment and the public.

Public executions were often rowdy affairs as this account of the execution of a Native American in Montana in 1854 reveals:

> Liquor was openly passed through the crowd, and the last moments of the poor Indians were disturbed by bacchanalian yells and cries. The crowd revealed the instincts of brutes and was composed of ruffians. A half drunken father could be seen holding in his arms a child, eager to see all; giddy, senseless girls and women chattered gaily with their attendants, and old women were seen competing with drunken ruffians for a place near the gallows. (Bessler 1996: 584–585)

The largest public mass hanging in the United States occurred in 1862, when thirty-eight Dakota Indians were hanged in Mankato, Minnesota, after a Sioux uprising. Originally more than three hundred had been sentenced to death after hasty trials, but the number was reduced when President Abraham Lincoln commuted all but thirty-nine of those sentences. One man received a last minute reprieve. Notice was given to the public that the mass hanging would take place in the public square at 10:00 a.m. Martial law was imposed, and a large number of troops were brought in to maintain order. Three thousand citizens watched the execution (Bessler 1996: 599–601).

Large crowds have been a feature of public hangings. For example, in 1824 a crowd estimated to be at least 50,000 strong gathered along the route to the gallows in New York, and in 1805 an estimated 12,000 people flocked into Cooperstown, New York, to witness the hanging of a schoolteacher who had beaten his young niece to death for not being able to pronounce a word. In 1827 a crowd said to be close to 30,000 collected in Albany, New York, to see the hanging of a field hand who had murdered the husband of his aristocratic lover (Madow 1995: 477). One of the last public hangings in the United States was the 1936 hanging of Rainey Bethea in Kentucky, which drew an audience of near 10,000. After the hanging many in the crowd tried to climb on the gallows wanting to obtain pieces of the dead man's shroud as souvenirs (Madow 1995: 465). In the northeastern states public executions were abolished quite early on. For example, they were no longer carried out in Connecticut by 1830, in Pennsylvania by 1834, and New Jersey and New York by 1835. In the South and West, however, public executions lingered on until much later, in some states until the 1930s (Madow 1995: 492).

Theorists who write about the changing nature of punishments over time argue that public executions were abolished or reduced in scale not because they were thought to be barbaric, or at least not principally for this reason, but because they were socially disruptive (see, for example, Masur 1989: 109). They agree that the purpose of public punishments generally was to display the authority of the state and encourage conformity to social values endorsed by the state. In 1777 Nathan Strong, writing *The Reasons and Design of Public Punishments,* explicitly gave the following as the purpose of public punishments: "Such awful exhibitions are designed that others may see and fear—Go not to that place of horror with elevated spirits, and gay hearts, for death is there; justice and judgment are there; the power of the government displayed in its most awful form is there" (in Masur 1989: 25). Masur points out that the ritual of a public execution also served to reinforce religious authority because ministers used hanging days to show that only God could save sinners (1989: 26). Ministers linked civil government with divine intervention, claiming that civil government had the blessing of God and ought to be revered as such, and that God had given civil powers the authority to punish sinners who offended against the norms and values of society (Masur 1989: 31). The ritual of hanging required that the condemned person show penitence and plea for God's mercy as proof of the saving grace of God, and the sermons given on such occasions promoted the notion of penitence (Masur 1989: 41). By the end of the eighteenth century public executions appeared to have taken on a carnival aspect and had become places of illegality where authorities were abused and people drank heavily and engaged in activities that were seen by those in authority as subversive and dangerous to the welfare of the state (Madow 1995: 494; Rothman 1990: xxiv). They occupied public space and threatened the interests of commerce (Masur 1989: 102). It was the political dangers posed by these crowds that caused the authorities to back away from public executions. It is argued that social control could no longer be achieved through public displays of this nature and new methods had to be devised that were more appropriate to an urban mobile society. It is interesting to note that Beccaria opposed the death penalty because he believed it lacked deterrent value. His view was that public executions provided only a transitory spectacle and were a less-effective means of deterrence than incarceration, where a person would represent a continuing example of what happened to criminals (Masur 1989: 53). Other theorists like Peter Spierenburg (in Madow 1995) and David Rothman (1990: xxiv) argue that the decline of public punishments ought to be attributed to the changing sensibilities and sensitivities of the middle and upper classes of the period, especially in relation to the infliction of pain. In this approach, Spierenburg follows the argument first propounded by Norbert Elias (1994), who contended that a "civilizing process" was at work in the later eighteenth and early nineteenth centuries that caused elites to become more empathetic to the infliction of pain and suffering and that this came about as states became more stable and settled. To this must be added the development of bureaucracies and forms and systems of ruling that displaced previously unstable ways of governing, which meant that punitive displays were no longer necessary (Madow 1995: 496). Masur stresses the concern with civility and privacy that developed in the nineteenth century and the way the middle and upper classes rejected the public sphere as disorderly (Masur 1989: 103).

In the United States the death penalty has come before the Supreme Court on a number of occasions. In 1972, the U.S. Supreme Court declared all but a few death penalty statutes unconstitutional (*Furman v. Georgia*) and each of the approximately 630 inmates then on death rows throughout the country were resentenced to life imprisonment. The Court was divided on the issue of whether capital punishment as then practiced violated the Constitution. Two in the majority said that capital punishment constituted cruel and unusual punishment, whatever form it took under state law. The other three justices of the majority said that capital punishment as it was then practiced under state laws was unconstitutional as it allowed for too much discretion (Marquart et al. 1994: x). Essentially, the court told the states to remedy the defects in their legislation, and the states promptly obliged so that by 1976 new or revised legislation authorizing capital punishment had been enacted in five states (Marquart et al. 1994: 129). A scant four years after *Furman* the Supreme Court reversed any notion of a permanent abolition of the death penalty by approving several recently enacted capital statutes (*Gregg v. Georgia*). That case and others endorsed legislation in the states that set out a series of aggravating factors in the commission of homicides to be weighed by a jury in choosing between the punishment of death and other available punishments. The aggravating factors vary by state but include whether the homicide was committed during the commission of other felonies, whether it involved torture, and whether the killing was done under a contract to kill (Zimring 2003: 9). The ability of legislators to add new aggravating factors to their death penalty laws means that the capital punishment net can be widened and the number of capital punishment offenses constantly expanded. For example, in 1996 several states amended their legislation to add new aggravating factors. For example, Florida added the aggravating factor of committing murder during the commission of a felony by a "criminal street gang member." Pennsylvania added as an aggravating factor the killing of a woman who was in her third trimester of pregnancy where the defendant knew about the pregnancy. South Carolina added the murder of a rescue worker, firefighter, or paramedic on official duty, and Virginia extended the net to catch those convicted of killing more than one person within a three-year period (Welch 1999: 164).

Public opinion over the past fifty years on the death penalty has varied. During the 1950s and until about 1966 support for the death penalty decreased to about 47 percent, but since 1982, about 75 percent have been in favor of it (Radelet and Borg 2000: 44). The reason for this support during the early 1970s was the perception that the death penalty operated as a deterrent, despite the fact that studies generally have failed to demonstrate that the death penalty is more of a deterrent than a long period of imprisonment (Radelet and Borg 2000: 45). Another basis of support is the idea that the death penalty incapacitates the offender. This it certainly does, because no executed offender has ever killed again. The argument is that we need the death penalty to protect society from murderers who might murder again; however, one study has found that among those whose death sentences were commuted, only about 1 percent killed again (Radelet and Borg 2000: 46). Even though life without parole is an option instead of death, an element of the public still supports the death penalty because they do not trust that political leaders will not release murderers sentenced to life. Thus a paradox exists: This group supports giving the government the ultimate right to take the life of a person but only because they distrust that same government to keep that person incarcerated (Radelet and Borg 200: 47). However, as Zimring (2003: 11) points out, what distinguishes the United States from other countries in relation to the death penalty is the intensity with which people identify with that penalty rather than the percentage that express support of it.

Studies have shown that having a modern day death penalty system is very expensive. Such a system costs considerably more than one in which the maximum penalty is life imprisonment without parole. One estimate can be considered typical: It costs $3.2 million to electrocute a prisoner as against $600,000 for imprisonment for life (Radelet and Borg 2000: 50). In 2000, Amnesty International reported that taxpayers in Texas were paying an average of $2.3 million for each execution, while incarceration for life cost between $800,000 to $1 million (Zimring 2003: 47).

In 1998 only five countries, one of which was the United States, were responsible for more than 80 percent of executions across the world. The other countries were China, the Congo, Iraq, and Iran, a group not normally allied with the United States on any issue (Radelet and Borg 2000: 55). By the end of 1998, sixty-seven countries had abolished the death penalty for all offenses, fourteen retained it for exceptional crimes, and twenty-four others had not executed anyone for at least ten years. All countries in the European Union have abolished the death penalty. In fact as

Zimring (2003: 17) points out, in Europe the death penalty debate is not only over, the issue of abolishing capital punishment is now orthodox criminal justice policy and abolition is "a moral imperative believed necessary to the status of any civilized modern state." This is despite the fact that polls show the public in many European states support the death penalty. In other words, in Europe, it is the political leaders and not public opinion that have set the standard on the issue of the death penalty. This could be because the average European citizen does not consider the issue a major one. Importantly, capital punishment is now regarded as an issue of human rights and not a matter of choice in criminal justice policymaking on punishments. European governments now believe that its practice ought to be governed by international minimum standards on human rights because capital punishment offends against the right to life (Zimring 2003: 27). This has had the effect of broadening the issue and thereby the constituency of abolitionists and also of sidelining all other arguments about the merits or demerits of the death penalty.

In his recent study of capital punishment in the United States, Franklin Zimring (2003) offers a number of explanations for this isolationist approach to capital punishment in the United States. At the heart of the death penalty question in the United States lies the fact that death penalty enforcement and practice varies enormously by state and by region. In twelve of the fifty states there is no law authorizing capital punishment, and several other states have legislation but have not conducted any executions for many years, for example, South Dakota and New Hampshire have death penalty laws but have not executed anyone in more than fifty years (Zimring 2003: 7). However, other states take a different path on executions. Of the seventy-one executions that took place in 2002, thirty-three were carried out in Texas, the next highest state being Oklahoma, with only seven executions. Of the total of seventy-one executions in 2002, fifty-four were performed in southern states even though that region makes up only about one-third of the U.S. population (Bonczar and Snell 2003). Unlike in the past, the death penalty system in the United States is now noted for large inmate populations on death row and the very long delays that occur between the sentence of death and the actual execution (Zimring 2003: 7). In 2002 those actually executed had on average been under sentence of death for ten years and seven months (Bonczar and Snell 2003).

In contrast to Europe, where most countries have abolished the death penalty, the issue of the death penalty in the United States is considered a justice policy issue to be decided upon in the same manner as other policy issues in the criminal justice field, taking into account state and federal roles and powers (Zimring 2003: 45). Zimring observes that the death penalty debate in the United States differs from that in Europe because Europeans do not focus on the families of homicide victims, who, in the United States, are allowed to appear at capital trials and become the center of public attention. He sees this stress on the victims of homicides and the media attention given to the need for victims to have "closure" as being core elements in differentiating the debates about the death penalty (Zimring 2003: 48). As he puts it, the death penalty "is regarded as a policy intended to serve the interest of the victims of crime and those who love them, as a personal rather than a political concern, an undertaking of government to serve the needs of individual citizens for justice and psychological healing" (Zimring 2003: 49).

Today, retribution is the most popular argument in favor of the death penalty. The argument is that those who commit the most heinous crime themselves deserve to be executed, and life without parole is simply not sufficient punishment (Radelet and Borg 2000: 52). Often this argument has been justified by reference to the position of the victim of a murder, and, to the extent that it represents a moral position, it is interesting to note that the moral leadership in the United States—that is to say the churches—all strongly oppose the death penalty.

In the United States there are two phases to a death penalty trial. In the first, the object is to present facts that prove that a crime has been committed that constitutes a capital case. If during the first phase, the jury finds the defendant potentially eligible for the penalty of death, a second proceeding, which is usually known as the penalty phase, commences. It is during the penalty phase that the jury must decide whether the defendant will be sentenced to the death penalty or some other punishment. This latter phase commonly provides an opportunity for the prosecution to offer evidence about the deceased, the crime itself, and about the harm suffered by the victim of the murder as well as that suffered by their family members. Often the prosecutor compiles a victim impact statement based on information supplied by the victim and his or her family, and this might be read to the jury, or the family members might testify during the penalty phase of the trial (Zimring 2003: 52–53). According to Zimring the effect of this process is to set up a "status competition" between the offender and those who have indirectly or directly been injured by the crime. In other words, the penalty phase has now become a competition between the claims of private parties. The role of the state in prosecuting the offender for a capital crime for which the state may have him or her executed has been sidelined. This refashioning of the role of the state in capital cases differentiates the United States from other countries and renders the impact of the death sentence more a matter of private redress than public act (Zimring 2003: 56–58).

The term *closure* was not employed in death penalty discourse until about 1989, and it refers to the feelings of satisfaction that one experiences when something unpleasant has finally come to an end. Unfortunately, closure is not a rapid process for the relatives of homicide victims because, as noted previously, the average time spent on death row before execution can be up to ten years. It can be difficult for victims' families to sustain a level of emotional intensity through the appellate process, and research suggests that family members often feel ambivalent about the execution by the time it does come about and that closure is not necessarily achieved (Foster 2001: 10). Zimring (2003: 61) observes how closure in death cases has now been adopted by politicians in their political rhetoric about getting "tough on crime" so that appealing for closure becomes, "a plea for executions as psychotherapy for survivors." In summary it can be said that as regards capital punishment in the United States, the concept of closure has replaced the notion of vengeance and the role of the state now focuses on providing a service for victims, thereby diminishing the effect of what is actually taking place, that is, the taking of a human life by the state. Nevertheless, the fact remains that in many states the death penalty remains largely symbolic and serves as a political statement of public willingness to take a tough stand on crime (Foster 2001: 10).

Zimring develops a further argument relating to the death penalty. He suggests that the federal system in the United States grants the states extraordinary power in the choice and administration of punishment and that this in itself differentiates the United States from other countries and in turn gives rise to wide variations in death penalty practice in the country (Zimring 2003: 65–66). Asking why it is that certain states have such strong records on executions, Zimring locates the explanation in their history of vigilante justice. His contention is that the states in the South, with their history of vigilante justice (see Chapter 1), are more likely to regard official executions as the will of the community. They will tend to identify more closely with the process of punishment and not perceive carrying out the death penalty to be the exercise of power by the distant federal government isolated from the community processes. Within the context of Western societies, Zimring argues that only in the United States do citizens believe that executions are an expression of the community as opposed to the government or the state. Accordingly, executing people for crimes is likely to find a higher level of acceptance in those states and executions are therefore more prevalent in those states. Thus he argues, "the propensity to execute in the twenty-first century is a direct legacy of a history of lynching and of the vigilante tradition," and he links modern execution rates to those states that had the highest rates of lynching in the past (Zimring 2003: 89). In contrast to these views, those most active in death cases—the lawyers—have expressed a different opinion. In 1997 the conservative House of Delegates of the American Bar Association called for a moratorium on the death penalty for several reasons: (1) lack of adequate defense counsel in capital cases; (2) prohibition of review applications by legislation; (3) the issue of racial bias; and (4) the refusal of states and courts to prevent the execution of juveniles and the mentally challenged (Radelet and Borg 2000: 56).

In terms of the argument on federalism, it was not until after almost 150 years of constitutional government that there were any federal restrictions on the death penalty. Up to that time the states made their own decisions and carried out their own practices concerning capital cases. In the mid-1930s the cases of *Powell v. Alabama* and *Brown v. Mississippi* introduced federal restrictions by requiring that indigent defendants must have legal counsel if a state sought the death penalty and by excluding evidence in the form of involuntary confessions (Zimring 2003: 69). By the mid-1960s, further restrictions both procedural and substantive had been introduced relating to searches and interrogations and then the *Furman* decision came in 1972. The outcome has been that the Supreme Court has had to fashion a detailed set of principles to apply in death cases that have been developed on a case-by-case basis. Zimring argues that this "micromanagement" by the Supreme Court is deeply resented by the states (Zimring 2003: 71) and is found equally objectionable by the justices. The result is huge delays in death cases because most of the central issues in such cases are federal questions, and before those can be examined a defendant must exhaust all remedies in state courts. Zimring points out that it is only in the United States that such tensions arise.

Data indicate that the states with a history of high lynching rates account for 85 percent of all executions in the present day, and the lowest lynching states make up only 3.2 percent of all such executions. States in the middle comprise 12 percent of recent executions (Zimring 2003: 96). By examining concealed weapons laws and notions of self-defense in the various states, Zimring seeks to link his argument to the present day while acknowledging that there is no reason to assume that the vigilante values of the past persist today. His research tends to show that there is a strong argument that this history of self-help in the South in the form of vigilantism and lynching does have a significant effect on death penalty cases today and on the intensity with which proponents of the death penalty maintain their position that it constitutes an acceptable penalty. Zimring also notes that there is no evidence that the vigilante tradition of the past has been rejected by the South, pointing to the romance associated with the issue of flying the Confederate flag and the modern activity of groups like the Ku Klux Klan and the general tradition that endorses the private use of force in the South (see Chapter 1) (Zimring 2003: 110). An alternative view is offered, but not fully explained, by Foster (Nelson and Foster 2001: 21) that suggests that states with the highest execution rates express small town and rural values as opposed to the conditions of big city life. This could correspond with Zimring's views about the expression of community will in those states.

Zimring concludes that the existence and history of federalism (with its associated distrust of government) and the vigilante tradition combine to grant the death penalty issue in the United States a political dimension that it lacks in Europe. Simply put, U.S. citizens care much more about whether or not the death penalty is provided as a punishment for criminality because they have a greater emotional investment in the issue. In the end, argues Zimring, the death penalty debate in the United States will be influenced more by the damage that can be done by the abolitionist campaign in Europe to the U.S. self-image of being a politically advanced state having a high regard for individual rights and freedoms (Zimring 2003: 183).

In terms of constitutional law relating to capital punishment, the Supreme Court remains in control but has deferred to the decisions of state courts in the sense that it requires clear evidence of constitutional violations that have prejudiced a defendant before it will reverse death sentences (Zimring 2003: 10). Attempts by legislators to reduce the ability of defendants to "delay" executions culminated in 1996 in the Anti-Terrorism and Effective Death Penalty Act. A condemned prisoner is now required to file an application for habeas corpus to the federal courts (arguing that he or she is being detained illegally) not later than 180 days after the final state court has affirmed his or her conviction. The law mandates that the state court's decision is presumed to be correct and that to obtain a review the defendant must produce clear and convincing evidence. Second or successive claims for habeas corpus are barred (Nelson and Foster 2001: 121–122).

Gender Issues

As of July 2001, fifty-four women in the United States were on death row. As Amy Pope (2002: 257) points out, women sentenced to be executed are also mothers, sisters, and wives, and looking at the death penalty from a feminist perspective raises issues that may otherwise be overlooked. Applying a feminist ethic of justice and of care to the practice of the death penalty brings a perspective that stresses emotion and the human element rather than the rationality emphasized in the masculine approach. Thus the process that leads to the imposition of the death penalty is fixed on judge-made law and statute law and this disregards individual circumstances. Pope sees rationality and objectivity, factors that are always in the forefront of legal argument, as reflecting a social order that is grounded in patriarchal beliefs and values (2002: 262). A feminist approach focuses on context and on relationships and asks questions that are normally considered outside the jurisdiction of the rational and objective legal system. A feminist approach aims to "formulate a criminal justice system that fits the individual defendant and addresses the needs of the victim and the community, as opposed to finding a way to fit the individual into the appropriate model" (Pope 2002: 263). At the same time, care must be taken to avoid reinforcing stereotypes of women as caregivers or as emotional and nonrational. Another critique of the male rational approach to punishment leveled by feminists is that male privilege is so entrenched in our legal system that it in fact can be said to represent the Rule of Law. Thus it is argued that male conceptions of gender neutrality and objectivity are so paramount that women are essentially required to adopt these principles.

Applying the feminist theories cited previously to the death penalty, Pope critiques the decision of the Supreme Court in *Furman,* arguing that the justices avoided coming to grips with the crucial and fundamental issue of whether the criminal justice system is biased against the already marginalized in society (Pope 2002: 270). Instead, the justices, in effect, tinkered with the role of the jury and its discretion in death penalty cases. Further, although there were suggestions in *Furman* that punishment must not be unacceptable in relation to current societal standards of punishment, Pope brings up the question of who speaks for society in deciding that issue. For example, many parts of the country support racial segregation, and many studies have shown that there is bias in capital cases against African-Americans. She suggests that a feminist approach would question assumptions about who is supposed to speak for society and to express its norms. It would also raise the issue of breaking out of the so-called black letter approach to the law, which resulted in Justice Blackmun in the *Furman* case deciding that his role was limited to passing judgment on the constitutionality of legislation rather than addressing the issue of a personal abhorrence of the death penalty.

Feminists argue that emotion and personal preference cannot be removed from the process of judging whether they emanate from the offender, the victim, or the court. In other words, concealing emotion behind a facade of objectivity and rationality as exemplified in the language and practice of the law denies the reality of society. That reality is that the function of the death penalty is to kill "mostly poor men without adequate representation" (Pope 2002: 272). For example, in Texas during the period 1923 to 1972 a majority of those executed came from a rural setting and the typical offender was a young (less than thirty years old), minority male who was single or divorced when the offense took place. Most were unskilled laborers with long histories of employment instability, the majority were functionally illiterate, and many had only marginal intelligence (Marquart et al. 1994: 69–71).

In criticizing the decision in *Furman v. Georgia* Pope notes that the court focused on the issue of the role of state legislatures as assessors of community sentiment and the limited sentencing role of juries. For the court these factors represented objective criteria by which it was proper to determine the public attitude toward a particular sanction. However, the court did not question the composition of state legislatures as so-called representatives of communities. Similarly, the court lauded the jury for its supposed impartiality and decided that a jury sentence reflected the view of the community on punishment, ignoring the fact that only those already predisposed to choose the death penalty would be selected to sit on a jury in capital cases. Ultimately, as Pope points out, the Court failed to question underlying assumptions about society, its composition, and the notion of objectivity itself.

Boot Camps

Are boot camps an effective form of punishment and what is the attraction of having offenders undergo military style training as a mode of punishment? Is the boot camp model an effective form of punishment? Those who believe in punishment as retribution applaud boot camps for their supposed capacity to save money that would otherwise be spent on housing offenders in prison and for their mode of punishment. This is argued to be appropriately severe, regimented, and likely to induce discipline and structure into the life of a young offender who lacks these qualities and values. Over the past ten years boot camps have become a notable addition to punishment options, much commented upon, and often figuring in media depictions of appropriate punishment.

Proponents of this form of punishment contend that young, nonviolent, and often first-time offenders will respond positively to the short, sharp shock of a boot camp. Thus, it is argued that punishment there will be more effective than incarceration and will be less expensive (Welch 1999: 108). In 1994 there were boot camps operating in thirty states, and throughout the nation more than 7,000 beds were dedicated to boot camp–type programs, where offenders are detained for between 90 and 180 days. In New York State the largest boot camp operates 1,500 beds (Welch 1999: 109).

Boot camps draw heavily on a military model, and this itself has been the subject of criticism. Critics ask why the model of a boot camp, designed to teach soldiers how to fight in war and other forms of conflict is appropriate for young nonviolent offenders. Is the notion of boot camp at all compatible with the ideal of rehabilitation? These questions have particular force when the military itself has discontinued the confrontational approach to teaching recruits military skills because of the adverse effects of training that is intended to demean and humiliate young men and women (Welch 1999: 110). The boot camp emphasis on masculine conduct and the corresponding debasement of images or behavior that is perceived to be feminine also raises questions about the appropriateness of such a regime for life outside the boot camp.

The effectiveness of boot camp programs as a form of punishment has also been questioned. MacKenzie and colleagues in a 1993 study note that boot camps have not reduced recidivism, and another study in 1995 of eight states concludes that participants at boot camps perform neither any better nor any worse than offenders undertaking other forms of punishment (Welch 1999: 111). Other criticism relates to the tendency to assume that boot camps are a good idea because of the fact that they privilege notions of discipline, routine, and military ethos, values that find much support throughout the United States, which has a high regard for its military forces. Other forms of punishment do not enjoy this kind of loyalty, and thus questions are asked about why citizens react to boot camps in this manner. Associated with this questioning is the notion, again generally accepted, that young men and women can be scared into being better and more law-abiding citizens. In this sense, many seem to regard boot camps as extensions of the discipline that was once imposed in the home but which is now considered out of line with modern thinking on parenting practices. For those who favor corporal punishment, such as paddling (see later in this chapter), the attraction of boot camps is that they reflect what are perceived as traditional disciplinary practices within the family which are no longer permitted or condoned by most citizens.

Welch (1999: 113) points out that boot camps also constitute "normalizing institutions," that is, they are intended to apply correction and bring persons into line with a set of standards judged to be "normal" and as such are not primarily to be seen as institutions inflicting punishment. Again, the question remains why the military model has been chosen as a normalizing standard and not, for example, the model of the family (chosen in the past, see Chapter 1), the hospital and clinical model (also chosen in the past), the school and educational model (see Chapter 1 and the Elmira Reformatory concept), or the factory, plantation, and corporate model (prison labor instilling the work ethic) (see Chapter 1, especially on the penitentiary). In addition to these models, Welch points to other seemingly more appropriate forms, such as athletics, with its connection to sports and notions of fair play, teamwork, moderation, and discipline, and even to martial arts, which again stresses discipline and self-control (Welch 1999: 116–117). One response to these issues is that boot camps are directed at satisfying middle-class notions of appropriate punishment, a middle class that has lost faith in the ability of the prison to correct and that favors images of strict militaristic-type discipline and masculinity (Welch 1999: 118).

The military has been a model for correctional practice in the past and continues to inform practice today. For example, in Chapter 1 we saw that Castle Island prison in Boston Harbor was an institution that was run very much on military lines. The essence of the early penitentiary was a military model that practiced marching and walking in lockstep and copied from the military other practices such as time scheduling and notions of supervision and control. Among the prison officers a military model was, and still is, followed in relation to the formal ranks of officers and their training and staff organization. Ultimately, the military represents an ideal of law and order and is associated with the process of bringing order out of chaos (Welch 1999: 122). Thus for many overlapping reasons the regime of the boot camp resonates within U.S. society, and boot camps will likely continue to retain adherents regardless of their value as deterrent or retributive institutions.

Mass Imprisonment

At year-end 2001, more than 5.6 million U.S. adults had served time in federal and state prisons. Assuming unchanged incarceration rates, 6.6 percent of U.S. residents born in 2001 will go to prison at some time during their lifetime (Bureau of Justice Statistics 2002). Overall, the United States had incarcerated 2.1 million persons at year-end 2002, a rate of incarceration of 476 inmates per 100,000 of population and an increase from the 1995 rate when it was 411 per 100,000. This means that 1 in every 110 men and 1 in every 1,656 women in the country were sentenced prisoners under state or federal jurisdiction. As of December 31, 2002, state prisons were operating at between 1 and 17 percent above capacity, and federal prisons at an extraordinary rate of 33 percent above capacity (Harrison and Beck 2003).

Criminologist Nils Christie (1993) has suggested that the increasing prison populations in western countries, especially in the United States, represent a move toward "Gulags western style." The term *gulag* became identified with the harshness and repression experienced in Soviet Russia symbolizing a secret zone run by bureaucrats where entire populations of "undesirables" were marginalized, brutalized, and terrorized. Christie argues that penal policymakers, who at one time saw prison as a punishment of last resort, now see it as almost the only viable option for punishment of offenses.

Since the 1970s, the rush to incarcerate has resulted in a rate of imprisonment in the United States that has increased from 230 per 100,000 in 1979 (Christie 1993) to a present rate of 476 per 100,000. This means that almost two million persons are being incarcerated in the United States at any given time. This is a remarkable development in the history of penal policy and practice. However, the phenomenon of mass imprisonment is not limited to the United States. In England, the rate per 100,000 increased from 93 in 1986 to 125 in 1998; in New Zealand the comparable rates are 75 to 160, and as a whole, the rate in Australia has increased from 65 to 106 over the same period (Pratt 2001: 284). Various explanations have been put forward for this situation, including political promotion of the need to get "tough on crime," which creates fears that unless we incapacitate offenders we will not be safe from them. The move toward mass imprisonment has been seen by many as something exceptional and unusual, but Nils Christie (2000: 178) suggests that this trend toward the increasing use of imprisonment might in fact be a normal feature of modern societies and that the mass imprisonment seen today in the United States is not an aberration at all. In support of his argument, Christie cites Bauman's (1989) contention that the Holocaust too was no aberration but simply a logical extension of society as it existed. Bauman identifies a number of conditions that contributed to the making of the Holocaust: the division of labor, modern bureaucracy, the rational mind, the stress on efficiency, the scientific mentality, and the relegation of values by sectors of society. He sees those same factors as contributing to the phenomenon of mass imprisonment in the United States today.

In a radical extension of Christie's argument, John Pratt (2001: 283) puts forward the view that we may in fact be moving further than Christie envisaged and entering into "a theatre of punishment that exists beyond the gulags" (2001: 285) where the punitive attitudes currently prevailing in some modern societies will take us beyond even the gulag. Bauman and Christie identify the routinization of control and moral indifference as central elements in this movement. The former condition emphasizes efficiency in moving and processing offenders through the criminal justice system and into penal institutions. Increasingly we see no real public involvement at all in the punishment process. It has become a bureaucratic routine invisible to the general public, taking on a life of its own and, as Christie has noted, crime control has now become an industry. Moral indifference is associated with the way punishment has become more private and invisible over the centuries to an extent that it is now possible for politicians to advocate still more incarceration of those who are now routinely described and treated as if they were no longer part of humanity. Separating criminals out and treating them as a special class of "others" began in the eighteenth century as described in Chapter 1, but that process has now reached a new level of indifference as citizens are bombarded with media stories (real and fictional) about the threat that crime and criminals present to themselves and their families. Media-induced panics about sexual predators and teen violence fuel the notion that to live risk free we have to become indifferent to the social and economic circumstances that contribute to criminality and that we must isolate these "others" from the rest of human kind.

In answer to the question of how this movement is to be stopped, Christie believes the main hope lies in replacing the present bureaucratic rationality about punishment with a revival of cultural values. In other words, he believes that human decency and conscience will prevail (Christie 2000: 182). Pratt, on the other hand, contends that we may already have moved beyond the gulag. He argues that the gulag is no longer able to function as a brake or control on our actions and that some societies have already created new possibilities for punishment. He identifies a number of themes that suggest this possibility. The first is that there has been a movement over time (see Chapter 1) away from the very public face of the prison built in grand and mass architectural style toward prisons that no longer bear the public distinguishing marks of prisons. In other words, prisons have now merged into the landscape and become disguised as ordinary buildings and have lost their identifiability. Second, and related to the disguise now worn by prisons, we have become indifferent to the very existence of prisons and of those people inside them. Increasingly, prisons are zones of complete indifference so far as the public is concerned. Third, bureaucratization has resulted in prisoners again being distanced from the public as prison administrators disdain the opinions of others about their work and operations, and the business of tending inmates is left to penal experts.

According to Pratt we are now seeing a "decline of indifference" as penal policy has come to be driven by populist politicians constantly urging a more punitive attitude toward offenders. Associated with this is the emphasis by politicians and the media on the pain experienced by the victims of crime and the statements by some states that there are limits to the extent to which it can intervene to protect the public in their daily activities. States have acknowledged that crime cannot be solved or eradicated and have declared limits to the protection they can offer the public. The decline of indifference is marked, for example, by proposals to reintroduce chain gangs (see Cruel and Unusual Punishment, this chapter) and the construction of registers for sex offenders who may be surveilled or even hunted down by communities that fear having them live in their midst. Even the prison has changed status because, in the United States in particular, it has become a desirable edifice to have in a locality, because it provides employment and job security for rural areas abandoned by other industries. Prison guards in California and elsewhere actively lobby for the prison establishment to be expanded. The investment of human and financial capital into the prison system means that increasing numbers of people are now seeing the inside of prisons and becoming involved in the prison system.

Pratt's argument is therefore that public sentiments are now spilling out of the gulag, which in the past contained them, and society is advancing toward a more expressive view of punishment, which could take the form of hostility, hatred, and massive intolerance (Pratt 2001: 304). This change in public sentiment is reflected not only in chain gangs but in other public forms of punishment that contain elements of shaming, such as local citizens putting up posters that shame those named and warn about delinquent persons returning to the area and the explosion of media programs that convey information about who is "most wanted" and how citizens can bring them to the attention of law enforcement.

As the state has declared its inability to eradicate crime and warned the populace to look after itself, the community has responded with gated communities staffed by private security guards functioning like police and supplementing the efforts of the state (sometimes even replacing them) to control crime. Public sentiment and emotion are now unleashed against crime and criminals at every opportunity, spurred on by media panics and outrages with televised trials and punishments, police pursuits along the freeways, and programs about the work of police, coming together to bring a new focus on crime and its control. Victims are very much in the forefront of this explosion of emotion. Their response to crimes and their views about how criminals should be punished are a staple in the news and crime reporting media.

It seems beyond argument that the penal system of today does not concern itself with preventing or stopping crime so much as administering and managing criminals and delinquents by placing them under control and supervision in an efficient manner (Garland 1985: 260). This modern function is often termed "warehousing" prisoners.

Prison and Amenities

What standard or amenities should be provided to inmates in prisons? In the history of the development of the prison, we noted in Chapter 1 that some researchers (for example, Rusche and Kirchheimer 1939) had suggested that deteriorating economic conditions were associated with changes in penal policy. They concluded that criminal punishment in any era must provide conditions that are worse than the living conditions of the poorest free people if such punishment is to be seen as a deterrent. This reflects the so-called doctrine of less eligibility, which determines that the standard of life of an inmate must be less than that enjoyed by a free laborer outside the prison (Garland 1985: 11). This principle was applied in the past, for example, by mandating that all prisoners be given a regular diet calculated to provide a minimum level of nutrition to enable the inmate to sustain life, taking into account the prison environment and the work expected of the prisoner (Garland 1985: 13).

The Philadelphia prison reformers of the nineteenth century often emphasized the cruelty of the correctional methods they were advocating as practice in the new penitentiaries. As we have seen, these included solitary confinement and the rule of silence. In stressing the severity of their methods of punishment they were responding to claims that incarcerating someone was a much less severe punishment than the public forms of punishment that preceded incarceration. In 1793 one of these reformers, William Bradford, wrote, "When he looks into the narrow cells prepared for the more atrocious offenders—when he realizes what it is to subsist on coarse fare—to languish in the solitude of a prison—to wear out his tedious days and long nights in feverish anxiety—to be cut off from his family—from his friends—from society—from all that makes life dear to the heart—when he realizes this he will no longer think the punishment inadequate to the offense" (Dubber 1998: 6).

Later, those supporting the notion of rehabilitating inmates argued that punishment was really treatment. Prison reformer John Howard who participated in the drafting of the English Penitentiary Act of 1779, which mandated a diet for inmates and directed they be provided with clothing (neither had previously been supplied in prisons), wanted to make the pains of imprisonment (in other words, suffering) more just but was not in favor of reducing the intensity of those pains. In his view, if humane treatment was allied with the strict regulation of activity, this would have the effect of improving the physical condition of inmates and their morals but would not prevent the prison regime being very "irksome and disagreeable" (Ignatieff 1978: 94).

The topic of amenities supplied to inmates periodically gains media attention. Politicians and others who want to show they are "tough on crime" complain that prisoners have access to television, are allowed to use weight-lifting equipment, and have radios, and "good" food. Their argument is that prisoners are there to be punished and if their standard of amenity is higher than that of the man on the street they can't be said to be suffering punishment. Those in favor of a reduced level of amenities or no amenities at all beyond the bare minimum seem to want to return to the conditions in the early penitentiaries described in Chapter 1. The media periodically adds fuel to this debate by running stories about prisons being resorts where inmates live a good life. For example one U.S. senator complained, "we've got to stop building prisons like Holiday Inns" (Lenz 2002: 500).

In 1996 the No Frills Prison Act was passed as an amendment to the Department of Justice's appropriation. It bans televisions, coffeepots, and hot plates in the cells of federal prisoners and also prohibits computers, electronic instruments, certain movies rated above PG, and unmonitored phone calls (Lenz 2002: 500). Among the states, in 1997, Alaska passed a similar bill that prohibited cable television, cassette tape players, tobacco use, and weight-lifting equipment (Lenz 2002: 510). The assumption underlying this approach is that making a sentence more punitive, that is, making the inmate suffer more, will have a greater deterrent effect on that particular inmate. He or she will be less inclined to reoffend knowing the harsh conditions in prison. However, there are no studies that support this claim. Correctional experts respond to claims of this nature by stating that removing or reducing amenities will not prevent recidivism. Some might argue that cutting back on amenities will save the state costs, but this is not necessarily so. For example, the thirty-one states that allow televisions in cells do not pay for them, because inmates or their relatives are required to purchase them, and cable television is usually funded through profits made by the prison commissary from vending machines and long distance phone calls (Finn 1996: 6–7).

There is a perception among some sections of the public that prisoners are being provided with amenities that the ordinary person cannot afford. In addition to the fact that taxpayers, as noted previously, do not generally fund such amenities, most prison wardens are against removing these amenities. Prison officials rely very heavily on a system of rewards and punishments to keep control in prisons. Educational programs, vocational training, and recreational activities, as well as televisions and radios are important means of rewarding good behavior (Lenz 2002: 506). So far as wardens are concerned, just keeping inmates busy is a major benefit that helps maintain prison order, and the level of amenities provided can have a good deal of influence on inmate activity. Of course, few citizens are fully aware of conditions in prison and even fewer have actually visited a prison and seen the prison environment. A statement from a prisoner in a state prison in south Michigan gives a sense of the prison experience:

> To describe what it means to be a prisoner, how it feels to be confined, is impossible for one who has not experienced it. The psychological state of complete passivity and

> dependence on the decisions of guards and officers must be included among the pains of imprisonment, along with the restriction of physical liberty, the possession of goods and services, and heterosexual relations. The frustration of the prisoner's ability to make choices and the frequent refusals to provide an explanation of the regulation and commands descending from the bureaucratic staff involve a . . . threat to the prisoners self image and reduce the prisoner to a weak, helpless, dependent status of childhood. The imprisoned criminal finds his picture of himself as a self-determining individual being destroyed by the regime of the custodian (Duguid 2000: 83).

Another prisoner put it like this, "Inside the walls nothing is certain, nothing can be taken for granted except the arbitrary exercise of absolute power. Rules engraved in stone one day will be superseded the next. What you don't know can always hurt you. And the prison rules are designed to keep you ignorant, keep you guessing, insure your vulnerability" (Duguid 2000: 83).

Corporal Punishment: Caning, Paddling, and Flogging

On 4 May 1994, Michael Fay, a U.S. teenager who had pleaded guilty to several acts of vandalism in Singapore was caned for those offenses. He was stripped, bent at the hip over a padded trestle, tied down at his ankles and wrists, and his buttocks were lashed four times with a four-foot-long half-inch-wide stick of rattan soaked in antiseptic. Fay, eighteen, had lived in Singapore since 1992. This sentence of corporal punishment gained huge media attention in the United States, with many expressing their views. President Clinton, in a personal letter to the Singapore president urged him to spare the rod and revoke the punishment, which Clinton described as "extreme." Also, twenty-four U.S. senators appealed to the president of Singapore to offer clemency. However, U.S. public opinion expressed support for the punishment, some even writing to the Singapore Embassy in Washington expressing their approval. In Dayton, Ohio, where Fay's father lived, citizens supported the punishment by a 2 to 1 margin. The Singaporean courts and government rejected the various appeals for clemency, except that the government agreed to reduce the number of lashes. A Home Affairs Ministry official stated that

Singapore was able to keep its society orderly and crime free because of its tough laws against antisocial crimes (Nygaard 2000: 1).

As Davis (2000: 198) reveals, the Michael Fay case prompted legislators in some states in the United States to introduce legislation providing for corporal punishment. In the 1994 to 1995 legislative sessions, seven different bills were sponsored in six state legislatures. They mandated public caning, paddling, flogging, and whipping. None of the bills became law, but their promotion in various states indicates a level of interest in the United States in reintroducing corporal punishment. Only a few weeks after Fay's punishment, an assemblyman in California announced that he planned to bring in legislation that authorized the paddling of juveniles for graffiti-related offenses (Davis 2000: 201). A bill in Mississippi was aimed at all persons committing criminal acts, but most bills like that from Tennessee singled out particular crimes such as trespassing, vandalism, mailbox tampering, flag burning, and burglary.

In California, New Mexico, and New York the proponents saw graffiti as the offense most suitable for paddling (Davis 2000: 204). Five of the seven bills mandated that the corporal punishment was to take place in a public setting, usually a courtroom, and one provided specifically that it should occur on the courthouse steps. Sponsors noted that location was intended to make the punishment especially degrading (Davis 2000: 206). Two bills spelled out the severity of the caning. The Tennessee bill required that the severity be comparable with the severity of the criminal act, whereas the bill from Louisiana required that a parent or guardian be ordered to stop paddling if the court thought it was being administered too severely (Davis 2000: 207). Justifications for the bills generally centered on the need to tame wild youth, and a number of sponsors lamented the passing of whipping as a punishment. Most thought that the corporal punishment would act as a deterrent and especially stressed the spectacle that the public whipping would produce. Some thought that only caning was a "real punishment" because they perceived it to be more humiliating and more painful than prison. Sponsors also indicated they had been paddled as children and had learned a lesson and suffered no ill effects. In this way they attempted to link childhood punishment with corporal punishment authorized by a court. Thus they attempted to confer legitimacy and legality on a practice that is generally considered to be brutal and humiliating and a form of state violence long since condemned as wholly inappropriate (Davis 2000: 211). Davis concludes that the bills were a response to media coverage and media themes arising out of the Michael Fay caning, affording those at the political level an opportunity to demonstrate how tough they were on crime.

Maximum and Super-Maximum Prisons

According to the National Institute of Corrections twenty-two states detain inmates in maximum-security facilities, and of those, twelve built "supermax" prisons in the 1990s. A number of the new supermax prisons provided no space for treatment programs because their sole function was to incapacitate offenders. For example, Maryland's supermax prison has 282 beds and was designed to hold violent prisoners with records of escape for short periods during which they would correct their prior behavior. Inmates were detained in sixty-five-square-foot cells for twenty-three hours each day with only an hour out of their cells for exercise. Costs at this supermax prison run at nearly twice the amount required to keep an inmate in a maximum-security facility (Associated Press 2003). The cost of keeping an inmate in a supermax prison is $75,000 a year compared with $24,000 for a maximum-security cell (Welch 1999: 202). The U.S. Penitentiary at Marion, Illinois, is a supermax unit holding 400 of the nation's most high-risk inmates who have been incarcerated within the federal prison system. One characteristic of this and other supermax prisons is the condition known as *lockdown* during which all inmates are confined to their cells for twenty-three hours each day. They are permitted to leave for only one hour a day for exercise and allowed to shower only two or three times a week (Welch 1999: 200). Inmates are routinely chained to their beds for several days at a time. The Pelican Bay Prison in California houses about 1,200 inmates in super maximum–security conditions. Again, inmates spend most of their time confined in their cells, in this unit for twenty-two and a half hours a day, within a cell measuring eight by ten feet, where the temperature is maintained at a steady 85 to 90 degrees. Inmates are not permitted to work or study.

Punishing Sex Offenders

Apart from being incarcerated for their offenses, sex offenders have now become subject to a range of post-incarceration identification and surveillance measures in most states of the United States, based on what has come to be known as Megan's Law. In 1994 New Jersey took only four months to legislate Megan's Law as a response to a massive community protest over the killing of a seven-year-old girl (Petrunik 2002: 483). Megan's Law contains no provisions relating to the treatment of convicted sex offenders (Simon 2000: 15); rather, it aims at surveillance and continuing control and long-term punishment through those measures. Megan was Megan Kanka, who was assaulted and killed by a sex offender who lived across the street, and her mother became a prominent figure in pushing for legislative action against sex offenders.

There has been a dramatic increase in the number of sex offenders under state control, and between 1988 and 1990 the number of incarcerated sex offenders increased by 48 percent in the United States, and by 1998 about one-third of inmates in some states were sex offenders (Petrunik 2002: 483).

There are variations among states, but the basic model of sex offender legislation is that the specified sex offenders are required to register certain information with local law enforcement agencies, sometimes for a period of years and in some cases for the rest of their lives. Additionally, some laws mandate that sex offenders give information about where they are living and perhaps other particulars to specified community groups and to certain citizens and institutions, for example, to schools, and to facilities for child care (Lynch 2002: 533). As well, a good deal of this sort of information about a sex offender can be located on the Internet. In at least thirty states access to sex offender registries is possible through Web sites sponsored by those states (Petrunik 2002: 484).

It is not only in the area of information that sex offenders have been subjected to punitive measures. At least fifteen states have legislation that permits "violent sexual predators" to be committed to prison under civil procedures. The constitutionality of such laws was endorsed by the Supreme Court in *Kansas v. Hendricks* in 1997 (Petrunik 2002: 484) and in *Smith v. Doe* and *Connecticut Department of Public Safety v. Doe;* both decided in 2003, the Supreme Court held that "Sex offenders are a serious threat in this Nation" and that registration laws are nonpunitive in nature (Levenson 2003).

In further moves to penalize sex offenders, a number of states, including California, Florida, and Georgia, have legislated for mandatory chemical castration as a condition of parole for repeat sex offenders against children (Petrunik 2002: 484).

Essentially, there is zero tolerance within the community for sex offenders, who have now earned the status of "monsters." These offenders are considered beyond humanity and incapable of being cured, and therefore they are perceived as a permanent danger to the community. Most recently, a number of states have introduced a shaming or "scarlet letter" component associated with notification by sex offenders. For example, in Louisiana, offenders must identify themselves and their status as a sex offender to community members, and the sentencing court has the power to require that an offender notify community members using signs, handbills, vehicle bumper stickers, or labels on clothing. In Texas a judge ordered fourteen sex offenders on probation to carry bumper stickers on their vehicles that read "Danger! Registered Sex Offender in Vehicle" and to place signs in front of their residences reading "Danger! Registered Sex Offender Lives Here" (Petrunik 2002: 493).

The federal government has also become involved in making policy on sex offenders. In 1994 it included in a crime bill a requirement that funds available for federal anticrime programs be withheld from those states that did not maintain sex offender registration systems. As a result of this legislation many states that did not possess such systems moved to install them, and by 1996, forty-nine states had systems in place (Lynch 2002: 533). In 1996 the federal government acted again, this time to provide for nationwide tracking of sex offenders in a database operated by the FBI under a federal Megan's Law (Lynch 2002: 535). Again in 1996 the federal government enacted the Pam Lychner Sexual Offender Tracking and Identification Act requiring lifetime registration for offenders convicted of one or more sexual offenses involving certain acts with victims younger than twelve years of age (Petrunik 2002: 494). Finally in 1998, legislation required that states identify those sex offenders considered to be "sexually violent predators." This group is required to give further additional information on registering and will be subject to notification requirements for the rest of their lives (Petrunik 2002: 494).

How did this focus on sex offenders come about, and what are the implications of punishing persons convicted of particular offenses far beyond normal limits of state control? As Petrunik (2002: 487) explains, the clinical approach to sex offenders relying on various treatment programs was cast in doubt in the 1970s and 1980s when a widely cited review of such programs questioned their effectiveness. These criticisms prompted an interest in a justice approach to these particular offenders advocating determinate sentences as opposed to the indeterminate sentences favored in the clinical approach.

The justice approach argues that sex offenders are not as dangerous as they are made out to be under the clinical approach and also that issues of rights and freedoms are raised with mandatory therapy that can have the effect of keeping offenders in custody for very substantial periods of time. In turn, the justice approach came under attack by victim advocates and groups, including in particular the women's movement and child protection organizations. Studies showed that sex offenders often committed repeat offenses (Petrunik 2002: 491), and in general the pressure from victims and other groups gave rise to a policy of zero tolerance toward sex offenders. This was exacerbated when sensational media coverage set in motion waves of moral panic about the risks posed by these offenders (Jenkins 1998). As these groups brought pressure to bear on political figures to legislate, sex offenses began to assume the dimensions of a national crisis. Thus, the justice approach to sex offenders became a community risk-management approach.

At the same time as these developments were occurring, advances in technology began to make possible forms of surveillance, monitoring, and control that had not previously been available. Risk measurement and risk management joined with technology and populist punitive justice to produce the first sex offender legislation in Washington in 1990 with the federal Jacob Wetterling Crimes against Children and Sexually Violent Offender Act of 1994 following soon after. This act targeted two classes of offenders: those convicted of an offense against a minor and those convicted of a sexually violent offense. Offenders were required to register for ten years, and states were mandated to release specified information about these offenders to the public. As of October 2001 there were some 3,888,000 registered sex offenders in the United States.

The current community risk-management approach to dealing with sex offenders raises a number of issues:

- The cost of legislation against sex offenders is said to be unduly high. For example, new bureaucracies are required at state and federal levels to implement the new laws, litigation costs increase with appeals and constitutional challenges, and the fees of experts and the cost of operating special facilities must also be factored in. One estimate is that Washington and California have been spending about $100,000 a year for each person committed as a sexually violent predator.

- The registration and notification provisions have serious funding implications also because of the need to ensure compliance with the new laws. Many states have no idea of the percentage of sex offenders in their jurisdictions who have actually registered, and some argue that law enforcement could spend all its time on registration and notification and still not fully implement legal requirements (Petrunik 2002: 499). For example, in Massachusetts there are hundreds of sex offenders who have failed to register with state authorities after arriving from other states, and these transient populations of offenders are difficult to track (Meyers et al. 2003).
- Unexpectedly, the laws have had an effect on the housing market because in at least one state, potential buyers have been issued a disclaimer warning them to check with local law enforcement about possible sex offenders living in the area. In one case in Wisconsin, a sixty-year-old offender confined to a wheelchair was forced to vacate his apartment when his landlord refused to allow him to continue living there. This person was even discouraged from using public transport provided specifically for the disabled (Petrunik 2002: 500).
- Some have contended that the sense of isolation and hostility that accompanies the risk management in the community approach renders ex-offenders a hopeless class, with the result that they have no motivation to change or accept treatment.
- There is the general concern that state policing of sex offenders through the many ways listed in the various laws gives sex offenders' civil rights a backseat to community rights and the rights of victims. The community demands total control of the life and movement of a sex offender, and no risks at all are considered acceptable. Recent developments include the placing of global positioning satellite (GPS)

monitors on sex offenders so they can be tracked anywhere in the world using GPS technology (Ramierez 2003).

Privatizing Punishment

Private prisons have been defined as "those that are privately owned, operated, or managed, under contract to government" (Logan 1990: 13), and states have been privatizing prisons over the last twenty years. The federal government is not new to privatization, because the Immigration and Naturalization Service has for many years contracted for the provision of facilities to hold illegal aliens. As well, some states began to privatize their juvenile facilities and community correction programs some time ago. For example, Massachusetts contracted out its juvenile programs in 1969. Nevertheless, embarking on a policy of privatizing institutions designed to carry out punishment imposed by the state does raise some ethical concerns. Those who oppose the concept of privatizing punishment generally raise the following arguments (Banks 2004):

- How do private prisons deal with the issue of the use of deadly force? It is one thing for employees of the state acting according to legislation that grants them custody over prisoners to use deadly force but quite another for the employees of a prison run by a private corporation to use such force.
- Is it right that imprisonment should be managed and administered by a private corporation, or must this role and function be left with the state and its authorities?
- Is the profit motive appropriate to the task of running a prison? In other words, will a private contractor cut corners and provide a reduced level of custody and treatment in order to maximize profit?
- Does the existence of private prisons actually create a demand for imprisonment that can only be satisfied by greater levels of imprisonment? That is, are private prisons a case of "if you build them, they (prisoners) will come, regardless of other alternative punishments"?

A central argument in the debate about private punishment is whether the state should abdicate its role in imposing punishment to a private entity. The contention is that punishment has always been seen as a function of the government (whether federal or state) since the earliest times and the state has always prohibited private punishment in such forms as self-help, vigilantism, and the like. If this view is correct then there is no place for privatizing prisons or any other form of correction.

As noted in Chapter 1, a punishment is imposed by an authority established by the state and for an offense that is created by the legislature of a state. The notion of a social contract involves citizens transferring their rights to the state with the state in turn providing protection and security to its citizens. It would be entirely inconsistent with this understanding for the state to abdicate its right to impose punishment and empower a private corporation to do so. In fact, contracting out the power to punish renders the role of the state minimal, and the state will be seen as surrendering its monopoly over crime control and punishment.

There is also the constitutional issue of whether the state may empower private agencies to punish lawbreakers. In 1986 the American Bar Association expressed the view that private prisons did not accord with the constitution, arguing that "incarceration is an inherent function of the government and the government should not abdicate this responsibility by turning over prison operations to private industry" (Shichor 1995: 52). Against this argument, advocates of private punishment point to the fact that privatization is already well established in the field of criminal justice. Another argument is that the uniform, style, and manner of operation of public prisons signify the state exercising punishment on behalf of all citizens against those who have breached the social contract. From this perspective, any action that would detract from this role would weaken the role of the state with regard to punishment. Advocates of privatization counter this view with the argument that what matters is substance and not symbolism.

The profit motive is clearly central to a private corporation in any business activity, and opponents of privatization argue this means that a private entity will be attempting to make a profit out of the punishment of citizens (Banks 2004: 194–195). This seems morally objectionable and intuitively wrong, and the American Civil Liberties Union (ACLU) has argued that, "the profit motive is incompatible with doing justice" (Logan 1990: 72). Will a private corporation put its own interest in making profits ahead of the interests of those entrusted to its custody? One answer to this question is that the prison system, especially in the United States, has had a long association with profit, because, since the nineteenth century prisoners have been leased out to, and performed labor for, private companies (see Chapter 1). Thus, there is nothing new in this linkage of profit with prisons, and having a contractor run an entire prison is simply a logical development from contracting for the labor of prisoners.

In response to the argument that privatization creates a demand for imprisonment, some suggest that those in the business of making money out of punishment will seek to expand their business interests and will lobby and influence policymakers and planners in the bureaucracy to ensure that private prisons continue to be built and that their capacity is always utilized to the maximum (Banks 2004: 195). Currently there is also an economic argument associated with prison building. For example, in upper state New York prisons are being built in areas where other industries have moved out and where jobs are sorely needed (Christie 2000). Sometimes the local prison will provide the only available form of employment in that area. In this period of mass imprisonment (see section entitled Mass Imprisonment in this chapter), will the economic benefit that prison employment brings to a depressed rural area result in the construction of more prisons in these areas that will have to be populated with inmates? Will this result in more citizens being incarcerated than would otherwise be the case? The number of private prisons under construction in 1998 was sixty (Christie 2000), and there is every reason to believe that private prisons are now an accepted part of the criminal justice system. In California, prison officers have become unionized and form a distinct and powerful lobby group when issues of prison building arise in government. To what extent will lobby groups such as this influence the level of incarceration in the nation?

Recently private companies have become involved in managing and operating maximum-security prisons, and this has raised the core issue of the use of deadly force (Harding 1998: 635). Is it morally acceptable that nonstate employees should have the right to use deadly force in controlling prisoners in a maximum-security prison, for example, if an escape is attempted? What controls and accountability exist to prevent abuse of any authority that is given to use deadly force? Some argue that private companies will seek to reduce costs by minimizing training for their staff in the use of deadly force and that their staff will be more ready to employ such levels of force than would be the case in a public prison. Questions arise about how the use of force is to be regulated and what mechanisms exist and can be implemented in practice to prevent the unlawful deployment of lethal force.

Generally, it is apparent that privatizing prisons has given rise to a set of legal and ethical issues that have yet to be fully addressed. Most importantly, will privatizing prisons distort the operations of the criminal justice system to such a degree as to significantly contribute to the mass imprisoning of citizens already taking place? It is easy to see the evolution of a circular process where prisons become overcrowded, prompting new prison construction by private contractors. In turn those private prisons become overcrowded (because they have to be filled), causing yet more private prisons to be built. Has a "prison-industrial" complex already developed to match the "military-industrial complex"? At year-end 2002 privately operated correctional facilities housed 93,771 inmates. This amounted to 5.8 percent of state and 12.4 percent of federal inmates (Harrison and Beck 2003: 1–14).

Mandatory Minimum Sentences ("Three Strikes and You're Out")

As we saw in Chapter 1, in the 1970s a movement against rehabilitation began and has continued into the present. The notion that rehabilitation no longer worked and the development of a more punitive approach to punishment found their ultimate expression in the mandatory minimum sentences enacted by many states and the federal government in the 1980s. The more punitive approach toward offenders included the formulation of policies intended to punish offenders through incapacitation, enhance the status of victims, and above all reassure the public that crime control measures were being adopted that would ensure their safety as well as that of their families.

Legislation seeking to punish violent felony offenders—called Three Strikes and You're Out, meaning commit three felonies and you will be incarcerated for a lengthy minimum period—was pioneered by the states of Washington and California. In 1993, the ballot in Washington State included a proposal mandating life imprisonment without parole for offenders convicted for a third time of specified violent or otherwise serious felonies (Austin and Irwin 2001: 184). The initiative came about when a convicted rapist, who had recently been released from prison, murdered a woman and when Polly Klaas was kidnapped in California and was later murdered. She was kidnapped by a felon with a long record of violent crime. These two events provided further impetus for the Three Strikes and You're Out movement. Voters in Washington and California passed their ballot proposals, and by 1997 twenty-four other states and the federal government has passed mandatory minimum penalties laws. The rationale for this kind of legislation was said to be deterrence. Its proponents argue that deterrence will be shown to be effective if severe and certain punishment is imposed on habitual offenders (Banks 2004: 178).

Opponents of mandatory minimum penalties argue, on the other hand, that it is unrealistic to expect a habitual criminal to be knowledgeable of the laws and to make a rational, conscious decision not to commit another crime, that is, it assumes that all offenders make calculated decisions about their future actions (Austin and Irwin 2001: 185). The measure also relies greatly on a high probability of arrest and conviction. Others argue that incapacitation is the correct approach to take with habitual criminals, but this assumes that they will always be criminals, whereas studies have shown that this is a difficult matter to predict. Also, it ignores the fact that criminal careers do not usually extend beyond a certain age.

Three strikes legislation commonly provides a list of offenses that carry minimum penalties, sets out the number of strikes that must be satisfied to invoke the minimum penalty, and sets out the actual ultimate penalties. In the California law, any felony can qualify as a strike if the offender already has one or two prior felony convictions that appear on a list of strikeable offenses. In the first case, the two strikes will warrant a minimum sentence twice that provided for the offense concerned and in the second case the automatic penalty is mandatory life in prison with no possibility of parole for a minimum period of twenty-five years (Austin and Irwin 2001: 187). This law is among the most severe in the nation. For example, the third strike need not be a violent felony, it can be any felony at all, and it provides a wide range of offenses that qualify as strike offenses. In California between 1994 and 1998 some 45,000 three strikes cases were sent to prison (Austin and Irwin 2001: 197), leading to some strange and anomalous situations. For example, one offender received a sentence of twenty-seven years to life for attempting to sell stolen batteries, the value of which was only $90 (Austin and Irwin 2001: 208).

Fortunately for the prison system (California initially was predicted to have to double its capacity for inmates), courts, and prosecutors have mitigated the rigor of three strikes laws, thus avoiding a penal crisis in the state. For example, a California prosecutor has the power to decide whether a third strike offense should be charged as a felony or a misdemeanor (Shichor 2000: 1). If the prosecutor chooses to prosecute for a misdemeanor, then three strikes is not invoked.

Is there public support for three strikes laws? The first law imposing this measure was approved in Washington in a referendum in 1993 by a margin of three to one and in another referendum in California by a margin of 72 percent for and only 28 percent against (Cullen et al. 2000: 38). In 1994, a Time/CNN poll found that 81 percent of adults favored mandatory life imprisonment for persons convicted of a third serious crime. However, like all public opinion polls the answers given depend greatly on the questions put. Thus when the public was given a chance in a 1995 study in Cincinnati, Ohio, to select sentences for specific offenses, ranging from no punishment and probation to life with and without parole, only about 16 percent chose a life sentence.

Currently, in the context of a depressed economy, mandatory minimum penalties are being assessed in some states in view of their impact on the size of the prison population. However, like the war on drugs it seems difficult for legislators to admit they might have made a wrong policy choice on a matter of law and order where no one wants to be seen as less than "tough on crime."

Cruel and Unusual Punishment

The Eighth Amendment to the American Constitution prohibits "cruel and unusual punishment." This principle can be traced back to the *lex talionis,* that is, the concept of "an eye for an eye, a tooth for a tooth." This Judeo-Christian principle essentially argues that punishment for a crime ought to correspond with the nature of the crime committed, that is, it ought to be proportionate with the crime. Nowadays we tend to focus on the rigorousness and harshness of this notion but the *lex talionis* actually fixed an upper limit to punishment and promoted the concept of proportionality expressed during the classical Greek period by Aristotle, who wrote that a judge should try to "make the parts equal by the penalty he imposes" (Gorman 1997: 459). Later, the Magna Carta prohibited excessive punishment declaring that offenses should carry punishments that reflected the nature of the offense. The expression "cruel and unusual punishments" first appeared in the Declaration of Rights of 1689 in England, but the meaning was never really clear. Some argued that it was intended to deal with the method of punishment and not the actual punishment, and these ambiguities carried over into the U.S. Constitution when the expression was incorporated into the Eighth Amendment in 1791.

One issue, the method and not the degree of punishment, is just what the framers of the Constitution intended the term to mean when they adopted it, but very little information is available on this aspect and again, some argue that they were concerned about issues like torture and barbarous punishments. Others argue that it simply repeated the English injunction against excessive punishment. This lack of historical specificity has made it a difficult task for the Supreme Court to apply the expression to particular cases coming before it. In the nineteenth century the Court applied the Eighth Amendment to compare methods of execution alleged to be cruel, and later such arguments were raised in relation to the penalty of electrocution. For example, in *Louisiana ex rel. Francis v. Resweber* (1947), the Court said that a second attempt at electrocution was not a violation of the Eighth Amendment, because the failure of the first procedure was the result of an accident and not an attempt to cause unnecessary pain. In *Wilkerson v. Utah* (1878), the Court explained the scope of the expression cruel and unusual punishment, holding that punishment should not involve "terror, pain or disgrace." The facts of that case were that a defendant had been convicted of murder and sentenced to death and, acting in accordance with state law, the judge directed that he be executed by shooting. The Court made it clear that the Eighth Amendment prohibited torture but held that shooting was an acceptable mode of execution because it did not amount to "cruelty." It based its opinion on the fact that shooting was commonly employed as a penalty in the military. In this case, the

Court specifically condemned practices like public burning, disemboweling, and drawing and quartering, which it considered offensive to acceptable standards of decency.

In another case the Court found that a punishment must be excessively cruel to be in violation of the Eighth Amendment, and the fact that a punishment was new or unusual did not in itself amount to excessive cruelty (*In re Kemmler* [1890]). In this case Kemmler challenged electrocution as being cruel and unusual punishment, and the New York Court of Appeals agreed with the state legislature that the then untested electric chair was "more humane" than hanging. Although the Court agreed that electrocution was unusual it had not been demonstrated to be cruel because there was "no reasonable doubt that the application of electricity to the vital parts of the human body, under such conditions and in the manner contemplated by the statute, must result in instantaneous, and consequently, in painless death" (Lumer and Tenney 1995: 3). In fact, the electrocution of Kemmler, the first in the nation, did not bear out the justices' faith in the new science of electricity. Even with the assistance of Thomas Edison, who personally wired the chair for the electrocution, Kemmler needed two jolts of electricity to kill him, and the second lasted seventeen seconds, a far from instantaneous process. In fact it was reported that the smell of burning flesh was so awful that the prosecutor ran from the room (Lumer and Tenney 1995: 3).

Concerning the issue of how to judge whether a punishment is excessively cruel, the Court held that a "common knowledge" test could be applied. In the 1910 landmark case of *Weems v. United States*, for the first time the Court addressed the notion that a punishment might violate the Eighth Amendment if it was excessive. Here the Court moved away from its earlier focus on cruel punishments to look at the degree of punishment. In this case, Weems was sentenced to a form of punishment by a court in the Philippines that required that he wear a chain at the ankle that would link up to his wrists and that he perform hard labor while chained in this way for fifteen years. He also lost certain personal rights and was to be subjected to lifelong surveillance. Even though the punishment was well established in that country, the Court said that this did not justify its imposition. The Court noted that the Eighth Amendment was a progressive measure, not fixed in the past, and that its meaning could be elaborated as times changed and public opinion became more enlightened and liberal about what kinds of punishment were considered acceptable. This decision set the tone for the future by indicating that the Eighth Amendment would be applied flexibly in line with changes in the times and the varying standards of society.

The Supreme Court has also considered nondeath penalty cases under the Eighth Amendment, and in 1962 in *Robinson v. California* the Court struck down a California law that declared that drug addiction was illegal and allowed persons to be sent to jail after being convicted of drug addiction even though he or she did not actually possess any drugs. The Court has also said that the term *punishment* may extend to include not just physical punishments but also punishments that have psychological impact. Ultimately the standard in such cases will usually be whether a particular punishment is inconsistent with "evolving standards of decency" (*Trop v. Dulles* [1958]). According to this test punishments must reflect changes in society and its values. For example, Tessa Gorman argues that the punishment of chaining prisoners together in chain gangs violates the Eighth Amendment because it does not reflect changes in society about standards and modes of punishment. She contends that having been abolished generally in the 1960s, in part because of its associations and links with the practice of slavery, the reintroduction of chain gangs in Alabama in 1995 was in violation of the Eighth Amendment. As she puts it, "using chains as punishment in a culture where chains are intimately connected with the subjugation of a race implicitly embraces slavery. The enslavement of people is unacceptable by any standard of decency" (Gorman 1997: 477).

In May 1995 Alabama reintroduced the chain gang as a punishment. In fact the sanction was soon withdrawn following suit brought against the state by the Southern Poverty Law Center. However, until withdrawal, chain gangs of about 700 prisoners were formed in Alabama. Most were sent there for breaking parole or prison rule violations. Those sentenced for parole violations were to spend a minimum of six months on the gangs, whereas those sentenced for disciplinary reasons spent between fifteen and forty-five days there (Anderson et al. 2000: 8). Male prisoners assigned to the chain gangs wore white uniforms with the words *CHAIN GANG* stamped across their backs (Gorman 1997: 442–443). They were required to kneel down before the prison guards, who shackled them for the day's work, chaining the men ankle to ankle. A day's labor, generally pounding big rocks into smaller rocks with sledgehammers, lasted ten hours.

Gorman (1997: 443) argues the "chain gang has largely been an instrument with which to terrorize, torture, and exploit Africans and African-Americans," emphasizing that chains have figured greatly in the history of slavery. Chains were employed to control and transport slaves to the colonies on board slave ships; on their arrival and having been made ready for sale, slaves were displayed in chains; and following their purchase, slaves traveled to their new owners' homes wearing chains. The link between chaining Africans and African-Americans during the period of slavery and chaining them on chain gangs is clear, and chaining, as a practice, can be seen as a visible symbol of slavery. The suit filed against the reintroduction of chain gangs by the Southern Poverty Law Center alleges, among other infringements of rights, that chain gangs constitute cruel and unusual punishment (Anderson et al. 2000: 8).

The then newly elected governor of Alabama, Fob James Jr., had suggested in his preelection campaign that he would reintroduce chain gangs in his state, and opinion polls showed overwhelming support for the idea (Gorman 1997: 453). Prison officials put four justifications for the reintroduction of chain gangs forward: They will reduce crime; they will reduce the number of repeat offenders; they will address disciplinary problems among inmates; and they will shame inmates into a life of conformity (Anderson et al. 2000: 9). Putting prisoners in chains and having them work in public created a spectacle, but Alabama welcomed the public and press attention, perhaps because the public wanted to see prisoners being punished rather than imagining punishment behind prison walls. In other words, Alabama was promoting the expressive aspect of punishment. Some residents of Alabama acknowledged the punitive nature of the punishment but argued that humiliation and hard labor are deterrents to crime (Anderson et al. 2000: 10).

Alabama's return to the inglorious past of convict chain gangs lasted only until June 1996, when, without any necessity for a court order, the state entered into a settlement with the Southern Poverty Law Center to cease the punishment (*Michael Austin et al. v. Fob James Jr. Governor of Alabama and Ron Jones, Commissioner of ADC*) (Anderson et al. 2000: 7). The state announced publicly that it had decided to end the practice owing to administrative concerns, arguing that individual chaining would be more effective than chaining prisoners to each other. Chaining prisoners together had in practice created major problems such as inmates fighting each other, with other inmates on the chain unable to escape the fighting and themselves being injured. However, Alabama did not entirely renounce chaining, because prisoners would continue to have their legs shackled. Only chaining prisoners together ceased.

Punishing White-Collar Crime

Among those who study the subject, there is no consensus about exactly how to define the concept of "*white-collar crime.*" Many continue to use criminologist Edwin Sutherland's working definition established in 1949. In his definition, white-collar crime comprises those offenses, "committed by a person of respectability and high social status in the course of his occupation" (Rosenmerkel 2001: 312–313). Generally, white-collar crime is seen as comprising categories of crimes that have been termed elite deviance, occupational deviance, and organizational or corporate offending (Rosenmerkel 2001: 313).

Many argue (see for example, Welch 2003: 229) that the public is presented with images of crime, chiefly through the media, which depict crime as being located mainly at the street level and as involving young, poor, black and Latino males. White-collar crime was, until quite recently, largely ignored because of such stereotypes. Thus, offenses such as fraud, embezzlement, and securities fraud, often under the jurisdiction of regulatory bodies like the Securities and Exchange Commission (SEC), have been punished in civil and administrative proceedings rather than by criminal law. Even when the SEC refers cases to the criminal law for a corporate regulatory prosecution, cases must be first directed to the Department of Justice, which refers them to the U.S. Attorney's Office, which has complete discretion over the decision to proceed with the prosecution or not. One study by Shapiro in 1984 found that U.S. attorneys declined to prosecute 26 percent of all cases referred to them for prosecution by the SEC and that a full 48 percent of cases that were referred for prosecution never went to trial (Griffin 2002: 260).

Additional barriers to the prosecution of white-collar crime include: The lower legal standard in civil cases makes complicated white-collar cases easier to prove; aware that jail sentences are not the outcome of civil cases, defendants are far more likely to cooperate with the legal system if the proceedings are civil; and there is a possibility of substantial fines (Griffin 2002: 260). There is a long history of leniency toward white-collar offenders, and their high socioeconomic status has generally protected them from prosecution. Moreover, complex fraud and corporate crimes require special skills not possessed by all state district attorneys, so that, with the exception of states like New York and California where such expertise exists, white-collar crime has generally been given less prominence than crimes of violence and property offenses. Of course, high-status persons involved in white-collar crime typically have the economic means to hire the best lawyers and experts in their defense, and this serves to ensure lengthy and hard-fought trials.

The Federal Bureau of Investigation reported that in 2002 white-collar crime accounted for 4 percent of reported crime, that the majority of such crimes were committed by individuals arrested for bad check offenses, that most white-collar offenders had contact with their victims, and that they were typically white males in their late twenties to thirties (Federal Bureau of Investigation 2002). The FBI also reports that 42 percent of white-collar crime in that year involved offenses committed with a computer. These figures demonstrate the usefulness of computer technology as a tool in this form of crime.

Recent corporate and other white-collar scandals include: the prosecution and conviction of personality and wealthy businesswoman Martha Stewart for obstructing justice by lying about a stock sale; indictments against officers of Enron Corporation for fraud and related charges; the prosecution of officers of the cable TV company, Adelphia Communications, for treating the company as their personal bank; charges against officers of WorldCom for accounting fraud that claimed $11 billion in false profit; and charges against former CEO of Tyco for looting $600 million from the company. This recent activity in the prosecution of white-collar crime comes after President George W. Bush promised a "crime blitz" against corporate crime in July 2002, when he called for a "new ethic of personal responsibility" among business leaders. The president signed an executive order creating a "financial crimes SWAT team" with the Department of Justice and called on Congress to toughen penalties for white-collar and corporate crimes. However, it remains to be seen whether the recent political initiatives focusing on white-collar crime, the increased media attention, and the accompanying public pressure will bring about the same high profile and crime control attention historically and currently enjoyed by street crime offenders.

Conclusion

This discussion of issues in punishment has shown how the concept of punishment itself is problematic and why it is vital to understand the social and cultural context in which punishments are formulated and changed as well as the philosophical basis for the state exercising a right to punish offenders. Most importantly, punishment should not be seen simply as a response to crime but as a complex process in society. Currently, issues in punishment in the United States center on the prevailing punitive approach to crime control and on the general perception that societies and social practices should be shaped in such a way as to minimize and even eliminate risk in the lives of citizens. Thus, rehabilitation as a goal of punishment has given way to incapacitation, and the state has enlisted science and technology on an extensive scale to monitor and supervise offenders of all kinds.

Increasingly, mass imprisonment has become the dominant face of punishment in the United States. For complex reasons the media has transformed some crime stories into moral panics that have in turn promoted political moves to "get tough on crime" and to wage "wars on crime" and "wars on drugs," actions that have fueled the prison crisis and prompted the ethically questionable business of privatizing prisons. Capital punishment continues to excite emotions both for and against and will be an issue as long as the country (for whatever reasons) continues its independent approach to this form of punishment. Some have argued that disciplining offenders using corporal punishment, recalling punishment practices of the past, is the solution to the problem of how to punish and deter, and so boot camps and paddling and caning have their adherents. Others promote the notion that shameful or degrading punishments, such as chaining inmates together in gangs, benefit society despite the lessons from the past that indicate otherwise.

Current debates about how to punish are reflections of the societal response to crime and punishment at a particular moment in time. If there is a cycle of punishment according to the pressures of social forces then we might expect that the present populist, punitive attitude will give way to another approach or perspective less disciplinary in tone. However, it is equally possible that the prevailing debates and policies might represent the beginning of a still more draconian approach to punishment that could lead back to the expressive and public punishments of the past.

References

Anderson, James, Laronistine Dysan, and Willie Brooks Jr. 2000. "Alabama Prison Chain Gangs: Reverting to Archaic Punishment to Reduce Crime and Discipline Offenders." *Western Journal of Black Studies* 24(1): 9–23.

Associated Press. 2003. "New Thinking on 'Supermax': Financially Strapped States Shifting Focus." http://www.msnbc.com/news/989755.asp?Ocv=CB20 accessed 11 May 2003.

Austin, J., and J. Irwin. 2001. *It's about Time: America's Imprisonment Binge,* 3rd Edition. Belmont, CA: Wadsworth.

Banks, Cyndi. 2004. *Criminal Justice Ethics: Theory and Practice.* Thousand Oaks, CA: Sage Publications.

Barnes, H. E. 1972. *The Story of Punishment: A Record of Man's Inhumanity to Man.* Mont Clair, NJ: Patterson Smith.

Bauman, Zygmunt. 1989. *Modernity and the Holocaust.* Ithaca, NY: Cornell University Press.

Bean, Phillip. 1981. *Punishment: A Philosophical and Criminological Inquiry.* Oxford: Martin Robertson.

Bessler, John D. 1996. "The 'Midnight Assassination Law' and Minnesota's Anti-Death Penalty Movement, 1849–1911." *William Mitchell Law Review* 22: 577–730.

Bonczar, Thomas P., and Tracy Snell. November 2003. "Capital Punishment, 2002." *Bureau of Justice Statistics Bulletin.* Washington, DC: U.S. Department of Justice.

Bureau of Justice Statistics. 2002. "Prevalence of Imprisonment in the U.S. Population 1974–2001." *Bureau of Justice Statistics Bulletin.* Washington, DC: U.S. Department of Justice.

Bush-Baskette, Stephanie. 1999. "The 'War on Drugs': A War against Women." In *Harsh Punishment: International Experiences of Women's Imprisonment,* edited by Sandy Cook and Susanne Davies, 211–229. Boston, MA: Northeastern University Press.

Christianson, Scott. 1998. *With Liberty for Some: 500 Years of Imprisonment in America.* Boston, MA: Northeastern University Press.

Christie, Nils. 1993. *Crime Control as Industry: Towards Gulags, Western Style?* London: Routledge.

———. 2000. *Crime Control as Industry: Towards Gulags, Western Style,* rev. ed. London: Routledge.

Cullen, Francis, Bonnie Fisher, and Brandon Applegate. 2000. "Public Opinion about Punishment and Corrections." In *Crime and Justice: A Review of Research,* edited by Michael Tonry, 1–79. Chicago: Chicago University Press.

Davis, Phillip W. 2000. "Get Tough Legislation as Represented Action: The Case of Caning, Paddling, and Flogging." *Studies in Symbolic Interaction* 23: 197–216.

Dubber, Markus Dirk. 1998. "The Right to be Punished: Autonomy and Its Demise in Modern Penal Thought." *Law and History Review* 16: 113.

Duff, Antony. 2001. *Punishment, Communication, and Community.* Oxford: Oxford University Press.

Duguid, Stephen. 2000. *Can Prison Work?: The Prisoner as Object and Subject in Modern Corrections.* Toronto: University of Toronto Press.

Elias, Norbert. 1994. *The Civilizing Process.* Oxford: Blackwell.

Federal Bureau of Investigation. 2002. Press Release—2002—White Collar Crime Study. 6 March 2002. U.S. Department of Justice. http://www.fbi.gov/pressrel/pressrel02/wc3030602.htm accessed 11 June 2004.

Feinberg, Joel. 1994. "The Expressive Function of Punishment." In *A Reader on Punishment,* edited by Antony Duff and David Garland, 71–91. Oxford: Oxford University Press.

Finn, P. 1996. "No-Frills Prisons and Jails: A Movement in Flux." *Federal Probation* 60: 35–44.

Foster, Burk. 2001. "Why Death Is Different: Capital Punishment in the Legal System." In *Death Watch: A Death Penalty Anthology,* edited by Lane Nelson and Burk Foster, 1–15. Upper Saddle River, NJ: Prentice-Hall.

Garland, David. 1985. *Punishment and Welfare: A History of Penal Strategies.* Aldershot: Gower Publishing.

———. 1990. *Punishment and Modern Society.* Oxford: Oxford University Press.

Glaze, Lauren. 2003. "Probation and Parole in the United States, 2002." *Bureau of Justice Statistics Bulletin.* Washington, DC: U.S. Department of Justice.

Gorman, Tessa. 1997. "Back on the Chain Gang: Why the Eighth Amendment and the History of Slavery Proscribe the Resurgence of Chain Gangs." *California Law Review* 85: 441–478.

Griffin, Sean Patrick. 2002. "Actors or Activities? On the Social Construction of 'White-Collar Crime' in the United States." *Crime Law and Social Change* 37: 245–276.

Harding, Richard. 1998. "Private Prisons." In *The Handbook of Crime and Punishment* edited by Michael Tonry, 626–655. New York: Oxford University Press.

Harrison, Paige, and Allen Beck. 2003. "Prisoners in 2002." *Bureau of Justice Statistics Bulletin* (July): 1–14. Washington, DC: U.S. Department of Justice.

Hudson, Barbara. 1996. *Understanding Justice: An Introduction to Ideas, Perspectives and Controversies in Modern Penal Theory.* Buckingham, UK: Open University Press.

Ignatieff, Michael. 1978. *A Just Measure of Pain: The Penitentiary in the Industrial Revolution, 1750–1850.* New York: Pantheon Books.

Jenkins, Philip. 1998. *Moral Panic: Changing Concepts of the Child Molester in Modern America.* New Haven, CT: Yale University Press.

Lenz, Nygel. 2002. "'Luxuries' in Prison: The Relationship between Amenity Funding and Public Support." *Crime and Delinquency* 48(4): 499–525.

Levenson, L. 2003. "The War on Sex Abuse." *National Law Journal* 25 (37: 30–35).

Logan, Charles. 1990. *Private Prisons: Cons and Pros.* New York: Oxford University Press.

Lumer, Michael, and Nancy Tenney. 1995. "The Death Penalty in New York: An Historical Perspective." *Journal of Law and Policy* 4: 81–.

Lynch, M. 2002. "Pedophiles and Cyber-Predators as Contaminating Forces: The Language of Disgust, Pollution, and Boundary Invasions in Federal Debates on Sex Offender Legislation." *Law & Social Inquiry* 27: 529–566.

Madow, Michael. 1995. "Forbidden Spectacle: Executions, the Public and the Press in Nineteenth Century New York." *Buffalo Law Review* 43: 461–562.

Marquart, James W., Jonathan R. Sorensen, and Sheldon Ekland-Olson. 1994. *The Rope, the Chair, and the Needle: Capital Punishment in Texas, 1923–1990.* Austin: University of Texas Press.

Masur, Louis. 1989. *Rites of Execution: Capital Punishment and the Transformation of American Culture, 1776–1865.* New York: Oxford University Press.

Meyers, Jack, Kevin Wisniewski, Jonathan Wells, and Maggie Mulvihill. 2003. "Special Report: Tracking Sex Offenders; Losing Track; Florida's Sex Offenders Flock to Mass., Then Disappear." *The Boston Herald,* 6 November .

Nelson, Lane. 2001. "The Great Writ—Re: The Condemned." In *Death Watch: A Death Penalty Anthology,* edited by Lane Nelson and Burk Foster, 120–127. Upper Saddle River, NJ: Prentice-Hall.

Nelson, Lane, and Burk Foster. 2001. *Death Watch: A Death Penalty Anthology.* Upper Saddle River, NJ: Prentice Hall.

Nozick, Robert. 1981. *Philosophical Explanations.* Cambridge, MA: Harvard University Press.

Nygaard, R. 2000. *Sentencing As I See It.* Incline Village, NV: Copperhouse Publishing Company.

Petersilia, Joan. 1998. "Community Corrections for Drug-Abusing Offenders." In *Community Corrections: Probation, Parole, and Intermediate Sanctions,* edited by Joan Petersilia, 111–113. New York: Oxford University Press.

Petrunik, Michael G. 2002. "Managing Unacceptable Risk: Sex Offenders, Community Response, and Social Policy in the United States and Canada." *International Journal of Offender Therapy and Comparative Criminology* 46(4): 483–511.

Pope, Amy. 2002. "A Feminist Look at the Death Penalty." *Law and Contemporary Problems* 65(1): 257–282.

Pratt, John. 2001. "Beyond 'Gulags Western Style'? A Reconsideration of Nils Christie's Crime Control as Industry." *Theoretical Criminology* 5(3): 283–314.

Prendergast, Michael, M. Douglas Anglin, and Jean Wellisch. 1998. "Treatment for Drug-Abusing Offenders under Community Supervision." In *Community Corrections: Probation, Parole, and Intermediate Sanctions,* edited by Joan Petersilia, 113–124. New York: Oxford University Press.

Radelet, Michael, and Marian Borg. 2000. "The Changing Nature of Death Penalty Debates." *Annual Review of Sociology* 26: 43–61.

Ramirez, Chris. "Parole Monitoring Goes Global." *Albuquerque Journal.* 29 July 2003.

Rosenmerkel, Sean. 2001. "Wrongfulness and Harmfulness as Components of Seriousness of White-Collar Offenses." *Journal of Contemporary Criminal Justice* 17: 308–327.

Rothman, David. 1990. *The Discovery of the Asylum: Social Order and Disorder in the New Republic,* revised edition. Boston, MA: Little, Brown and Company.

Rusche, Georg, and Otto Kirchheimer. 1939 (reprinted 1968). *Punishment and Social Structure.* New York: Russsell and Russell.

Shicher, David. 1995. *Punishment for Profit: Private Prisons/Public Concerns.* Thousand Oaks, CA: Sage Publications.

———. 2000. "Penal Policies at the Threshold of the Twenty-First Century." *Criminal Justice Review* 25(1): 1–30.

Simon, Jonathan. 2000. "Symposium Introduction: Law, Democracy, and Society: Megan's Law: Crime and Democracy in Late Modern America." *Law and Social Inquiry* 25: 1111–1150.

Spohn, Cassia. 2002. *How Do Judges Decide? The Search for Fairness and Justice in Punishment.* Thousand Oaks, CA: Sage Publications.

Ten, C. L. 1987. *Crime, Guilt, and Punishment: A Philosophical Introduction.* Oxford: Clarendon Press.

von Hirsch, Andrew. 1994. "Censure and Proportionality." In *A Reader on Punishment,* edited by Antony Duff and David Garland, 112–132. Oxford: Oxford University Press.

Walker, Nigel. 1991. *Why Punish?* Oxford: Oxford University Press.

Welch, Michael. 1999. *Punishment in America: Social Control and the Ironies of Imprisonment.* Thousand Oaks, CA: Sage Publications.

———. 2003. "Force and Fraud: A Radically Coherent Criticism of Corrections as Industry." *Contemporary Justice Review* 6(3): 227–240.

Zimring, Franklin E. 2003. *The Contradictions of American Capital Punishment.* Oxford: Oxford University Press.

Zimring, Franklin E., and Gordon Hawkins. 1991. *The Scale of Imprisonment.* Chicago: University of Chicago Press.

Cases Cited

Brown v. Mississippi, 297 U.S. 278 (1936)
Connecticut Department of Public Safety v. Doe, 123 S. Ct. 1160 (2003)
Furman v. Georgia, 408 U.S. 238 (1972)
Gregg v. Georgia, 428 U.S. 153 (1976)
Kansas v. Hendricks, 521 U.S. 346 (1997)
In re Kemmler, 136 U.S. 436 (1890)
Louisiana ex rel. Francis v. Resweber, 329 U.S. 459, 464 (1947)
Michael Austin et al. v. Fob James Jr. Governor of Alabama and Ron Jones, Commissioner of ADC, Case No. 95-T-637-N (1996)
Powell v. Alabama, 287 U.S. 45 (1932)
Robinson v. California, 370 U.S. 660 (1962)
Smith v. Doe, 123 S. Ct. 1140 (2003)
Trop v. Dulles, 356 U.S. 86, 101 (1958)
Weems v. United States, 217 U.S. 349 (1910)
Wilkerson v. Utah, 99 U.S. 130 (1878)

3

Worldwide Perspective

We have seen in Chapter 1 how punishment for criminal conduct in the United States was shaped by a series of complex social, economic, and political forces. Although many countries have followed the British and U.S. patterns and forms of punishments, some have pursued a different approach to punishment. For example, some Islamic states have their own unique systems of law and punishment that reflect and implement the tenets of Islam.

In this chapter we will explore punishment from a worldwide perspective in order to provide a larger context to punishment practices in the United States. Do most countries follow U.S. practices in the same way that the United States adopted British practices in the early colonial days? What divergences exist worldwide, and are there any punishments that are radically different to those generally adopted by Western nations? These and other questions will be addressed in this chapter, which explores the issue of punishment in different countries and will also draw attention to commonalities and differences.

Themes and Divergences

Robert P. Weiss and Nigel South (1998), in a wide-ranging review of penal developments among industrialized countries (including the United States), outline several common themes: the development of a hard-line approach to punishment favoring just deserts, debates about the use of labor in prisons and conditions in prisons generally (the "less eligibility" argument as discussed in

Chapter 2), the growth of a managerial approach to crime and punishment with the aim of identifying and isolating groups considered to pose a greater risk, a policy of selective incapacitation with only the most serious offenders going to prison but for longer periods (this policy does not seem to be operating in the United States), the increase in the number of maximum security facilities (a feature that again points to a harder approach to punishment), and the policy of privatizing prisons that seems to go hand in hand with a general global trend toward privatization in many fields of activity.

One expert on sentencing compares U.S., Michael Tonry, sentencing policy to that of western European states and emphasizes that in the United States, "crime and punishment are central issues in ideological and partisan politics" (Tonry 1999: 48–49). Alternatives to imprisonment are not often accepted in the United States, because they are thought of as being insufficiently tough on criminals, whereas western European nations are more tolerant of noncustodial sanctions. For example, the punishment termed *day fine* was established early in the century in Scandinavia. The basic concept is that the court can reflect the severity of an offense in a monetary penalty by ordering payment of a larger or smaller number of day fines according to the seriousness of the crime. Also, the fine can be further adjusted to take account of the actual income and assets of an offender. Day fines are considered most appropriate for minor offenses and can replace short terms of imprisonment, relieving the stress on prison capacity.

In the United States, a pilot day-fine project was introduced in New York and produced positive results, although with some qualifications, including the lack of an intention to use day fines as a substitute for short prison sentences. This led to the project being extended to four other states, but in one of them, Arizona, day fines came to be employed as a substitute for probation. A similar path was followed in England, but day fines became embroiled in adverse publicity, and the hostile media presentations finally resulted in their removal from punishment options (Tonry 1999: 53). In practice, this punishment has only become established in Europe excluding England, and the United States and other common-law countries have not continued with early pilot schemes.

Community service as a form of punishment is another area where U.S. punishment policy diverges greatly from that of western Europe. By the early 1990s community service punishments were being widely used in Europe as well as Australia, New

Zealand, and Canada (Tonry 1999: 56). This punishment was conceived as an alternative to a prison sentence in minor-offense cases, where, for example, a sentence of less than six months would have been imposed. Typically, community service requires an offender to perform some kind of service in the community for a fixed number of hours over a fixed period of time. The punishment is supervised, and those who fail to comply can be imprisoned. As Tonry points out, the idea originated in California but has not been taken up in any large-scale way as a penal policy in the United States (Tonry 1999: 58). Usually, community service in the United States is made a condition of probation and is not ordered in its own right. It is viewed, not as an alternative to imprisonment, but as an alternative to a fine or as a condition to be imposed to make a probation sentence a more severe sanction. Tonry suggests that the reason for the divergence between the United States and other countries in the use of this sanction is that in the United States any punishment other than imprisonment is regarded as insufficiently punitive. Therefore, the notion that community service is an adequate penalty for an offense that might carry a maximum sentence of imprisonment for up to six months is simply not accepted.

Sometimes, for social and historical reasons punishments in countries that would ordinarily be aligned quite closely can show significant divergences. An example is the punishment for *infanticide* in the United States and Britain. The United States punishes this crime as though it were a category of homicide, but Britain treats it as a unique form of criminality where medical and psychological factors must be taken into account in sentencing and this results in a nonpunitive approach. The crux of this issue is whether infanticide should be regarded as a unique phenomenon and as the product of the physical and mental effects of childbirth or be regarded simply as an evil, murderous act. Britain and most European countries take the former approach, and the United States adopts the latter. Daniel Maier-Katkin and Robbin S. Ogle (1997) point out that in the United States, no statistics are collected on this type of crime (it is simply recorded as a homicide), whereas many European countries do collect statistics on it as a unique category and as a product of postpartum psychosis. Viewing it in this way, European states separate it from other forms of homicide.

The U.S. perspective, therefore, tends to view this crime, like all others, as a matter for individual accountability and responsibility despite that fact that seven separate studies conducted on two continents between 1846 and 1975 all agree that a syndrome called postpartum psychosis exists and can affect women who have recently given birth, and that this psychosis can constitute a causal factor in this crime (Maier-Katkin and Ogle 1997: 308).

As long ago as 1938 the British passed an Infanticide Act that established a presumption that mothers who kill their children within twelve months of birth are suffering from an imbalance of the mind. The legislation does not specify the actual condition suffered by the mother—that is left to medical evidence—but infanticide was then categorized as a special kind of homicide requiring unique treatment and punishment (Maier-Katkin and Ogle 1997: 309). One effect of this law is that between 1982 and 1988, of the fifty-seven cases of infanticide in Great Britain that resulted in convictions, 79 percent of the women convicted were given probation and treatment as punishment, 7 percent were hospitalized, and only 14 percent were sent to prison. In a study between 1987 and 1997 conducted by Maier-Katkin and Ogle (1997) of infanticide cases in the United States, the researchers found great diversity in punishment. Of the twenty-four cases they identified, ten were resolved in favor of the accused, who were found not guilty by reason of insanity or mental defect, three women were found guilty but mentally ill, and the remaining eleven women were convicted of various forms of homicide or manslaughter and received prison sentences ranging from one to three years to life imprisonment (Maier-Katkin and Ogle 1997: 312). This suggests that, although there is some support in the United States for treating infanticide as a special crime, U.S. policy on crime and punishment has yet to adopt this approach.

Imprisonment

What is the overall picture of imprisonment throughout the world? Brian Tkachuk and Roy Walmsley (2001) note that in 2001 over eight and a half million persons were in prisons throughout the world, resulting in an average rate of incarceration of 140 per 100,000 of population. Although this might not seem especially high, prison populations worldwide grew during the 1990s, and this has put great pressure on capacity and resources for incarceration, which in turn has resulted in a serious downturn in prison conditions. In Latin America and the Caribbean, Elias Carranza (in Tkachuk and Walmsley 2001: 5) states that among twenty-six states in this region, prison overcrowding was a critical factor, and the same situation prevails in Asia. Mikinao Kitada (in Tkachuk and Walmsley 2001: 6) similarly reports that prison overcrowding was the principal concern along with overreliance on imprisonment as the sole or main form of punishment. For Africa, Eric Kibuka notes (in Tkachuk and Walmsley 2001: 6) that harsher penalties are being imposed and that these longer periods of imprisonment are contributing to prison overcrowding, yet little new prison construction is taking place.

At the beginning of 2000, Russia enjoyed the distinction of having the highest imprisonment rate in the world, about 730 per 100,000, followed by the United States with 690 per 100,000. Worldwide, however, there are great divergences among prison populations, with Africa having a rate in the south that is five times the rate for Central and West Africa, whereas in the Americas, the rate for the Caribbean is nearly three times that for South American states. Similarly, in Asia the average rate for the central Asian states is about six times that of Southeast Asia. In Europe, central and eastern European rates are three times those for southern Europe. In Oceania the median rate is just below the world average (Walmsley 2001: 15–16).

Charting the growth in prison populations worldwide Walmsley notes that in the 1990s growth has been more than 20 percent in Europe, but for the United States, Mexico, Argentina, Brazil, and Colombia, the rate has been from 60 to 85 percent (Walmsley 2001: 15–16). There is a general trend toward growth in prison populations worldwide, and in only two of the states surveyed—Sweden and Finland—has there been a downward trend. What explanation can be found for this increase? Contrary to expectations, the cause is not a rise in crime rates, because in many countries these rates have been stable or have even decreased. The increasing reliance on incarceration seems to result from fear of crime, loss of confidence in the state's means of controlling crime, and the attraction of "get tough" policies that stress retribution and not rehabilitation. Generally, more people worldwide seem to believe that prison is a better alternative than any other punishment.

Some might argue that locking up criminals worldwide is good policy and the more people you lock away the less crime there will be. Unfortunately, this is not the case. Research has pointed out that for incarceration to have a significant effect on crime levels would mean locking up more people for longer periods of time than occurs even now in those states that are most supportive of mass incarceration (Walmsley 2001: 18). Thus, the public cost of imprisoning sufficient numbers of criminals in order to achieve an effect on the crime rate would be enormous. On a practical level, states would have to initiate enormous prison-building programs such as has occurred in the United States, but no other state can afford the accompanying costs. There is also the public-policy dimension to consider. As Roy Walmsley puts it, "what does it say about the nature of a country when it finds it necessary to lock up a high proportion of its people? . . . What does this say about the crime prevention in these countries? Does social cohesion matter? Should the emphasis be more on promoting social integration and less on locking people up?" (Walmsley 2001: 18).

In comparative terms, the United States now incarcerates its citizens at a rate that is five to eight times that of other industrialized nations (Mauer 2003: 2). In terms of specific crimes, it seems that the United States imprisons property crime offenders for much longer periods and more often than similarly placed nations, and this is also true for drug offenses. For violent offenses, U.S. rates of incarceration are comparable to those of other similar industrialized nations (Mauer 2003: 8), although length of sentences might vary.

Australia

Although employing a federal system of government the federal government in Australia does not maintain its own prison system. If charged under federal laws, accused persons are tried in state courts and sentenced to state prisons. Each state maintains its own prison system, and there are considerable variations in penal policies and practices, many owing to historical and social factors. In a number of states, Aboriginal populations suffer disproportionate imprisonment rates, as in Canada and the United States. In 1996 the national imprisonment rate was 120 per 100,000, but some states imprison at rates far in excess of this rate, such as Western Australia, with a rate of 170 per 100,000 and the Northern Territory, with a staggering rate of 388 per 100,000 (Brown 1998: 372). It is noteworthy that Japan with a population much larger than that of Australia has an imprisonment rate about one-third of that in Australia. These disparate rates indicate the importance of special political, legal, and cultural factors in sentencing practice in Australia (Brown 1998: 373). As already indicated, the massive Aboriginal overrepresentation is one of the distinguishing features of Australian punishment practice, and in 1993 Aboriginal men were imprisoned at the massive rate of 2,749 per 100,000 throughout Australia, as compared with a rate of 197 for non-Aboriginal men (Brown 1998: 376).

Prison privatization has gained a foothold in Australia, with Queensland being the first state to experiment with this option in 1990 (Brown 1998: 380). Research tends to show that private prisons do not turn out to be less costly than public prisons. Other states are moving to adopt privatization, and as of 1994, 8 percent of inmates were incarcerated in private prisons. Penal policy has taken much the same course as in the United States and in Western European countries, with just-deserts approaches gaining favor. The main forms of punishment are unsupervised release, monetary penalties, supervised releases, and imprisonment (Brown 1998: 383).

Canada

Although policy and practice on crime and punishment in Canada is influenced in many respects by U.S. models, the Canadian approach to punishment differs significantly from that in the United States and follows a strategy more like that of European states. Nevertheless, in common with other countries, Canadian imprisonment rates have increased, sentences have lengthened, and parole rules have been made stricter (Gaucher and Lowman 1998: 63). In spite of these policy shifts away from a perspective favoring rehabilitation and toward a more punitive approach, Canadian imprisonment rates are far short of those prevailing in the United States (see Chapter 2 for current U. S. rates).

Prison building in Canada has expanded beginning from the late 1950s when there were only nine federal prisons, to a total of sixty prisons by 1993, at which time the average prison population in federal and provincial prisons reached about 34,000 (Gaucher and Lowman 1998: 67). This increase is largely accounted for by the growth in longer-sentence prisoners serving sentences for drug and sex related crimes. The increase in the rate of imprisonment has prompted calls for the implementation of policies to reduce the prison population on grounds of cost and that prison be used only as a last resort to confine the most serious offenders (Gaucher and Lowman 1998: 68). In fact, with Canada now having the second highest imprisonment rate among the Western democracies, it was considered that unless a policy of de-incarceration was adopted, the financial and social costs to Canada would produce a crisis (Gaucher and Lowman 1998: 69).

The legislative framework for the operation of Canadian prisons calls for the Correctional Service in Canada to provide "humane custody" and to assist in rehabilitating offenders and in their reintegration into the community. Prisoner rights are formally recognized as well as the principle of fairness in dealing with offenders who are incarcerated (Gaucher and Lowman 1998: 74). Like those in the United States, Canadian prisons have adopted a cognitive skills/social learning approach to treatment, and case management teams create programs of control within the prison environment; but as Bob Gaucher and John Lowman point out (1998: 79), over the past 150 years, there have been numerous reports following inquiries into the lawlessness of guards and prison administrators and, as recently as 1994, an enquiry into events at the women's prison in Kingston, Ontario, pointed out deficiencies in programs, violent confrontations between guards and prisoners, hostage taking, and attempted suicide by inmates. One of the most serious problems within the prison system is overcrowding, with up to 25 percent of federal prisoners being double bunked (Gaucher and Lowman 1998: 83).

The incarceration of minorities is a particular problem in Canada, as it is in the United States. In Canada visible minorities make up 19 percent of the federal prison population. Aboriginal people who comprise only 3 percent of the Canadian population make up 12 percent of the male and 17 percent of the female federal prison population. In the Prairie Provinces where the Aboriginal population makes up 5 percent of the total, their rate of incarceration rises to a staggering 32 percent. This disproportionality in inmate population is a serious concern for Canadian penal policymakers.

China

Prisoner labor is a feature of the Chinese prison system. In a bid to modernize the country in the final days of the nineteenth century, the Chinese dynasty imported a range of new ideas and technologies from the West, and one such idea was reforming criminals through labor. Subsequently, with the Communist state came great reliance on the concept that labor could transform offenders, and after 1956, prison labor and its production were included in the state economic plan (Dutton and Xu 1998: 295).

In the People's Republic of China, labor reform camps for prisoners were an economic enterprise conducted on behalf of the state, and the products of prison labor were sold both domestically and internationally and constituted a vital part of the national economy. The Chinese argue that penal labor is not discriminated against as it is in the West where it is reduced to a menial condition for little or no pay (Dutton and Xu 1998: 290). The Chinese perspective is that labor can be reformative. Only the Chinese have introduced a fully structured, complete program of thought reform connected to labor. In this respect the Chinese system differs from the Communist Soviet system, which was less planned and depended more on ad hoc approaches to punishment (Dutton and Xu 1998: 291).

Michael Dutton and Xu Zhangrun (1998: 292) contend that the Chinese system is not entirely wedded to or a product of Marxist-Leninism, but is an amalgam of both the Communist way of punishing and traditional ways and values, which also incorporates aspects of Western models of punishment. This can be seen, for example, in Chinese notions that manual labor signifies class difference and that only lower classes perform manual labor, whereas higher classes labor with their minds (Dutton and Xu 1998: 297). Chinese penal philosophy traditionally advocates the use of prison and punishment as a means of moral education in norms of behavior (Dikotter 2002: 242). Specifically this means that prisons are expected to aim for the complete reformation of the offender and not focus on the infliction of pain and humiliation (Dikotter 2002: 245). Thus, prison was seen as a "place of change by persuasion" (Dikotter 2002: 246).

The free-market reforms post-1978 in China have significantly affected the society as a whole, and in penal policy, the main effect has been to reduce the importance and morality of thought reform through labor. Nevertheless, the penal system has not developed as the economy has changed but is still locked in the pre-reform days.

Pre-reform China maintained strict policing over persons' movements and reinforced a strong sense of community to such an extent that released prisoners were able to reintegrate into the local economy while still being monitored and supervised (Dutton and Xu 1998: 303). Their labor was seen to be continuing postrelease as a contribution toward national production. Changes in economic production with the development of a new private sector have affected these patterns of employment and reintegration so that by 1990 state ownership of industry had been reduced to only about 50 percent of all enterprises (Dutton and Xu 1998: 303). With a private sector free to hire those it wanted, released prisoners found that reintegration was no longer a smooth progression, and many were not selected as employees by the new nonstate enterprises. In response to this, some prisons set up local enterprises to employ ex-prisoners, but again they must now compete with the new private industries and many will not survive in economic terms (Dutton and Xu 1998: 304–305).

The problem of employing ex-prisoners has become particularly acute on prison farms (Dutton and Xu 1998: 308). These were located away from areas where they might compete with local farmers, and so they are found in sparsely populated areas, where the land is poor or where access is difficult owing to remoteness. It is doubtful that many prison farms will be able to compete in the new economy, and the result has been that they have contributed to the breakdown of the previously active and vibrant prison enterprise sector. Thus, overall the prison system has yet to cope with the new economic conditions, which have rendered the collectivist notions of the past irrelevant to the future development of the state.

Social change in China has also produced a weakening of state control over movement internally—previously strictly controlled—and an increase in people's overall freedoms has meant that incidence of crime has rapidly risen, with an increase of 32 percent between 1985 and 1991 and with a 40 percent increase in violent crime (Dutton and Xu 1998: 309). Mobility has meant that criminal elements have moved to the increasingly rich population centers and there has been an overall increase in the level of serious crime. Policing has yet to change to meet this new challenge, but one development has been the emergence of new ad hoc institutions to deal with crime and to impose punishment. Dutton and Xu (1998: 311) identify three types of detention centers—the local jails, city jails, and lockups—used to detain those who have been charged but are yet to be convicted.

There is also a growing distinction between forms of criminal and administrative detention (Dutton and Xu 1998: 312). Those convicted of crimes can receive sentences from one year to life imprisonment, with light offenders going to prison camps and those sentenced to ten years or more going to prisons. In contrast, there is labor education, which is administrative and noncriminal and imposed through a management committee. Labor education does not result in a criminal record but does involve punishment and deprivation of liberty. Sentences of up to three years can be imposed under this sanction and system. This system, unlike that of the prisons, which must provide their own resources, is funded by local governments and by the state itself. Incarceration in an administrative manner provides police with a convenient method of dealing with the new problems they face, and the committees that impose this kind of detention do not operate independently of the police (Dutton and Xu 1998: 313). Another form of detention in China exists to deal with prostitution, and in 1983 police were given power to impose punishments in areas where prostitution was rampant. A form of detention known as female education and fostering centers was developed to meet this issue.

There is dispute about the number of persons incarcerated, but like Dutton and Xu (1998: 324), some believe that there are 3 to 4 million in the prison sector, whereas one official figure is 1.2 million in prison and another 150,000 persons in administrative detention.

One aspect of punishment found in China and not in the West is the *public sentencing rally* (Trevaskes 2003). Since 1983 anticrime campaigns have been conducted using a policy of "severity and swiftness" in pushing offenders through the criminal justice system (the elements of which are the public security bureau, the procuratorate, and the courts) (Trevaskes 2003: 359). The public sentencing rally is a particular feature of these campaigns, and the rally held in 2001 was a public spectacle at which many criminals were displayed before being executed. The rallies draw attention to the crime situation and highlight the government's efforts to maintain social order in a very public way.

As Susan Trevaskes observes (2003: 360), the sentencing rally is intended to shame the offender and deter others at the spectacle from criminal activity, but it is a judicial event and not simply a display or spectacle. The audience at a rally can range from a few dozen to more than one hundred thousand, and at the rally the judgment of the court is announced and a shaming ritual acted out. Places such as stadiums, market places, and community halls are used for these rallies, and the size of the criminal group brought forward varies from a few to large groups. The ritual followed at a rally involves offenders being brought in succession onto a platform or stage (Trevaskes 2003: 361). They will generally be handcuffed and in the custody of police and sometimes wear placards around their necks showing their name, the crimes committed, and the sentence. Government officials and senior police are usually seated on the stage, and after a series of speeches, a senior judge or president of the court declares the sentences, after which the offenders are taken away to their deaths (Trevaskes 2003: 361). The audience applauds as the sentences are read out to "show support for and confidence in the justice meted out by the judicial organs" (Trevaskes 2003: 364).

In many respects these sentencing rallies appear to resemble the public spectacles conducted historically in the West (see Chapter 1), including public corporal punishments like whipping and public executions. As indicated in Chapters 1 and 2, these public events, like the sentencing rallies of China, were designed to display the power of the state and reassure the citizens that the state was in control of the social order. In fact, in China, public sentencing rallies have been part of the state apparatus for maintaining control over people's conduct and thinking since the 1950s when the mass trials of the revolutionary period were first staged (Trevaskes 2003: 362).

The rallies can be seen as a development away from a more public presentation of violent punishment. For example, prior to the introduction of sentencing rallies, public executions were common but were condemned in the 1980s, and the courts were advised to display less violence and to adopt a more "civilized" approach to punishment (Trevaskes 2003: 369–370). Changes in that period include banning public processions of soon-to-be-executed criminals through the streets to the place of execution (Trevaskes 2003: 370).

England and Wales

The trend to increase the punitiveness of punishment found in the United States has been matched by developments in England and Wales since the 1970s. The prison population has expanded by some 70 percent since 1971 (65,298 in 1998 compared with 38,040 in 1971) (Ashworth 2001: 62). Three factors have been identified as implicated in the expansion of the prison population: a rise in the proportion of cases determined by the courts to warrant imprisonment, an increase in the length of sentences imposed, and the greater length of time spent on remand and awaiting trial. The prison population is now more than 50 percent higher than it was in the early 1990s, and the use of custodial punishment has risen by 40 percent, with sentence lengths increasing by more than 10 percent (Walmsley 2001: 17).

In 1993 this surge toward greater use of incarceration was given a significant boost when a government minister declared, "prison works," and called for tougher sentences. As well, judges have felt impelled to impose longer sentences and make greater use of incarceration believing these necessary to reflect their understanding of public opinion. However, public-opinion surveys have shown that the reason people tend to criticize court sentences for leniency is that they lack knowledge about sentencing, often assuming it is much less severe than is in fact the case (Ashworth 2001: 83).

Political rhetoric on crime and criminals has spurred the expansion of prison construction, and a hard-line approach to penal policy has adopted a focus on privatization and managerialism so that by 1995 there were five private prisons operating in the United Kingdom. Requests were made to double the budget of the Prison Department, and the government itself contributed to the focus on imprisonment when in 1996, it published a set of policies containing sentencing proposals that could only contribute to the increase in prisoner numbers (Ryan and Sim 1998: 193–194). For example, policy proposals were created to bring automatic life sentences for offenders over eighteen years of age convicted of a serious crime for the second time, to abolish forms of early release, and to introduce mandatory minimum sentences of seven years for drug offenders with two or more previous convictions.

Unlike in the United States, there are no sentencing guidelines in England and Wales, and judges are free to fix sentences with the legislature setting only the maximum term of imprisonment. The judiciary has always been aware of the need for consistency in sentencing, and recent developments in this direction include the use of the guideline judgment, where the judgments of the Court of Criminal Appeal have incorporated general guidance to other judges on the appropriate penalty for an offense, taking into account the circumstances of that offense (Ashworth

2001: 73). One problem, however, is that these guideline judgments tend to focus only on the most serious offenses, so that offenses like burglary and theft are not the subject of any guidelines (Ashworth 2001: 74). A further new development since 1998 has been the advent of the Sentencing Advisory Panel, which was set up to advise the Court of Appeal on sentencing (Ashworth 2001: 75).

One interesting aspect of the debate on sentencing in England is the presence of the judiciary in public debates about sentencing. Although judges have sometimes taken public stands on issues, they have not previously made use of the media to the extent that they have since the 1980s. The judges have taken a stand that argues that the legislature should not "interfere" in their role as sentencers (Ashworth 2001: 76). In fact judges have acted to neutralize legislation that has attempted to curb their sentencing discretion, for example, by interpreting legislation in such a way as to override provisions intended to override their discretion (Ashworth 2001: 78–79).

Germany

Under the German system of government the federal government makes penal legislation that is implemented and administered by the states, and the federal government has no control over the states in this respect. The result is that there are considerable variations in penal practice among the states. The traditional punishment philosophy is retribution, but the prevalent legal regime emphasizes rehabilitation. These two notions have been combined in legislation that specifies that not only must the guilt of the offender be a factor in assessing punishment but also the judge must take into account the effects of the punishment on the future life of the offender (Feest and Weber 1998: 235–236). The emphasis remains on guilt and accountability, but rehabilitation is recognized as a proper factor to take into account.

Traditionally, German penal law provides for very long sentences, and judges have been accustomed to imposing lengthy sentences. In terms of penal policy, Germany has had to cope with the reunification of East and West Germany (Feest and Weber 1998: 240). In the East, prisons were not run in accordance with the minimum acceptable international standards, but prisoners were given the right to work, and this right was exercised in practice. Prisoners were paid wages, which, while below market levels, were well above those paid in other prison systems. Following reunification in 1990 all prisoners now receive the same low wages for work in prisons.

West Germany always maintained a high prison population in comparison with other western European states, and even during the liberal period of the 1960s the rate was above 100 per 100,000 (Feest and Weber 1998: 241). By 1994 the rate had fallen to 88 per 100,000, still high compared with Scandinavian countries (Feest and Weber 1998: 242). Prisoners are given certain rights under law, including the right to seek a court review if they believe their rights have been violated. Local courts, which deal with these complaints, also adjudicate whether or not a prisoner should be released before the end of the period of sentence, much like parole boards in other countries (Feest and Weber 1998: 251–252).

Traditionally, German prisons were run on strict military-type lines, but from the 1970s more liberal regimes were introduced with home leaves and work furloughs, and now administrators have the discretion to allow inmates to be released on home leaves for up to twenty-one days a year (Feest and Weber 1998: 249). Use of this provision led to a decrease in the number of attempted escapes, but some prisoners such as drug addicts and nonnationals were not able to take advantage of this favorable condition, because they were judged to be high risk. Also, long-term prisoners have great difficulty in securing home leave, and the law envisages a minimum period of ten years' incarceration before home leave may be granted (Feest and Weber 1998: 250).

One interesting punishment option in Germany is the *prosecutorial fine.* In 1970 legislation was passed discouraging the courts from imposing prison sentences of less than six months unless there were exceptional circumstances (Tonry 1999: 54). Since 1975, German prosecutors have had the option to invite the accused to pay a sum of money to the victim, or to the state or a charity, in exchange for the dismissal of the charge (Tonry 1999: 55). The accused does not have to enter a guilty plea but must pay a fine equivalent to that which would have been ordered on a conviction. This option proved so popular that by 1989 conditional dismissal incorporating this punishment made up 27 percent of all court-imposed sanctions.

Italy

According to Vincenzo Ruggiero (1998: 208), the legacy of the thinking of Beccaria, an Italian, is that Italy is perceived in official rhetoric as the country of rational, nonvindictive punishment with an emphasis on rehabilitation. In Ruggiero's view, however, the Italian prison system, while superficially maintaining a focus on rehabilitation, in fact practices a different penal strategy.

In 1995 there were some 50,000 prisoners in Italian prisons, with about half of that number on remand awaiting trial (Ruggiero 1998: 209). The number of prisoners has tended to fluctuate quite widely over the past ten years, largely because of the arbitrary use made of imprisonment by the courts, but significantly, for the last decade, prisoners serving sentences of less than two years have made up more than 80 percent of the prison population (Ruggiero 1998: 209). Penal tradition in Italy advocates the release of prisoners when they are judged to have been rehabilitated, the contention being that therapy is most successful when carried out outside the confines of a prison. Added to this, the Italian Constitution clearly stipulates that prison is to be used as a last resort and not for punishment. In other words, retribution is unconstitutional and if custody does not produce rehabilitation, it has no rationale or justification ((Ruggiero 1998: 210–211). Thus, Italy stands almost alone among the western European countries in not reviving a policy of just deserts or retribution, at least not in official rhetoric.

Measures of rehabilitation are pursued in prisons under the supervision of judges, who are charged with the regulation of prisons and base their decisions on the reports of prison administrators who are required to observe the behavior of prisoners and to identify those deserving of noncustodial treatment (Ruggiero 1998: 214). Thus all decisions about probation and other forms of early release from confinement are in effect made by prison staff and by the executive government. Ruggiero (1998: 214) notes, however, that prison staff lack the training and skills to actually make these decisions. Contrary to this focus on rehabilitation and early release from custody, is the notion of "social defense" provided for by a law that allows rehabilitation to be interrupted in the face of overriding security concerns where there are exceptionally serious circumstances. Social defense measures may only override normal rules for a period of three months, but they can be extended if prison administrators considered this action warranted because of continuing security concerns (Ruggiero 1998: 216). Permitted social defense measures include suspending treatment, censorship of correspondence, high visitor surveillance, and banning certain activities directed at rehabilitation.

In using this provision, Italy has established high-security prisons initially in response to political struggles. These institutions are not, however, described as secure institutions but rather, as having an emphasis on security, which applies not to the institutions, but to individual prisoners (Ruggiero 1998: 217). In practice, each prison now includes a high-security facility where the notion and goals of rehabilitation are suspended for prisoners incarcerated there (Ruggiero 1998: 218). New rules have designated some offenders (associated with the Italian Mafia [Ruggiero 1998: 219]) as not being capable of rehabilitation except in exceptional circumstances, thus reversing the focus away from the goal of rehabilitation to one of security for this group.

By 1994 the prison population had reached 55,000, double the official capacity of all prisons in the country, and about 20 percent of this prison population constituted nonnationals, the majority being citizens of African states (Ruggiero 1998: 221). The incarceration of immigrant populations at rates far out of proportion to their representation in the population has emerged as an issue in Italian penal practice, as it has in other western European states.

Japan

Compared with the rates of imprisonment in the United States, rates per 100,000 of the population in Japan are very modest, ranging from a high of 96 in the 1950s to lows of about 30 for the period from 1970 to 1990 (Johnson 1998: 338). Elmer Johnson (1998: 339) notes that Japan has managed to avoid the usual problem of overcrowded prisons and that Japanese prisons are peaceful, quiet places where the inmates are submissive to authority and far less likely to oppose and resist prison staff than are prisoners in other countries.

The Japanese cultural context is vital to an understanding of the distinctness of punishment in Japan. Basically, there is reluctance for cultural reasons to punish through the use of incarceration, and both prosecutors and judges are inclined to be lenient with offenders (Johnson 1998: 340). Most offenders display contrition and repentance during the criminal justice process and submit their cases to the authorities without defending the charges brought against them. This stance can only encourage an attitude of leniency and is coupled with structural and societal forces that impose their own sanctions on offenders. It is mainly because of these cultural factors that leniency is an easy option for judges in Japan. Like other societies, the Japanese subordinate the self to the group and even today this is reflected in the offender's restitution and expressions of regret to the victim (Johnson 1998: 343).

Traditional notions of morality themselves urge offenders toward an attitude of contrition and guide judges and prosecutors in that direction also (Johnson 1998: 343). For the defense attorney in Japan, the best advice that can be given to the offender is that he or she should negotiate with the victim, plead for forgiveness, and offer compensation (Johnson 1998: 345). If the victim indicates that lenient treatment is acceptable, the defense attorney will so advise the prosecutor, and this will be fully taken into account in the exercise of the prosecutorial discretion. The court will also take such matters into account on sentencing.

It is common for sentences of not more than three years to be suspended in Japan, and no supervision is generally ordered during the period of suspended imprisonment. The statistics bear out the success of this approach, as only about 10 percent of suspended sentences come back before the court for revocation (Johnson 1998: 347).

In Japan the total inmate population has sharply declined since 1950, and prisons actually have surplus capacity, with the average daily inmate population in 1992 being about 45,000 (Johnson 1998: 351). The notorious yakuza—the Mafia of Japan—have taken increasingly large proportions of the prison capacity, at almost 30 percent in 1991 (Johnson 1998: 358). Prison officials claim that most prisoners are satisfied with their sentences and the Japanese socialization toward persons of superior social positions reinforces an attitude that is compliant toward prison discipline and control (Johnson 1998: 359).

Japan has a well-developed system of volunteer probation officers who assist the professional probation officers (Sakai in Tkachuk 2002: 10–11). There are about 48,000 such volunteers drawn from various sections of society, including retired persons and homemakers as the largest group, with an average age being about sixty-three years. There is a long tradition of volunteerism in the community-based treatment of offenders that began in 1939 with legislation that established rehabilitation workers who later became renamed volunteer probation officers. Living in the same community as the probationer, the volunteers are able to contact the probationer daily and in emergencies, and can be seen by the probationer as a friend in the community and not a government representative.

Mexico

Like Canada, Mexico is also influenced by events in the United States in penal affairs, but here the influence is not so much connected with penal practice but is a result of the "war on drugs" in the United States. This "war" has impacted Mexico to the extent that the majority of those incarcerated in Mexican prisons along the border with the United States are there for drug-related offenses, mainly drug trafficking (Olivero 1998: 106).

Imprisoning persons in one form or another dates back as far as the Spanish conquest of Mexico, and even the Mayans and Aztecs maintained buildings for the purposes of confinement and detention (Olivero 1998: 99–100). However, it was the Spanish who first introduced incarceration as a form of punishment. Information about prisons in Mexico is hard to come by, because no statistical information is published or central records maintained, and prison officials are very reluctant to allow access to researchers (Olivero 1998: 100). However, it is recorded that in 1994 there were a total of 438 correctional facilities of various types in the country housing around 89,000 prisoners, with each of the thirty-one states maintaining its own prisons alongside a federal prison system (Olivero 1998: 101–102).

Prison guards lack education and training, and the ratio of guards to prisoners is far below the levels experienced in Western countries. Moreover, guards are poorly paid, have no standard uniform, and usually maintain complete separation from inmates by patrolling the prison entrances or the surrounding walls and never entering the prisoners' living areas (Olivero 1998: 102). Prison society and environment mirror the social worlds outside the prison, with those having wealth able to secure privileges and amenities that other prisoners can only dream of acquiring. It is possible to bring in most goods by paying off guards. Prisoners wear their own clothes and provide their own bedding. Cells are commonly purchased from guards and can range from those with air-conditioning to others that essentially comprise a space on a ledge. Similarly, family members bring in food, and those without are forced to beg or eat poor-quality prison food. As with the food service, medical services are grossly deficient and have to be purchased from the outside (Olivero 1998: 103). *Conjugal visits* are a feature of the Mexican prison system, and in some prisons, an entire family is permitted to visit and live for an extended period within the confines of the prison.

Overcrowding is the main problem for prison administrators, and there is an especially serious problem of overcapacity along the border with the United States. Although the general lack of resources in the country prohibits any program of prison expansion or construction, Mexico's border with the United States generates a constant supply of prisoners. Additionally, significant numbers of Mexicans are incarcerated in U.S. prisons for illegally crossing the border or for drug-related offenses, many awaiting deportation.

The Netherlands

In the postwar period, the Dutch prison system became a byword for a liberal and humane approach to punishment, with the prison population being reduced to a figure of only 25 per 100,000 of the population (Downes 1998: 143). As well, the Dutch emphasized the need for high levels of amenities in the experience of prison and its conditions, contrary to the practice of most other similar countries at the time. For example, Holland still adheres to the rule of housing only one inmate per cell. However, social change has now impacted these early policies and practices to such an extent that from the 1970s onward these achievements have largely disappeared from the penal system (Downes 1998: 144), and since the 1980s, imprisonment rates have risen faster in this country than in any other European country (Tak 2001: 151).

The most significant social change in Holland has been the lack of social integration, because second-generation immigrants have been generally excluded from employment and citizenship, and, therefore, David Downes (1998: 152) argues, have become involved in street crime out of all proportion to their representation in the population. Contemporary Dutch feel besieged by crime and criminals as never before, and this has fed through to the political process (just as in the United States), and calls for tough action and harsher forms of punishment have been heeded by politicians.

By 1984, study groups were recommending an expansion of the prison capacity to match projected rises in crime, especially at the level of drug offenses. However, the overall approach was to continue to reserve incarceration for the most serious offenses and to use community penalties and crime prevention to abate what was seen as a crisis in crime trends (Downes 1998: 155). In 1990 a further study resulted in a shift away from the offender to the victim, whose protection was seen as the highest goal of the criminal justice system. By 1994 a further report (Downes 1998: 156) focused on prison labor, signaling a move to toughen up prison regimes in order to reassure the public that all necessary measures of protection were being taken for their safety, and in the early 1990s fourteen new prisons were opened.

By the end of 1996 it was expected that prison capacity would rise to 13,000, a rate of imprisonment of 78 per 100,000 compared with the previous rate, 44 per 100,000 in 1990. This represents the largest rise of any west European country, almost doubling the prison population (Walmsley 2001: 17). Thus, after some three decades of minimal use of incarceration, the Dutch have changed policies and adopted the prevailing Western approach of penal punitiveness. In spite of this, prison conditions in the Netherlands remain generally good with the one-prisoner-per-cell policy being regarded as the only humane and acceptable standard. In line with concerns about the immigrant population, the number of non-Dutch prisoners has sharply increased from only 12 percent in 1981 to 26 percent in 1992 (Downes 1998: 164). This is in contrast, for example, to the United Kingdom, where only 6 percent of male and 20 percent of females were foreign prisoners.

Another new development for the Netherlands has been the growth in maximum-security facilities for those who represent a high risk of escape. This development was prompted by a number of escapes involving hostage-taking between 1991 and 1993 (Downes 1998: 166). Maximum-security regimes, like those of the United States, follow a lockdown policy with only limited periods of activity outside the cell allowed, and all cells have letterboxes through which prisoners must be handcuffed before exiting their cells (Downes 1998: 167). This system is in contrast to the relative humanity shown elsewhere in the Dutch prison system.

Like those in Germany, Dutch prosecutors are authorized to resolve a criminal case by permitting the accused to pay a sum of money to the state in exchange for no trial, and this power can be used in any case where there is a potential prison sentence of up to six years (Tonry 1999: 55). In recent years up to one-third of criminal prosecutions have been resolved using this approach. In addition, prosecutors have the power not to prosecute based on an expediency principle found in the law that authorizes waiver of prosecution for "reasons of public interest" (Tak 2001: 155).

Poland

In 1989, Poland became the first country in Central and Eastern Europe to attain a postcommunist democratic government. Before 1989 Poland, with a population of 40 million, had a high rate of imprisonment—almost 300 per 100,000—but the average sentence was only between twenty-two and twenty-seven months (Plateck 1998: 265). Prisons were regarded by the Communist regime as a place where manpower could be obtained to support the state economy, and forced prison labor became important during the 1970s, in particular when almost all prisoners were employed in labor schemes at no cost to the state in state-run enterprises (Plateck 1998: 268). Those not so employed were engaged in work in the prison system in prison-run enterprises. Most prison enterprises had contracts with important state industries, and so prison production became part of the state economy.

Following freedom from Communist control, new prison directors were appointed who declared a policy of rehabilitation within the Polish prison system. Amnesties were declared to free political prisoners or simply to reduce the numbers of inmates, but in Poland major riots occurred when the hopes of many prisoners for immediate release under an amnesty were raised and then dashed (Walmsley 1995: 7). Highly qualified persons were brought into the prison to run treatment programs, and the management structure radically changed, but these changes were accompanied by a steady increase in the rate of incarceration. Thus, after the first wave of reductions in prison population owing to amnesties, the rate per 100,000 began to rise, and, although the rate in January 1991 was 130 per 100,000, by 1994 it had risen to 160 per 100,000 (Walmsley 1995: 9). By 1994 Poland had a prison population of about 64,000 in some 210 institutions (Walmsley 1995: 37).

Monika Plateck reports that a harsher approach to punishment has been adopted in Poland as well, with talk of a looming crime problem in the face of an increase in violent crime brought about by the social changes within the country. Increased incarceration rates have put pressure on prison capacity and administrations and have led Poland to turn away from a liberal prison regime toward a more paramilitary style of management. Nearly all prison staff other than specialists in the treatment field are required to enforce a military style of discipline (Plateck 1998: 272–273). As well, there is an absence of alternatives to prison, and this tends to exacerbate the problem of overcapacity.

Plateck (1998: 276) argues that harsh punishment as a policy is something that the Polish people grew used to under the Communist regime, and so it is not difficult for them to accept its continuance now. This is reflected in a 1996 prison law, which sets security and costs as the prime factors (Plateck 1998: 277). Thus, the enthusiasm for a liberal approach to punishment that arose in 1989 lasted only a brief time and was focused mainly on political prisoners. Thereafter, penal policies have reflected those in most of Western Europe. In particular, there is concern among the Polish people whose standard of living has fallen significantly, that prisoners are enjoying much better conditions than the average Pole. Thus, "less eligibility" is an overriding concern for the Polish public so far as prisoners are concerned.

South Africa

In spite of the changes that have taken place in South African society with the ending of the system of apartheid, the prison system maintained during apartheid has not fundamentally changed its shape or goals. It continues to hold about the same number of inmates as during the period when the law was used by a minority government to impose a restrictive system based on explicitly racial criteria (Van Zyl Smit 1998: 401). During apartheid prisoners were rigidly segregated, and white guards outranked black guards. Prisoner rights were restricted, and this was even more so in the case of those detained on political grounds. The position changed with the adoption of the interim South African Constitution in 1993 that contained a bill of rights applying to all persons detained in the Republic of South Africa (Van Zyl Smit 1998: 403).

The prison system in South Africa is highly centralized and until quite recently was operated on military lines. Now military ranks have been abolished, but there has yet to be a fundamental appraisal of the goals and purposes of corrections in the country and a reorientation of the responsible department away from past practice.

Prison labor has always been a feature of the penal system, and its decline in agriculture especially outside the prison has been dramatic since the ending of apartheid (Van Zyl Smit 1998: 406). For example, although 68 percent of prisoners were employed in some form of prison labor in 1972, only 25 percent were so employed by 1995 with almost all the job losses occurring in the agricultural sector for work outside the prison (Van Zyl Smit 1998: 418).

High rates of imprisonment have also been a feature of the system. In 1976 prisons housed some 94,000 prisoners with a rate of 326 per 100,000 of population. This compares with figures for 1996 at 117 per 100,000, with the rate of black imprisonment having declined dramatically from 350 per 100,000 in 1976 to 198 per 100,000 by 1996 (Van Zyl Smit 1998: 417). Current concerns about escalating crime in the cities of South Africa make it unlikely that imprisonment rates will change any time soon. In fact, early release schemes are likely to be abandoned, and a major program of prison construction appears likely (Van Zyl Smit 1998: 420).

Punishments under Islamic Law

Islamic law has two main sources. The first is Sharia, which is based on a code revealed by the prophet Mohammad and written down in the Quran and Sunna (the acts of the prophet) (Souryal, Potts, and Alobied 1994: 252). Sharia means literally "a pathway" and defines what is right and what is wrong, illegal or illegal, and proper and improper in Islamic life. Sharia therefore operates to regulate human behavior by prohibiting or authorizing certain kinds of conduct. The Sharia also deals with issues of crime and punishment known as Huddud, or divine limitations. Huddud operates like a constitution, penal code, and criminal procedure code rolled into one. Crimes that fall into the category of Huddud are offenses against God's community, and penalties for these crimes are absolute, because God decrees them. Such crimes are seven in number and they must always be prosecuted to the fullest extent. No mercy or mitigation is permitted, nor may such penalties be judged by man or interpreted by judges.

The second source of Islamic law includes customs and principles of Western law that have been adopted through codes imported by colonizing powers in many Islamic states. For example, in the case of Egypt, its legal system was originally wholly based on Islam, but in 1882, the modern Egyptian Criminal Code was introduced, having origins in French law, and it was later revised drawing on Belgian, Italian, and Indian law (Mohsen 1990: 15). Thus while Islam plays an important role in legal systems in Islamic countries, its impact varies greatly. As compared with the United States, lawyers are relatively unimportant in Sharia law cases; the litigants and judges are the main actors, and there are no juries (Dwyer 1990).

It is crucial to understand that in Islam, religion and daily life and behavior are not separate categories, as they tend to be in the West. Rather, Islam permeates every aspect of life and of course that includes crime and punishment. Non-Huddud crimes are called quesas, or retaliation crimes, and include the crime of murder and may in fact be considered more serious than Huddud crimes. Punishment for these crimes follows the *lex talionis* (see Chapter 1), and although these crimes are mentioned in the Quran, penalties are not prescribed for them. Prosecution for such crimes is required, but the punishment can be negotiated or even forgiven in part or in full by the victim or his or her family.

As Sam Souryal, Dennis Potts, and Abdullah Alobied (1994: 254) put it, "punishment in Islamic justice is designed to be so severe as to deter the most corrupt in the community, but also so magnanimous as to accommodate their reintegration into the society of believers."

Theft is considered a particularly serious crime for cultural and historical reasons. For example, it was the practice in early times for people not to close or lock doors as a sign of hospitality. Thus, it is the element of stealth associated with theft that most troubles Islamic jurisprudence because it is seen as violating the integrity of the community (Souryal et al. 1994: 260).

Sharia laws endorse forgoing punishment by offering restitution when part of the punishment can be waived or through confessing and admitting the act before being apprehended, in which case, the entire punishment can be forgone (Souryal et al. 1994: 254). Sharia punishment is naturally harsh because the community of believers must always take precedence over the individual. Muslims expect harsh punishments, and Western assumptions about proportionality have no place in Islamic law

(Souryal et al. 1994: 255–256). Muslims are not concerned about the severity of the punishment so long as it equates to the harm suffered by the victim. Historically and traditionally the notion of retaliation in this form was also considered a far preferable option to the possibility of a tribal raid, which would have punished the offender, his family, and tribe.

The effectiveness of punishment that is itself harsh is increased by having the punishment carried out in public. Thus, Western concepts of retribution are present in notions of appropriate punishment, but notions of community and social cohesion are also incorporated. Examples of Islamic punishments include: beheading for robbery and murder, stoning to death for adultery, and receiving eighty lashes for public drunkenness (Souryal et al. 1994: 254).

The crucial point to understand is that appropriate punishment is believed to both purify society and redeem the individual offender and that the interest of the individual must always be sacrificed for the good of the whole community.

In a discussion of the penalty of hand amputation for theft under Sharia law Souryal et al. (1994: 255) note that this punishment is usually performed in the town square and within sight of the mosque when worshippers are finishing their Friday noon prayer. The process involves bringing out the offender, reading the sentence out loud, stretching the offender's arm out on a table, and in a rapid movement, a professional executioner, acting in the presence of at least one male physician and a male nurse, pulls the hand away from the wrist and severs the hand at the joint using a knife. At the point of excision the physician immediately stops the bleeding and bandages the wound. The punishment is performed in an atmosphere of solemnity (unlike the various forms of corporal punishment practiced previously in the West). Muslims argue that compared to a lengthy prison sentence this punishment is more appropriate and effective as a deterrent. Moreover, it allows the offender to resume his life with his family within the society within a short space of time.

It might be argued that punishments decreed by Sharia law such as hand amputation for theft shock the human consciousness and are expressions of a barbaric and backward society. The fact remains that within their cultural context (and such punishments are by no means practiced in most Islamic countries) these punishments are expected and accepted and that the levels of crime in such societies fall far below those experienced in the West. Souryal et al. (1994: 256) argue also that compared to punishments like chemical castration and capital punishment itself, these Sharia punishments are not repulsive or inhumane and that many would find castration and the death penalty more inhumane.

Muslims in different countries disagree about the emphasis to be placed on Sharia laws and conservative Muslims believe, like Christians who advocate the absolute truth of the contents of the Bible, that the Sharia principles are always applicable, and they refuse to accept that these principles could ever be affected by the passage of time and changes in society. Reformist Muslims, on the other hand, see a need for interpretations of Sharia that make it meaningful in the present day (Tucker 1998).

It is also important to be aware of the high standard of evidence that is to be met in cases of alleged theft, where hand amputation is the proscribed punishment. In fact, the rules of evidence in cases of theft are more stringent than those in a case of murder (Souryal et al. 1994: 262). To make sure that the case against the accused is as substantial as possible, only two kinds of evidence are acceptable: eyewitness evidence and a confession. A confession must be voluntary and must detail the events that constituted the crime, and it may be withdrawn at any time, even during the court proceedings themselves. The number of eyewitnesses required varies according to the particular crime charged. For example, in cases of adultery and slander, four male witnesses are required to establish guilt, and witnesses must themselves meet stringent criteria relating to their moral integrity, maturity, and background (Souryal et al. 1994: 262).

Punishment in Developing Countries

As a result of colonization many, if not most, developing countries follow Western models of punishment, with most employing imprisonment as the chief or only form of punishment. A good example of this colonial inheritance is Jamaica. When Britain abolished slavery in its colonies in 1833 it sent out instructions to colonial governors to make substantial changes in their criminal justice systems. Abolishing slavery meant that slave owners would no longer be able to punish their slaves in their own fashion and the colonies therefore needed to develop new models of punishment to meet this new situation (Paton 2001: 275). Naturally, most adopted the colonial punishment model of prison, and in Jamaica, a program of prison construction began and legislation was passed echoing the British rhetoric of reforming inmates through labor and religion (Paton 2001: 277). In 1854, legislation was passed that allowed for the release of convicts to serve as agricultural laborers anticipating the convict lease system that was developed in the United States (see Chapter 1) (Paton 2001: 288).

Colonial models were therefore introduced even though many colonized countries had their own systems of justice and punishment that had operated before colonization and were permitted to continue during the period of colonial rule. Thus for example, Egbeke Aja, writing of the Igbo society of Nigeria, comprising some ten million people, points out that in precolonial Igbo society, each community was self-supporting and had little outside contact; that persons were members of extended families, and punishments like exile carried severe consequences; that ownership of private property was rare, and so therefore was the crime of theft; and that in crimes like manslaughter or accidental killing, the offender was given a chance to flee the community for some specific period, and if he then returned he would have to pay compensation to the victim's family in order to rejoin the society (Aja 1997: 357). In this society sophisticated punishments had been developed that usually involved not just the individual offenders but the extended family as well, so that the community itself became involved in keeping the peace and in punishing offenders. Colonization eroded traditional systems of social control, including traditional punishments, replacing them with Western models regardless of their appropriateness to social and cultural contexts.

In 1996 a meeting was held in Kampala, Uganda, at which representatives from forty African countries discussed prison conditions in Africa. The outcome was the Kampala Declaration, which sets out a penal reform agenda calling for improved prison conditions, fewer remanded prisoners, better staff development for prison officers, and the development of alternatives to imprisonment (Stern 1999: 231). Many African states now face the prospect of maintaining colonial systems of punishment that are under severe strain because of resource constraints. Conditions inside prisons are often below international minimum standards, and there are huge numbers of prisoners awaiting trial, many of whom can expect to spend up to five years in prison before they are brought to trial. Some countries have taken the lead in reforming their penal systems, and Zimbabwe, for example, has established a community service scheme after a research study had revealed that up to 80 percent of those in prisons were serving sentences of six months or less, did not pose a risk to society, and could safely be placed in a community service program (Stern 1999: 231). Generally, reforms of this nature have a common element in that they seek to involve the community in crime prevention and punishment so that they will better reflect indigenous systems of social control.

Industrialized countries will continue to compare their laws, practices, and statistics about punishment even though each country will ultimately follow its own policies and practices. Nevertheless, comparative statistical sources indicate that this group of nations adheres to similar trends and that since the 1970s and 1980s the pattern has been to impose harsher punishment and move way from rehabilitative ideals. In the developing world most countries struggle with inherited systems of punishment, and some are trying to recover traditional ways of punishment. Ironically, in the West, notions of restorative justice and reparation have attracted interest, and these processes are often hybrid versions of traditional forms of punishment. In nations like China, punishment is an aspect of social and political life and is seen as a means of restoring adherence to social norms, whereas in many Islamic countries punishment is an integral part of the Islamic way of life and not a secular policy issue.

References

Aja, Egbeke. 1997. "Crime and Punishment: An Indigenous African Experience." *The Journal of Value Enquiry* 31: 353–368.

Ashworth, Andrew. 2001. "The Decline of English Sentencing and Other Stories." In *Sentencing and Sanctions in Western Countries,* edited by Michael Tonry and Richard Frase, 62–91. New York: Oxford University Press.

Brown, David. 1998. "Penality and Imprisonment in Australia." In *Comparing Prison Systems: Toward a Comparative and International Penology,* edited by Robert Weiss and Nigel South, 367–400. Amsterdam: Gordon and Breach Publishers.

Dikotter, Frank. 2002. "The Promise of Repentance: Prison Reform in Modern China." *British Journal of Criminology* 42: 240–249.

Downes, David. 1998. "The Buckling of the Shields: Dutch Penal Policy 1985–1995." In *Comparing Prison Systems: Toward a Comparative and International Penology,* edited by Robert Weiss and Nigel South, 143–174. Amsterdam: Gordon and Breach Publishers.

Dutton, Michael, and Xu Zhangrun. 1998. "Facing Difference: Relations, Change and the Prison Sector in Contemporary China." In *Comparing Prison Systems: Toward a Comparative and International Penology,* edited by Robert Weiss and Nigel South, 289–336. Amsterdam: Gordon and Breach Publishers.

Dwyer, Daisy Hilse, ed. 1990. *Law and Islam in the Middle East.* New York: Bergin and Garvey Publishers.

Feest, Johannes, and Hartmut-Michael Weber. 1998. "Germany: Ups and Downs in the Resort to Imprisonment—Strategic or Unplanned Outcomes?" In *Comparing Prison Systems: Toward a Comparative and International Penology,* edited by Robert Weiss and Nigel South, 233–262. Amsterdam: Gordon and Breach Publishers.

Gaucher, Bob, and John Lowman. 1998. "Canadian Prisons." In *Comparing Prison Systems: Toward a Comparative and International Penology,* edited by Robert Weiss and Nigel South, 61–98. Amsterdam: Gordon and Breach Publishers.

Johnson, Elmer. 1998. "The Japanese Experience: Effects of Decreasing Resort to Imprisonment." In *Comparing Prison Systems: Toward a Comparative and International Penology,* edited by Robert Weiss and Nigel South, 337–365. Amsterdam: Gordon and Breach Publishers.

Maier-Katkin, D., and R. Ogle. 1997. "Policy and Disparity: The Punishment of Infanticide in Britain and America." *International Journal of Comparative and Applied Criminal Justice* 21(2): 305–316.

Mauer, Marc. 2003. "Comparative International Rates of Incarceration: An Examination of Causes and Trends." The Sentencing Project, Washington, DC.

Mohsen, Safia. 1990. "Women and Criminal Justice in Egypt." In *Law and Islam in the Middle East,* edited by Daisy Dwyer, 15–34. New York: Bergin and Garvey Publishers.

Olivero, J. Michael. 1998. "The Crisis in Mexican Prisons: The Impact of the United States." In *Comparing Prison Systems: Toward a Comparative and International Penology,* edited by Robert Weiss and Nigel South, 99–114. Amsterdam: Gordon and Breach Publishers.

Paton, Diana. 2001. "The Penalties of Freedom: Punishment in Postemancipation Jamaica." In *Crime and Punishment in Latin America,* edited by Ricardo Salvatore, Carlos Aguirre, and Gilbert Joseph, 275–307. Durham, NC: Duke University Press.

Plateck, Monika. 1998. "Penal Practice and Social Theory in Poland before and after the Events of 1989." In *Comparing Prison Systems: Toward a Comparative and International Penology,* edited by Robert Weiss and Nigel South, 263–288. Amsterdam: Gordon and Breach Publishers.

Ruggiero, Vincenzo. 1998. "The Country of Cesare Beccaria: The Myth of Rehabilitation in Italy." In *Comparing Prison Systems: Toward a Comparative and International Penology,* edited by Robert Weiss and Nigel South, 207–232. Amsterdam: Gordon and Breach Publishers.

Ryan, Mick, and Joe Sim. 1998. "Power, Punishment and Prisons in England and Wales 1975–1996." In *Comparing Prison Systems: Toward a Comparative and International Penology,* edited by Robert Weiss and Nigel South. Amsterdam: Gordon and Breach Publishers.

Souryal, Sam, Dennis Potts, and Abdullah Alobied. 1994. "The Penalty of Hand Amputation for Theft in Islamic Justice." *Journal of Criminal Justice* 22(3): 249–265.

Stern, Vivian. 1999. "Alternatives to Prison in Developing Countries." *Punishment and Society* 1(2): 231–241.

Tak, Peter. 2001. "Sentencing and Punishments in the Netherlands." In *Sentencing and Sanctions in Western Countries,* edited by Michael Tonry and Richard Frase, 151–187. Oxford: Oxford University Press.

Tkachuk, Brian. 2002. *Criminal Justice Reform: Lessons Learned: Community Involvement and Restorative Justice.* Heuni Paper No. 17. Helsinki: The European Institute for Crime Prevention and Control, Affiliated with the United Nations.

Tkachuk, Brian, and Roy Walmsley. 2001. "World Prison Population: Facts, Trends and Solutions." Heuni Paper No. 15. Helsinki: The European Institute for Crime Prevention and Control, Affiliated with the United Nations.

Tonry, Michael. 1999. "Parochialism in U.S. Sentencing Policy." *Crime and Delinquency* 45(1): 48–65.

Trevaskes, Susan. 2003. "Public Sentencing Rallies in China: The Symbolizing of Punishment and Justice in a Socialist State." *Crime, Law and Social Change* 39: 359–382.

Tucker, Judith. 1998. *In the House of the Law: Gender and Islamic Law in Ottoman Syria and Palestine.* London: University of California Press.

Van Zyl Smit, Dirk. 1998. "Change and Continuity in South African Prisons." In *Comparing Prison Systems: Toward a Comparative and International Penology,* edited by Robert Weiss and Nigel South, 401–426. Amsterdam: Gordon and Breach Publishers.

Walmsley, Roy. 1995. *Developments in the Prison Systems of Central and Eastern Europe.* Heuni Paper No. 4. Helsinki: The European Institute for Crime Prevention and Control, Affiliated with the United Nations.

———. 2001. "World Prison Population: Facts, Trends and Solutions." In *World Prison Population: Facts, Trends and Solutions*. Heuni Paper No. 15, edited by Brian Tkachuk and Roy Walmsley, 14–24. Helsinki: The European Institute for Crime Prevention and Control, Affiliated with the United Nations.

Weiss, Robert P., and Nigel South. 1998. *Comparing Prison Systems: Toward a Comparative and International Penology*. Amsterdam: Gordon and Breach Publishers.

4

Chronology

This chronology covers specific years and also periods in time when important events took place in the history of punishment. Reading through the broad chronology helps bring a sense of the ebb and flow of societal movements and concerns relating to the issue of punishment.

Before A.D. 700 Early forms of punishment involve acts of private vengeance, and during the pre-A.D. 700 period, disputes between tribal societies are usually settled through processes such as blood feuds.

From A.D. 700 Private dispute settlement through violence is replaced by demands for compensation for injuries, and codes of law evolve such as the Justinian Code of A.D. 529, which lays down a scale of punishment and compensation for specified injurious acts.

Twelfth and Thirteenth Centuries Three basic methods of settling the issue of guilt or innocence and therefore, of whether punishment ought to be imposed, develop. These are trial by battle, the ordeal, and compurgation.

Twelfth Century In England, by 1166 the grand jury has taken form and a number of country gentlemen are summoned before the king's agents to inform them about any offenses that have occurred against the king's peace in their community.

1215 Lateran Council condemnation of the ordeal leads to the emergence of trial by jury throughout Europe.

Fourteenth Century The advent of trial by jury puts an end to other forms of determining guilt. This form of trial is of relatively recent origin and did not appear in the highly developed legal systems of Greece or Rome. Its origin can be traced to the late medieval period when the king used the procedure known as an inquisition, during which he sought to establish his rights, especially to land.

1400–1700 Feudalism declines, and the new nation-state consolidates its role as the authority in England. As capitalism develops and economic transformation occurs, vagrants and beggars become a concern to those in power, leading them to legislate in an attempt to control the poor and those who want to sell their labor for the highest price. The poor begin to be seen as constituting a criminal class because they do not work, and idleness begins to be equated with immorality.

1500 The workhouse appears as a means of confining the poor and vagrants, and the first workhouse begins operation in England in 1557. Workhouses, or houses of correction, begin to appear about the middle of the sixteenth century in Europe and are used to confine vagrants and paupers but not to house convicted felons. The workhouse aims to transform those whose character is thought immoral through the use of labor and discipline. In this era we see the beginnings of the notion that criminal characters can be reformed and rehabilitated through confinement and work under a regime of strict discipline.

1597 The law of England authorizes transportation as a punishment for the first time, providing for banishment "out of this Realm and all the dominions thereof." Returning after banishment without license or warrant is a capital offense.

1607–1775 During this period, beginning with the establishment of the colony of Virginia in 1607 and ending in 1775 with the rebellion against the English, many punishments in America have their source in English practice simply because the majority of colonists are of English descent. From the time that the colony of Virginia gains a new charter in 1619, it most closely follows English practice in punishment, and English common law and statutes form the basis of local law. Communities are close-knit and fearful and wary of strangers, and the expectation is that members will conform to local norms and rules in order to maintain cohesion. The two central values of the community are maintenance of community order and obedience to God. Religion permeates all aspects off life, including ideas about crime and punishment. Crime is regarded as sin and as an offense against God. Traditional Puritan conceptions of crime look upon punishment as a process that should be tailored to the individual offender and should have, as its aim, the integration of the offender back into the community.

1635 In Massachusetts, the Boston jail opens and remains the only place of confinement in Boston for eighteen years until 1776 when Massachusetts is split into twelve counties, and each is legally mandated to establish its own jail.

1641 Servitude, or slavery, is enacted as a punishment in the Body of Liberties of Massachusetts.

1682 Pennsylvania maintains a mild criminal code compared with other colonies, with murder alone carrying the death sentence. This reflects Quaker belief in the reformation of even the worst offenders and their view that causes of crime can be located in social and economic conditions such as poverty and unemployment. Restitution is mandated for property crime, and rape is punished with a combination of whipping and

1682 *(cont.)* imprisonment; and for a second offense, by life imprisonment. Adulterers are required to wear the letter *A* on their clothing after being whipped.

1713 Legislation in Connecticut calls for the establishment of a house of correction declaring that state concern is for "persons who wander about," and the vagabond is placed first on the list of those who might be confined in the workhouse.

1717 England establishes the legislative framework for transportation to America. The law notes that present laws are ineffective in deterring crime and that there is need for servants in the colonies and plantations in America. Its operative part reads that a person convicted of an offense for which he is liable to be whipped or branded on the hand or delivered to the workhouse might be sent to the colonies and plantations in America. By 1775, England is transporting about two thousand convicts each year to America, usually as indentured servants. In 1776 the American Revolution puts an end to transportation to America.

1748 Montesquieu, in *The Spirit of Laws,* argues against severe punishments, contending that extreme violence violates the rights of citizens and shows a government to be unfit. He declares that excessive punishments are inappropriate for republics.

1764 Beccaria publishes his famous *Essay on Crimes and Punishment.* At the time he writes his essay, criminal procedure is extremely adverse to an accused. The use of torture, the extensive number of crimes that are punishable by capital punishment, and the inability of an accused to call witnesses on his or her behalf characterize a criminal justice system that penalizes an accused from the outset. Beccaria recommends changes to this criminal justice system and to its social framework, which will alleviate many of its adverse effects. His work represents the most important advance in the history of crime and punishment and sets the scene for the advances that will occur during the next century and a half.

1770–1794 William Bradford, justice of the Supreme Court of Pennsylvania and attorney general of the United States, designs the reformed Pennsylvania Criminal Codes. He believes that imprisonment in solitary confinement or with hard labor will deter crime. He argues that the objective of punishment is to prevent crime and that penalties ought to be proportionate to the crime committed.

1776 The new Constitution of the state of Pennsylvania directs that there be a speedy reform of the criminal law with the aim of replacing the various types of corporal punishment with imprisonment. It calls for "punishments [to be] made in some cases less sanguinary, and in general more proportionate to the crimes." In 1786 a law is passed to give effect to the aims of the Constitution, and this law expresses the underlying justice and rationale of punishment as "the wish of every good government to reclaim rather than to destroy."

1779 The term *penitentiary* appears for the first time in law in the English Penitentiary Act 1779, which mandates hard labor in place of transportation. This act provides for the construction of two penitentiaries in the area of London in which prisoners are to be incarcerated for a maximum of two years. At night they would be imprisoned in solitary confinement and in the day would engage in congregate labor of "the hardest and most servile kind."

1780 A new punishment is employed in Pennsylvania and involves sentencing offenders to hard labor in public in supervised work gangs. These prisoners are known as wheelbarrow men and are often harassed and abused by the public. The wheelbarrow men are not always harassed by the public; in some cases ordinary people provide

1780 *(cont.)* them with alcohol, tobacco, and food, and the men fight their guards and conspire to escape. By 1790 the state determines that the scheme is a failure and instead places these convicts in the Walnut Street Jail.

1785 In New York a bill passes, applying only to the city, permitting officials to substitute up to six months hard labor in the workhouse for corporal punishment. The law refers to pressure on society by vagrants and "idle persons."

Castle Island in Boston Harbor is designated as a place of confinement for "thieves and other convicts to hard labor." Here convicts live under military-style discipline.

1787 Jeremy Bentham's *Panopticon* is published. In his work Bentham designs a penitentiary that he calls the Panopticon modeled on a factory his brother constructed in Russia. The structure is circular and allows guards at the center to constantly keep under view all the prisoners located in cells around the circumference of the building. Bentham reasons that constant observation of the inmates' conduct will instill a habit of obedience, good industry, and conformity in prisoners.

The Philadelphia Society for Alleviating the Miseries of Public Prisons is formed on 8 May 1787, and its aims include extending compassion to inmates, preventing them from suffering illegal punishments, and devising punishments that would restore inmates to the path of virtue and happiness.

1787 The *Federalist Papers* contend that the administration of justice in both its criminal and civil forms is the paramount purpose of government. The authors perceive punishment to be an important and necessary function of government, arguing, "every government ought to contain in itself the means of its own preservation" and warning that without punishment there might be sedition.

1790–1830 The population of Massachusetts doubles, that of Pennsylvania triples, and the population of New York increases fivefold. Towns begin to develop, followed by cities. There is a high degree of labor mobility, and the expansion West begins. The former communal lifestyle broadens out into an individualistic perspective. Property crime begins to increase, and its cause is perceived to be this shifting population. This in turn leads to the view that offenders should be regarded as a separate and distinct criminal class. Traditional sanctions, designed to work in a small community where everyone knew each other, are no longer regarded as effective.

The Enlightenment in Europe elevates the status of man, emphasizing rational thought and perspectives and the ability of science to define the universe for man. God is seen as a benevolent power interested in promoting the good and happiness of man. Notions of utilitarianism, equality, and liberalism transform earlier beliefs about man, society, and God.

1794 The Walnut Street Jail, built in 1773 as a county jail, is converted into a state prison and adapted to give effect to what comes to be known as the Pennsylvania system of prison discipline. Under this system those convicted of the most serious crimes are kept in separate cells in solitary confinement. However, at Walnut Street only hardened criminals are regularly placed in solitary confinement at night, and the punishment of solitary confinement is otherwise reserved for use as a disciplinary measure for serious breaches of prison rules, such as refusing to work. By 1815 the jail is overcrowded because commitments for imprisonment have increased substantially. This contributes to an increase in the number of escapes, and assaults on guards also multiply.

1794 *(cont.)* On a visit to Pennsylvania, Thomas Eddy and John Schuyler meet with members of the Philadelphia Society for Alleviating the Miseries of Public Prisons and are shown the new system in operation at the Walnut Street Jail. They believe it is a model worth emulating and promote a bill in the state legislature to substitute imprisonment for corporal punishment for non-capital crimes and to provide for the construction of two penitentiaries in the state at Albany and New York City.

1797 Newgate Prison is built in Greenwich Village, New York. Newgate Prison is unsuccessful because of its small size and use of the aggregate confinement model that makes classification and discipline very difficult. Due to space limitations it proves necessary to pardon a number of criminals each year to keep the population within the physical capacity of the prison.

End of the Eighteenth Century By this time the public has developed a distaste for the public spectacle of punishment and the "civilizing process" works to increase the level of human sensitivity to such events.

1805 In Massachusetts, all crimes become punishable by fine, incarceration, or the death penalty only, reflecting the modern system of penalties.

Massachusetts opens a new state prison with a massive stone frame and a capacity for three hundred inmates. Prisoners begin their sentences in isolation and then move into shared cells where they work from dawn to dusk.

1816 A law is passed authorizing the construction of a new prison at Auburn, New York. The first warden of the prison, William Brittin, a carpenter by trade, is also in charge of its construction. The structure was built using the congregate method of confinement, with both double cells and rooms capable of accommodating ten or more inmates. Initially, the Auburn model opts for solitary confinement in a single, small, inside cell without labor and with no provision for exercise. Not surprisingly this model proves a failure and causes sickness and insanity in inmates in solitary confinement.

1818 The Western Penitentiary is established, modeled on Jeremy Bentham's Panopitcon.

1820 By this date, most U.S. states have amended their criminal codes to replace the death penalty with incarceration.

Corporal punishment ceases to be the most common method of punishing crime. The most commonly employed methods of corporal punishment had been: flogging, mutilation, branding, the stocks, and the pillory.

1823 The Cherry Hill Prison (Eastern State Penitentiary) is established in Philadelphia. It takes the form of a massive stone construction with a thirty-foot-high wall looking like a medieval castle and with individual wings of cell blocks radiating out from a central core. Each cell is connected to a small, walled courtyard. Inmates are completely alone at all times and wear hoods when they leave their cells. At Eastern State Penitentiary labor is deemed a privilege or a reward. Convicts come to fervently desire any kind of work to replace the alternative of continuous inactivity.

1828 In New York, another prison is constructed, replacing Newgate Prison in Greenwich Village. It later becomes known as Sing Sing Prison and from the outset operates according to the Auburn system. Sing Sing (also known as Mount Pleasant Prison) occupies 130 acres, and the keeper's house is a three-story mansion commanding a good view of

1828 *(cont.)* the Hudson River. The prison cell block is five stories high and contains one thousand individual cells measuring only six feet to seven feet high, seven feet long and three feet three inches wide. Other than blankets, each cell contains only a Bible, a cup, and a spoon.

1829 The so-called Auburn system of confinement and discipline, comprising congregate work during the day and separation at night, accompanied at all times by enforced total silence on the part of inmates, comes into being. Auburn warden, Captain Elam Lynds, works on the new plan assisted by his deputy John Cray. The new Auburn model allows inmates to work in groups in the prison yard and shops during the day, and at night they are locked in individual cells. Silence is enforced at all times, and strict discipline is imposed through measures such as the lockstep, special regulations in the dining room, and through the use of whipping to enforce obedience to prison rules. The overall goal of the Auburn system of penalization is breaking the prisoners' spirit and engendering a state of complete submission to authority.

1830 An investigating committee in the state of New Jersey reveals that convicts are being strapped on their backs to a plank and left there for up to twenty days as a form of disciplinary punishment in the state penitentiary.

1831 France sends Gustave Auguste de Beaumont and the Versailles judge Alexis de Tocqueville to the United States to inspect the two systems of Auburn and Pennsylvania. During this visit, de Tocqueville collects material for his work *Democracy in America.* In their report comparing the two systems they write that the Pennsylvania system is considered to be more expensive to construct and operate, whereas the Auburn system is seen as difficult to successfully administer by the often-mediocre officials employed in penal administration. The authors consider that the Pennsylvania system produces "the deepest impressions on the soul of the convict," whereas the Auburn system, while being less intensive, also achieves prisoner reform. The difference between the two systems is perceived as follows: Although the Pennsylvania system produces more men of honesty, the Auburn system produces citizens who were more obedient. The severity of both models is noted, and the authors remark on the contrast between the "complete despotism" of the prisons to the "most extended liberty" in the rest of U.S. society. The Frenchmen favor the Auburn system, largely because it is more cost effective.

1832 William Crawford of the London Society for the Improvement of Prison Discipline is sent to the United States to report on the two systems at Pennsylvania and Auburn. He favors the Pennsylvania system, which is later adopted by England with some modifications principally in the form of the great Pentonville Prison modeled on the Eastern Penitentiary.

1837 In England, the pillory ceases to be used as a form of punishment.

1842 Writer Charles Dickens visits Eastern Penitentiary and is shocked by what he considers the inhumanity of the system and its psychological tortures.

1845 The Prison Society of New York is formed and becomes a proponent of the Auburn system.

1849 The governor of Virginia announces that putting black and white races together in the state penitentiary "can be productive of nothing else but mischief: It necessarily makes the Negro insolent, and debases the white man; it is offensive to our habits and prejudices as well as to our feelings and policy, and ought to be discontinued." The solution eventually arrived at is to lease free blacks to work outside the penitentiary.

1850 Penitentiaries reach the point of failure, and stagnation, debt, corruption, and an almost total failure of the integrity of the two competing systems of Pennsylvania and Auburn occurs.

In the South, experiments with prison industries produce little or no return for most states, and, dismayed at having to spend money on convicted prisoners, Virginia, Georgia, and Tennessee consider the idea of leasing their penitentiaries to businessmen.

The principal period of vigilantism begins in the United States.

1858 Virginia decides to take its convicts out of the prison system and lease them out to railroad and canal companies. This scheme is the forerunner of other convict leasing systems that will be found throughout the South after the Civil War.

1860 After this time, the controversy between the Pennsylvania system and the Auburn system dies away with the introduction into the United States of the Irish model. This model, as later developed by Frank Sanborn around 1865 and by others into the Elmira Reformatory system, came to be seen (by 1875) as far more sophisticated in contrast to the crude and elementary systems evolved at an earlier period.

1865 North and South Carolina build penitentiaries. Previously they continued to use whipping and shaming punishments as well as the gallows. Crime in South Carolina is believed to be exclusively caused by blacks, the majority of whom are slaves, and consequently private justice through vigilantism and punishment on plantations takes the place of the formal criminal justice system.

1866 The report of the Board of Inspectors of the Pennsylvania Western Penitentiary notes that prisoners in solitary confinement kept in silent conditions express feelings of despair and hopelessness and that prisoners suffer acute loneliness and depression, never seeing faces other than those of the guards.

The first chain gangs appear in Georgia when the legislature devolves the punishment of convicted offenders from the state penitentiary to the local counties who are empowered to use convicts to build roads or lease them to private interests. As a result, those convicted of vagrancy-type offenses and work-related crime, as well as theft, are sentenced to periods on the chain gangs where they can be whipped by guards if they slack in their work efforts or attempt to escape.

1867 The governor of Arkansas offers a temporary two-year lease of state convicts to buy time within which to plan a better system for offenders. Southerners claim that the convict lease system has one reforming effect, that is, it teaches blacks how to work. As well, according to some, the system trains and turns out good workers who are disciplined and skilled and who can command good wages and jobs after release from incarceration.

1868 Seventeen percent of leased-out Alabama convicts reportedly die, and the rate increases to 41 percent in 1870. By 1883 one doctor reports that in Alabama most leased convicts die within three years. Terror appears in the South in the form of the Ku Klux Klan operating between 1868 and 1871. The Ku Klux Klan intends to violently resist any attempts by blacks to gain political power in the aftermath of the Civil War. The Klansmen, unlike most vigilantes in other parts of the United States of that period, wear strange garb, comprising white sheets and cone-shaped hats, and ride at night on horses. The Klan uses all methods to achieve its objectives, including whipping, burning, raping, and even killing their victims.

1870 A meeting of the American Prison Society held in Cincinnati, Ohio, agrees on the form of a Declaration of Principles that explicitly accepts the premise that individualized care and scientific treatment of offenders based on a medical model will reform offenders. The recommendations of the meeting include establishing adult reformatories linked with indeterminate sentencing, classification systems, intensive academic and vocational training, labor, parole, and humane disciplinary regimes.

1876 The Elmira Reformatory system is introduced into New York State. Elmira houses first-time felons aged between sixteen and thirty who have received indeterminate sentences. This system adds to the notion of the indeterminate sentence the practice of classifying inmates into groups of ascending grades through which each inmate must pass in order to earn parole. The U.S. reformers who establish the Elmira Reformatory follow the model set by the Irish prison system. The Irish and the Elmira models relate the term of a sentence of incarceration to progress made by an inmate on the path to ultimate reformation. Both systems emphasize reformation as opposed to retaliation or deterrence. This represents an important landmark in the development of punishment in the United States, and by 1923 almost one-half of all offenders admitted to prisons in the United States receive an indeterminate sentence. The golden age at Elmira runs from 1883 to 1899 so that by the turn of the twentieth century it is regarded with awe and as the most important penal institution in the United States.

1877 The Florida legislature abolishes its state penitentiary, replacing it with a system of hiring convicts out to private contractors. A similar move occurs in South Carolina, and other states also expand leasing, thus leaving their prisons to run down and house the small number of white and infirm black convicts.

1878 Boston implements a professional probation service. Probation's origin seems to have been the efforts of John Augustus, a businessman in Boston, who, between 1841 and 1859, personally posted bail and served as guardian to about two thousand offenders.

1879 Virginia becomes the first state after Pennsylvania to build a penitentiary modeled on Bentham's Panopticon. When convicts arrive there they undergo a period of solitary confinement from one-twelfth to one-half of their sentence. The Virginia penitentiary is unsuccessful because, apart from the severe conditions for prisoners, the workshops fail to make a profit. Also, several successful escapes are made and few prisoners show any signs of being reformed.

1880 By this time, except for Virginia, all the southern states have leased out all or part of their convicts to private enterprises.

The high point of lynching as an extralegal practice of punishment occurs after 1880 as any perceived resistance to white supremacy in the South makes a man a target for the mob.

1890 From this time, the convict leasing system begins to decline owing to changes in the labor market, subleasing, and the state's demands that contractors pay them high fees. These adverse factors reduce the comparative advantages of convict labor as opposed to free labor, but only Tennessee, North and South Carolina, and Louisiana actually abolish convict leasing before 1900.

Death by electrocution is first used in New York State on 6 August.

1900 The early part of the twentieth century sees the birth of the eugenics movement and associated genetic theories of crime. The movement can be seen as part of a battle against immorality and vice.

1900 *(cont.)* It links to fears about the effects of large-scale immigration into the United States, seen as threatening the values of those already established in the country and polluting the nation with inferior peoples. The proponents of eugenics believe that "defectives" and "degenerates" will engulf "true Americans" and their values, and the only solution is to sterilize them. The rationale is that this will prevent them breeding and overwhelming the nation. From this time the movement views the individual offender as both a victim of his past heredity and as someone who perpetuates that inherited criminality.

1901 Louisiana ends its practice of leasing out its prisoners and puts prisoners to work on its own plantations.

1907 Indiana becomes the first state to give legislative effect to a policy of sterilization when it declares sterilization to be official state policy and pronounces heredity to be a major player in the transmission of crime. The law requires every institution in Indiana that contains criminals, "idiots, rapists, and imbeciles" to add two surgeons to its staff. Inmates can be referred to the surgeons for assessment about whether, in light of their condition, they should be prevented from procreating. If it is considered inadvisable for an inmate to procreate, the surgeon is empowered to operate to sterilize the inmate.

1909 California passes legislation that allows for the sterilization of prisoners who have twice committed sexual offenses, have three convictions for any other crime, or who are serving a life sentence if there is evidence that the inmate is "a moral and sexual pervert."

1910 Katherine Bement Davis begins psychological testing at Bedford Hills State Reformatory for Women in New York, and John D. Rockefeller creates a Laboratory of Social Hygiene at Bedford Hills, where female inmates are taken to be measured and tested and probed for the causes of their criminality. Their intelligence is tested, their family history explored and tabulated, and their physical characteristics as compared with those of noncriminal women are documented.

1919 The NAACP reports on the toll of men and women lynched over the previous thirty-year period. On average more than one hundred blacks a year have been lynched by whites and 78 percent of all those lynched are black.

1920 Following a transcontinental tour of U.S. prisons, a prison investigator reports that prisoners are flogged, routinely placed in solitary confinement for periods ranging from a few months to a few years, and that it is common for men to be confined in dark cells, fed only bread and water, and handcuffed to the wall or cell bars. Others are placed in an iron cage that encloses their entire body and prevents them from bending their knees or leaning against the cell bars or even turning around, so that they are forced to stand continuously, straight like a post. In some older prisons, underground cells are found that are pitch black, unventilated, dirty, and so cramped that a man cannot stand up in them. Men are kept in such conditions up to thirty days at a time.

By this time only Florida and Alabama still maintain the practice of leasing out prisoners, and gradually state farms begin to replace convict leasing altogether.

1921 The frontier state of Nevada, with a population of less than eighty thousand, passes a Humane Death Act, which provides that a condemned man should be approached in his cell while sleeping and executed by a dose of lethal gas.

1923 By this time, one-half of all releases from prison are under parole.

1924 At the Carson City prison, Gee Jon becomes the first person to be legally executed by lethal gas in the form of cyanide crystals.

1927 The United States Supreme Court upholds eugenics legislation that endorses the sterilization of a white woman in Virginia who is eighteen years old and "feeble minded." Justice Oliver Wendell Holmes Jr., in his judgment, writes that it is better for society not to delay "to execute degenerate offspring for crime" and that society should deny the ability to procreate to those who are "manifestly unfit."

1929 The Federal Bureau of Prisons declares rehabilitation to be the fundamental aim and purpose of incarceration, reflecting a new emphasis on treatment and rehabilitation.

1930 By this time, the federal government and about thirty-six states have established probation systems.

1936 In this year one of the last public hangings in the United States occurs, with the hanging of Rainey Bethea in Kentucky. This hanging draws an audience of ten thousand. After the event, many in the crowd try to climb on the gallows wanting to obtain pieces of the dead man's shroud as souvenirs.

1942 The United States Supreme Court strikes down an Oklahoma statute that permits the forced sterilization of a person who has been convicted of three or more felonies involving moral turpitude. The court finds that the law violates the equal protection clause because it draws irrational and unjustifiable distinctions. The court also warns that marriage and procreation are basic civil rights and will be protected.

1946 The practice of flogging prisoners is discovered in the state prison farm at Angola, Louisiana, and floggings continue into the 1950s.

1950 Parole evolves into a system that, like the treatment provided in prisons, emphasizes the professional ability of parole agents to design treatment programs responsive to an offender's individual needs for reform.

1954 The American Prison Association changes its name to the American Correctional Association, reflecting a new emphasis on treatment and rehabilitation.

1960 Chain gangs disappear from all the southern states. However, the actual conditions imposed in leasing and on chain gangs continue in the tough conditions prevailing in southern prisons in the modern day.

1967 It is revealed that in Georgia labor camps, inmates are chained together and required to break rocks. Working conditions become so bad that some inmates begin breaking, not rocks, but their own legs to escape the brutal conditions. The incidents come to national attention, and the labor camps are abolished.

1968 The Omnibus Crime Control and Safe Streets Act is passed, establishing the Law Enforcement Assistance Administration intended to implement a national strategy to wage the war on crime in the United States.

For the first time since the start of polling on public issues in the United States, Americans rate crime as the top domestic issue in the country.

1972 The "war on drugs" begins, and produces a vast increase in the number of persons incarcerated for drug offenses, especially women.

The United States Supreme Court declares all but a few death penalty statutes unconstitutional (*Furman v. Georgia*), and each of the approximately

1972 *(cont.)* 630 inmates on death rows throughout the country is resentenced to life imprisonment.

1974 Many commentators attribute the demise of the ideal of rehabilitation to an article published in this year by Martinson and some colleagues at the City University of New York. After evaluating a number of rehabilitation programs, they publish a study called "What Works? Questions about Prison Reforms," concluding that "with few and isolated exceptions, the rehabilitative efforts that have been reported so far have had no appreciative impact on recidivism." The call that "nothing works" becomes a rallying cry for penal conservatives, and an increased political emphasis on crime control and punishment is taken up by the media.

1975 Indeterminate sentencing using parole begins to be replaced in almost every state with determinate sentencing.

1976 Only four years after *Furman,* the Supreme Court reverses any notion of a permanent abolition of the death penalty by approving several recently enacted capital statutes (*Gregg v. Georgia*).

1977 The publication of *Discipline and Punish* by Michel Foucault revolutionizes thinking about punishment and discipline in society. In a complex analysis of these topics Foucault explains how inflicting pain on the body through early forms of punishment gave way to new forms of power by way of disciplining the individual through institutions like the factory and the prison and how such practices created a class of "delinquents." Foucault argues that the prison should be seen not as an instrument of punishment alone but as an institution where modern techniques of control are seen in their fullest extent.

1979 By this time the average caseload of a parole officer is seventy-nine, leaving only a few minutes each month for each parolee after having dealt with administrative duties.

1980 Intensive supervision is adopted as a form of punishment for probationers and parolees by most states. Penal conservatives want a way of showing toughness on crime that will also avoid more prison overcrowding, and therefore increasing prison expenditure, while at the same time preserving the policy of punishment in the community. The answer is to develop the use of intermediate sanctions, that is, penalties falling somewhere on the continuum between parole and probation that emphasize intensive supervision and compliance with conditions. Essentially, they provide a higher level of supervision and control of probationers and parolees. This form of punishment proves to be most effective at ensuring that offenders are returned to prison for punishment for technical violations of the conditions of their release into the community. The resulting issue faced by policymakers was one of whether or not to return them to prison for technical violations, and thereby contribute to further overcrowding in prisons, or ignore the technical violation and minimize the supposed effect of intensive supervision. Most states choose the former approach and prison populations increase even more.

1986 The Anti-Drug Abuse Act is introduced, penalizing drug trafficking and drawing a line between the offense of possessing crack cocaine and the offense of possessing powder cocaine. A person found guilt of possessing five or more grams of crack cocaine is liable to a mandatory minimum sentence of five years imprisonment and a maximum of twenty years imprisonment. On the other hand, possession

1986 *(cont.)* of five hundred grams of powder cocaine is required before a mandatory minimum sentence applies. This differentiation in treatment largely impacts the African-American population, since the cheaper crack cocaine is preferred over powder cocaine by drug users. The latter substance is used mainly by the white middle-class users.

The American Bar Association expresses the view that private prisons do not accord with the Constitution, arguing that "incarceration is an inherent function of the government and the government should not abdicate this responsibility by turning over prison operations to private industry."

1989 Privatization of prisons has become widespread throughout the United States, and privatization becomes an economic lobbying point for many rural communities. Competition to have a new prison constructed in one's locality grows fierce, and some communities offer free country club memberships and other benefits to prison administrators and guards as an incentive to site the prison in their community.

1994 Boot camps operate in thirty states, and throughout the nation more than 7,000 beds are dedicated to boot camp–type programs, where offenders are detained between 90 and 180 days. In New York State the largest boot camp operates 1,500 beds.

Federal law in the form of the Crime Bill requires that funds available for federal anticrime programs be withheld from those states that do not maintain sex offender registration systems.

1995 Proving that chain gangs still retain their attraction, in this year Alabama announces it will reintroduce the chain gang.

By this time the penal system comprises more than five thousand correctional institutions, including local jails.

Federal spending on waging the "war on drugs" reaches $13.2 billion, and the result of this enormous expenditure is a corresponding increase in the number of persons imprisoned for drug offenses. Between 1982 and 1988 convictions for drug offenses increase by more than 50 percent, and although in 1985 drug offenders make up 34.3 percent of the federal prison population, by 1995 this increases to 60.8 percent and to 72 percent by 1996.

1996 Enactment of the Anti-Terrorism and Effective Death Penalty Act. A condemned prisoner is now required to file an application for habeas corpus to the federal courts (arguing that he or she is being detained illegally) not later than 180 days after the final state court affirms his or her conviction. The state court's decision is presumed to be correct, and clear and convincing evidence must be produced by the defendant to obtain a review. Second or successive claims for habeas corpus are barred.

The No Frills Prison Act passes as an amendment to the Department of Justice's appropriation. It bans televisions, coffeepots, and hot plates in the cells of federal prisoners and also prohibits computers, electronic instruments, certain movies rated above PG, and unmonitored phone calls.

The federal government enacts the Pam Lychner Sexual Offender Tracking and Identification Act, requiring lifetime registration for offenders convicted of one or more sexual offenses involving certain acts with victims younger than twelve years of age.

Without any necessity for a court order, the state of Alabama enters into a settlement with the Southern

1996 *(cont.)*	Poverty Law Center to cease their use of chain gangs as punishment introduced one year earlier (*Michael Austin et al. v. Fob James Jr. Governor of Alabama and Ron Jones, Commissioner of ADC,* Case No. 95-T–637-N). The state announces that it has ended the practice, owing to administrative concerns arguing that individual chaining would be more effective than chaining prisoners to each other.
1997	By this time twenty-four states and the federal government have passed mandatory minimum penalties laws.
2000	Voters in California overwhelmingly approve a proposition that would give drug treatment instead of prison to first- and second-time drug offenders who are not charged with any other crimes.
2002	At year-end some 753,141 persons are on parole in the United States, and in this year the nation's parole population expands by 2.8 percent, a rate almost double the average annual growth since 1995. More than 2 out of every 5 persons placed on parole and discharged from parole supervision are returned to prison because of a rule violation or a new offense.
	At year-end, 3,995,165 persons are on probation in the United States and 50 percent of those have been convicted of a felony. Twenty-four percent are on probation for a drug offense.
	At year-end in the United States, 2.1 million persons are incarcerated. During the period 1975 to 1990, the number of persons under correctional supervision increases by 203 percent, and between 1980 and 1992 the number incarcerated in jails and federal and state prisons increases from 330,000 to 883,000, an increase of 168 percent.

At year-end 3,557 inmates are on death row, with California holding the largest number of 614, followed by Texas with 450.

At year-end state prisons are operating at between 1 percent and 17 percent above capacity and federal prisons at an extraordinary rate of 33 percent above capacity.

5

Biographical Sketches

John Augustus (1785–1859)

It is generally agreed that the idea of placing convicted persons on probation originated in the efforts of John Augustus, a businessman in Boston, who, between 1841 and 1859, personally posted bail and served as guardian to about two thousand offenders. Boston institutionalized Augustus's practice by implementing a professional probation service in 1878, and in 1891 a further law in the state of Massachusetts authorized a statewide system of probation. Other states later followed suit.

Cesare Beccaria (1738–1794)

Cesare Beccaria produced the most influential work in the reform of criminal jurisprudence and was an enormous influence in the development of thinking about crime and punishment both in Europe and the United States. From 1768 to 1770 he was professor of political economy in Milan, and in his later life he served on occasion as a magistrate and as a member of various investigating commissions. His famous *Essay on Crimes and Punishments* was published in 1764. Beccaria was not a professional lawyer, jurist, or criminologist, but he wrote as an intelligent outsider. At the time he wrote his essay, criminal procedure was extremely adverse to an accused. The use of torture, the extensive number of crimes that were punishable by capital punishment, and the inability of an accused to call witnesses on his behalf characterized a criminal justice system that penalized an accused from the outset. Beccaria recommended changes to the criminal justice system and to its social framework that would alleviate many of its adverse effects. These proposals included the idea that crime ought to be seen as an injury to society and the extent of the injury would be the measure of the crime committed. In other words, he promoted the notion of proportionality in punishment. He thought that punishment could only be justified if it helped to deter criminal conduct (the theory of deterrence). Before Beccaria, most had thought that deterrence was linked only to the severity of punishment as an act of revenge. He also argued that imprisonment as a punishment should be employed much more widely but that better facilities should be provided for prisoners and they should be separated and classified according to age, sex, and nature of offense. The *Essay on Crimes and Punishments* had an enormous influence on Beccaria's contemporaries and his successors in the field of criminology and was a great influence in the reform of the criminal law in the United States after 1776.

Jeremy Bentham (1748–1832)

After John Howard, the most influential prison reformer in terms of prison conditions and prison law was Jeremy Bentham. He wrote widely on many aspects of prison reform and administration, as well as on criminal jurisprudence, and was an intellectual catalyst for the reform of the English criminal law between 1775 and 1850. He was a utilitarian who believed in the theory of deterrence and who advocated fixing penalties as punishment that would impose a degree of pain just in excess of the pleasure that might be derived from the criminal act. He believed that the prospect of deriving more pain than pleasure from a crime would operate to deter future crime. At the same time, he appreciated that social and economic conditions also played a part in criminality, and he therefore advocated improved social conditions for all.

William Bradford (1755–1795)

Justice of the Supreme Court of Pennsylvania and attorney general of the United States, William Bradford designed the reformed Pennsylvania Criminal Codes of 1790 to 1794. In 1793 he described his mission as that of transforming the inherited English codes of criminal law, which he saw as severe and unsupported by many citizens. He believed, like Montesquieu that "as freedom advances, the severity of the penal law decreases." Bradford argued that imprisonment in solitary confinement or with hard labor would act as a deterrent to crime. He contended that the objective of punishment was to prevent crime and that penalties ought to be proportionate to the crime committed.

Zebulon Brockway (1827–1920)

After a career as a prison warden managing institutions that promoted reform, Brockway was appointed the first superintendent of the Elmira Prison Reformatory in 1876. Brockway expressed his conviction that prison should be more like a college or a hospital if it was to truly succeed in the task of reforming criminals, and Elmira was his testing ground for those ideas. Brockway graded prisoners at Elmira who were held there for indefinite periods; their release on parole depended on earning sufficient points or grades. There were three grades of offenders, each with different colored uniforms. In 1879 Brockway added a "School of Letters" to Elmira in which selected inmates were trained in skills like brush making. He also used a printing press to produce reports highly laudatory of the institution that helped persuade other prison administrators that Elmira was the model to follow in prison reform. However, by 1893, Elmira had become seriously overcrowded and Brockway's views were coming under greater scrutiny when he declared, for example, that physical degeneracy was the leading cause of crime and claimed that persons of low intelligence were incapable of becoming law-abiding members of society. His methods of practice at Elmira were also criticized in official reports and through special investigations, especially his habit of whipping those he considered immoral or defective.

Katharine Bement Davis (1860–1935)

As superintendent of the State Reformatory for Women at Bedford Hills, New York, Davis assisted in the establishment of the Laboratory of Social Hygiene for evaluating female inmates through extensive psychological testing. Researchers tested women inmates for intelligence and recorded and analyzed their family histories, looking for eugenic clues of their criminality. A believer in heredity as a factor in influencing criminal conduct, Davis rejected the eugenicist view that immigrants and African-Americans were "natural" criminals because of their heredity.

Davis and the work of the laboratory exemplify the scientific approach that sought to identify the causes of criminality in personality so that punishment could be graduated according to intelligence and family history.

Robert L. Dugdale (1841–1883)

In 1874 Dugdale visited thirteen county jails for the Prison Association of New York, and while visiting one rural county he found six persons in jail, four male, and two female, under four family names that suggested they were blood relatives. He attempted to trace their family history to explain their disproportionate involvement in crime and later claimed to have traced the family's roots to a colonial frontiersman descended from early Dutch settlers. In his book *The Jukes: A Study in Crime, Pauperism, Disease, and Heredity,* Dugdale demonstrated how he followed the bloodline back over five generations, during which 1,200 Jukes had been produced or had married Jukes. Of that number, he claimed to have identified 280 adult paupers, 60 habitual thieves, and 140 other criminals, 7 murderers, and 50 prostitutes. According to Dugdale, one member of the family in particular had shown strong criminal tendencies, and he therefore labeled its founder as "Margaret, Mother of criminals." His genealogy of degeneracy made good reading, and his pseudoscientific arguments gave support to the eugenics movement and to the claim that crime is inherited and could be identified in family histories and distinct physical features.

Louis Dwight (1793–1854)

Dwight founded the Boston Prison Discipline Society in 1826 and was an advocate of the Auburn system of punishment. He urged that the strict system at Auburn be employed throughout society in families, schools, and factories. In his role as advocate of the Auburn model, Dwight became the main critic of the Pennsylvania system, arguing that it could never be cost effective because of the need for solitary cells in large numbers and because working only to produce crafts rather than volume production made the system less economically viable. In favor of the Auburn system, he argued that it would fill the state's coffers while also reforming criminals. Naturally this argument appealed greatly to state legislators.

Thomas Eddy (1758–1827)

Eddy was brought up as a Quaker in Philadelphia and became interested in prison reform during his own incarceration after the Revolution. His interest also lay in the fact that as a merchant he wanted to see a penal code in force in New York that would better protect the property of citizens. He thought that prisoners could be redeemed through humane but strict treatment processes. From about 1785, Eddy lobbied the state legislature for the next eleven years to support a state-run penal establishment. His foremost patron at the political level was General Philip Schuyler, Alexander Hamilton's father-in-law. In 1796, they finally succeeded in having the state legislature abolish the death penalty for most crimes and to replace all other punishments for felonies with long prison sentences. The legislation permitted judges to set the length of prison terms and called for the construction of two state prisons where convicts would be provided with "coarse clothing" and "inferior food." Eddy supervised the construction of the penitentiary in Greenwich Village, which he named Newgate and which he modeled after the Walnut Street Jail. He was the first agent of the penitentiary, a position similar to that of warden. He issued instructions at Newgate that inmates could not be struck by guards and prohibited corporal punishment at the prison. The most severe punishment available was solitary confinement on reduced rations. Eddy favored reformation through a system of labor that would engender habits of industry and sobriety.

Eliza Wood Farnham (1815–1864)

Eliza Wood Farnham was appointed the matron of the Mount Pleasant Prison for Women in 1844, part of the men's prison at Sing Sing, New York. She introduced phrenology as a determinant of inmate treatment in the belief that the women could not be fully responsible for their crimes and that their criminal tendencies had been formed by their inherited characteristics. She advocated and practiced using positive incentives rather than harsh punishments and used education as the primary method of achieving reformation. By 1848 she had been forced from her position as matron of the prison by penal conservatives who did not believe in any diminution of the harsh treatment afforded by the Auburn system of incarceration. She was especially criticized for relaxing the strict rule of silence.

John Howard (1726–1791)

The most important reformer in England in the field of the treatment of criminals in the second half of the eighteenth century was John Howard. He had been orphaned as a young man and had inherited a large fortune. While leading a life of leisure he was taken from a ship on which he was traveling by French pirates and held as a prisoner for several months. From that time he became concerned about prison conditions. In 1773 he was appointed high sheriff of Bedfordshire, and in that capacity he visited prisons and observed their conditions, and this provoked his pity and interest in prison reform. The public awareness he created about prison conditions was a very powerful influence in the reform process. In 1775 and 1776 he visited more than one hundred prisons throughout Great Britain. He criticized prisons and jails for being places where idleness and vice were taught, urged that free clothing be provided to indigent convicts, that all inmates be given adequate food, and that rooms be properly ventilated. He recommended strict separation of male and female prisoners as well as the separation of youth from hardened criminals and advocated having prisoners sleep alone at night, arguing that solitude and silence were likely to engender reflection and might lead to repentance. He also thought that jailers should act humanely and be paid an adequate wage and ought not to accept fees or favors from inmates. He doubted that prison labor would ever turn a profit but thought that it might provide enough funds to enable an institution to at least become self-sufficient. Howard visited two institutions in Rome and Ghent that anticipated some of the conditions of the modern prison system. Both prisons followed a process of classifying inmates and also separated them in individual cells. Howard's writings contain descriptions of both institutions and their disciplinary practices and administration. It was through Howard's writings that Americans gained a knowledge and understanding of how these institutions operated. In 1777 Howard published the most comprehensive study at that time on English prisons, a volume of 489 pages entitled *The State of Prisons in England and Wales, with Preliminary Observations and an Account of Some Foreign Prisons.*

Cesare Lombroso (1835–1909)

Lombroso's focus was on the individual criminal as an animal and, using methods adopted from physical anthropology, made measurements of thousands of offenders and compiled lists of their physical abnormalities, which he linked with his argument about the existence of "the criminal type." By 1887 he had catalogued many "suspicious" traits such as possessing an excessive jaw or a receding forehead, which typified, in his view, a criminal personality. Lombroso's theories were widely accepted in the United States, especially in the new field of criminology. Researchers naturally turned to the prisons to test out his theories, and experiments were conducted in a number of penitentiaries. From about 1880, the field of physical anthropology gained a respectable following in academic and professional journals, focusing their attentions on criminals, arguing that the individual offender was both a victim of his past heredity and someone who perpetuated that inherited criminality.

Colonel Charles Lynch (1736–1785)

The term *lynching* immortalizes the name of Colonel Charles Lynch of Bedford County, Virginia, a justice of the peace, who, in the 1780s organized an extralegal group to catch suspected Tory sympathizers in the period of the Revolutionary War, conduct trials, and inflict punishment, mainly in the form of whipping. Later, lynching came to be seen not as a form of vigilantism but as the murder of men and women by mobs with no regard to the justice system. Essentially lynching represented a savage method of social control supported by large sections of society. The term *lynching* refers to groups of citizens killing one or more other citizens without the sanction of government. In the South, lynching was not an isolated event but a systematic, organized, and coherent expression of the social structure of that time.

Elam Lynds (1784–1855)

Elam Lynds was the originator of the Auburn system of discipline, and his background in the militia provided the military model for that system. Lynds was an extremely disciplined man and required that others conduct themselves in the same way. He prided himself on being self-made and on his determination and iron will, and he was quite convinced of his moral correctness. He was appointed agent and principal keeper of the Auburn penitentiary in 1821 and, along with his deputy John Cray who also had a military background, began to experiment with patterns of drill and marching and routines to create a stable disciplined prison regime. Many features of the Auburn system, including marching in lockstep, congregate work groups, and imposing total silence among the inmates, were developed at Auburn in the early 1820s. Lynds supervised the construction of Sing Sing Prison from 1825 to 1828, which was built with prison labor and which replaced Newgate Prison. He became the first warden of Sing Sing. He believed that whipping as a punishment was most effective and humane because it did not cause injury to health, but he regarded solitary confinement as dangerous and unhealthy. He did not believe that prisoners could be completely reformed except, perhaps, for those who were very young delinquents.

Benjamin Rush (1746–1813)

Dr. Benjamin Rush signed the Declaration of Independence and was the surgeon general of the Continental Army. He had previously been a medical student at the University of Edinburgh, Scotland. Observing the chaos that prevailed in the mid-1780s, Rush saw the need to instill virtue into citizens so that they would become self-controlled and self-disciplined. Rush applied medical principles and techniques to the study of criminals for the purpose of treating their moral faculties so they would develop the capacity to distinguish between virtues and vice. He thought this could be achieved by controlling their environment and their bodies. According to him, vice caused by idleness could be cured with work, and vice caused by vicious motives called for the separation of the debilitated mind from bad company. Where vice resulted from exciting the passions, this, he argued, could be regulated by the routine of labor. These remedies were termed "moral remedies," and Rush believed that it was possible to transform a person's moral character through the application of medical techniques. He is remembered especially for his "tranquilizer," a chair with straps for the hands, arms, legs, and feet and a structure for holding the head in place in a fixed position. The prisoner could be placed in the chair in a state of complete confinement and this allowed separation of the prisoner from the overload of sensory perceptions that he would otherwise be subject to. By the 1830s this chair would become a common instrument of punishment in penitentiaries. Rush also assumed that prisoners could be removed from sensory overload through solitary confinement. He considered solitude a valuable tool in the process of reformation and in fact used it on his own son who later became insane. He supported the abolition of corporal punishment and the death penalty, repudiating strict Calvinist principles that emphasized a stern and vengeful God and advocating a more liberal theology. In his *Enquiry into the Effects of Public Punishments upon Criminals, and Upon Society,* of March 1787, Rush argued that public punishments removed any sense of shame from criminals, destroyed their characters, and did not endure long enough to reform them.

Alexis de Tocqueville (1805–1859)

Along with Gustave de Beaumont, de Tocqueville toured U.S. prison systems in 1831 on behalf of the French government. Later he was to incorporate his observations in his work *Democracy in America.* With de Beaumont he wrote *On the Penitentiary System in the United States and Its Application to France* (1832), pointing out that, although U.S. society offered the most extended form of liberty, this freedom stood in great contrast to the utter despotism offered by the prison system. Alexis de Tocqueville noted the importance of work regardless of whether or not an inmate was reformed through the prison experience saying, "Perhaps, leaving the prison he is not an honest man, but he has contracted honest habits. He was an idler, now he knows how to work."

Roberts Vaux (1786–1836)

With his family background of Quaker beliefs, Vaux pursued altruistic aims and projects, including the abolition of slavery, a movement for the moral uplift of prostitutes, serving in the presidency of the state temperance society, and making major contributions to the construction of an insane asylum as well as an institution for the deaf. Through a relative who was governor of Pennsylvania at the time, Vaux was able to influence the plan for Eastern Penitentiary and was a member of the penitentiary's building commission.

Frederick H. Wines (1838–1912)

Reverend Wines was the secretary of the Illinois Board of Public Charities and a great collector of criminal statistics as well as a prominent criminal law reformer. He did not accept the notion that crime could be inherited, and he did not believe in the criminal type. For many years he led the opposition to the eugenics movement that promoted these theories. He noted that all the character and physical traits attributed to criminals covered a wide range of attributes, some even claiming that criminals were hypersensitive to climate and that criminals did not blush. He attacked the methodology of the physical anthropologists, accusing them of failing to compare so-called criminal characteristics with those of noncriminals in controlled studies.

Richard Wistar (1756–1821)

The origin of prison reform in Pennsylvania is associated with the name of Richard Wistar, a Quaker, who, as a visitor to the provincial jail in Philadelphia, had seen the misery of the inmates, some who had recently starved to death through administrative neglect. Wistar had acted to relieve the situation there by having soup prepared at his own house, which was then distributed to the inmates. He and others formed the Philadelphia Society for Assisting Distressed Prisoners in 1776.

6

Facts and Data

This chapter contains useful statistical information about punishment in America and elsewhere.

The following chart shows that at the end of 2002 more than 54 percent of federal prisoners were serving time for drug offenses. This compares to only about 16 percent in the 1970s.

Table 6.1
Federal Prison Population, and Number and Percent Sentenced for Drug Offenses, United States. 1970–2002

	Total sentenced and unsentenced population	*Sentenced population*		
			Drug offenses	
		Total	*Number*	*Percent of total*
1970	21,266	20,686	3,384	16.3%
1971	20,891	20,529	3,495	17.0
1972	22,090	20,729	3,523	16.9
1973	23,336	22,038	5,652	25.6
1974	23,690	21,769	6,203	28.4
1975	23,566	20,692	5,540	26.7
1976	27,033	24,135	6,425	26.6
1977	29,877	25,673	6,743	26.2
1978	27,674	23,501	5,981	25.4
1979	24,810	21,539	5,468	25.3
1980	24,252	19,023	4,749	24.9
1981	26,195	19,765	5,076	25.6
1982	28,133	20,938	5,518	26.3
1983	30,214	26,027	7,201	27.6
1984	32,317	27,622	8,152	29.5
1985	36,042	21,623	9,491	34.3
1986	37,542	30,104	11,344	37.7

(continues)

Table 6.1
Federal Prison Population *(continued)*

	Total sentenced and unsentenced population	*Total*	*Sentenced population drug offenses*	
			Number	*Percent of total*
1987	41,609	33,246	13,897	41.8
1988	41,342	33,758	15,087	44.7
1989	47,568	37,758	16,852	49.9
1990	54,613	46,575	24,297	52.2
1991	61,026	52,176	29,667	56.9
1992	67,768	59,516	35,398	59.5
1993	76,531	68,183	41,393	60.7
1994	82,269	73,958	45,367	61.3
1995	85,865	76,947	46,669	60.7
1996	89,672	80,872	49,096	60.7
1997	95,513	87,294	52,059	59.6
1998	104,507	95,323	55,984	58.7
1999	115,024	104,500	60,399	57.8
2000	123,141	112,329	63,898	56.9
2001	131,419	120,829	67,037	55.5
2002	139,183	128,090	70,009	54.7

Note: These data represent inmates housed in Federal Bureau of Prisons facilities; inmates hosued in contract facilities are not included. Data for 1970–76 are for June 30; beginning in 1977, data are for September 30. Some data have been revised by the souce and may differ from previous editions of Sourcebook.

Source: U.S. Department of Justice, Federal Bureau of Prisons. Available: http://www.bop.gov/fact0598.html (Sept. 9, 2003)

The following graph shows the huge disparities in drug admissions according to race, with African Americans being imprisoned at a significantly higher rate than any other race.

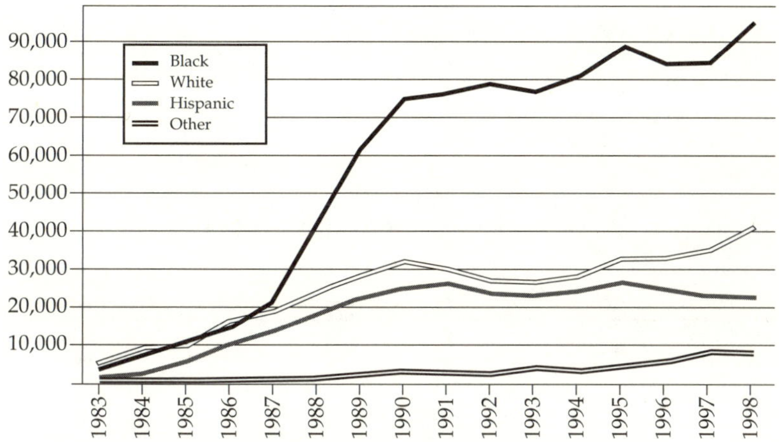

Figure 6.1 Prison Drug Admissions by Race, 1983–1998

Source: Iguschi, M.Y., J.A. London, N.G. Forge, L. Hickman, K. Riehman. 2002. "Elements of Well-Being Affected by Crimalizing the Drug User: An Overview." *Public Health Reports*, 117, (Suppl 1): S146–S150.

The following chart reveals the increase in the rate of imprisonment according to the five highest and five lowest states.

Table 6.2
Prisoners in 2003

Prison population	*Number of inmates*	*Incarceration rate, 12/31/03*	*Inmates per 100,000 residents**	*Growth, 12/31/02 to 12/31/03*	*Percent change*
5 highest:					
Federal	173,059	Louisiana	801	North Dakota	11.4%
Texas	166,911	Mississippi	768	Minnesota	10.3
California	164,487	Texas	702	Montana	8.9
Florida	79,594	Oklahoma	636	Wyoming	7.8
New York	65,198	Alabama	635	Hawaii	7.5
5 lowest:					
North Dakota	1,239	Maine	149	Connecticut	-4.2%
Wyoming	1,872	Minnesota	155	New York	-2.8
Vermont	1,944	North Dakota	181	Michigan	-2.4
Maine	2,013	Rhode Island	184	New Jersey	-2.3
New Hampshire	2,434	New Hampshire	188	Ohio	-1.9

*Prisoners with a sentence of more than 1 year per 100,000 in the resident population.

Source: Harrison, Paige, and Allen Beck. 2004. "Prisoners in 2003." *Bureau of Justice Statistics Bulletin*, NCJ 205335.

The following chart reveals the number of offenders registered in state sex offender registries between 1998 and 2001. The three states with the largest number of offenders registered are Florida, California, and Texas.

Table 6.3
Offenders in State Sex Offender Registries

By State, 1998 and 2001

State	*Offenders in registry* 1998	2001	*Percentage change 1998 to 2001*
Total	263,166	386,112	47%
Alabama	440	3,338	659
Alaska[a]	3,535	4,107	16
Arizona	9,200	11,500	25
Arkansas	958	2,935	206
California[a]	78,000	88,853	14
Colorado	4,326	8,804	104
Connecticut	(b)	2,030	X
Delaware	800	1,688	111
District of Columbia	50	303	506
Florida	9,000	20,000	122
Georgia	1,200	4,564	280
Hawaii	1,000	1,500	50
Idaho	1,710	1,778	4
Illinois[a]	14,300	16,551	16
Indiana	9,500	11,656	23
Iowa	2,240	3,921	75
Kansas	1,200	1,794	50
Kentucky	800	2,000	150
Louisiana	3,455	5,708	65
Maine	275	473	72
Maryland	400	1,400	250
Massachusetts	7,004	(c)	X
Michigan	19,000	26,850	41
Minnesota	7,300	10,610	45
Mississippi	1,063	1,512	42
Missouri	2,800	7,500	168
Montana[d]	1,739	2,088	20
Nebraska	640	1,120	75
Nevada	1,500	2,519	68
New Hampshire	1,500	2,168	45
New Jersey	5,151	7,495	46
New Mexico	450	1,171	160
New York	7,200	11,575	61
North Carolina	2,200	5,922	169
North Dakota	683	766	12
Ohio	1,294	5,423	319

(continues)

Table 6.3
Offenders in State Sex Offender Registries *(continued)*

By State, 1998 and 2001

State	*Offenders in registry* 1998	*Offenders in registry* 2001	*Percentage change 1998 to 2001*
Oklahoma	2,303	4,020	75
Oregon	7,400	9,410	27
Pennsylvania	2,400	4,533	89
Rhode Island	273	1,424	422
South Carolina	2,500	4,924	97
South Dakota	800	1,182	48
Tennessee	2,800	4,561	63
Texas	18,000	29,494	64
Utah	4,733	5,192	10
Vermont	877	1,509	72
Virginia	6,615	9,306	41
Washington	1,400	15,304	993
West Virginia	600	950	58
Wisconsin	10,000	11,999	20
Wyoming	552	682	24

Note: In March 1998, the U.S. Department of Justice, Bureau of Justice Statistics (BJS) established the National Sex Offender Registry Assistance Program (NSOR-AP). Several factors in each State's authorizing legislation significantly influence the size of a State's registry. Among these factors are the number of different offenses requiring registration, the date that triggers the registration mandate, and the duration of the registration requirement.

[a] Number includes more than just registered offenders (for example, never registered but required to do so, offenders in jail, registered but not in compliance).
[b] At the time the survey was conducted in 1998, Connecticut did not have a centralized sex offender registry.
[c] The 2001 count is not included due to a superior court injunction against the Sex Offender Registry Board, prohibiting registration without first providing the offender a hearing. At the time of the survey, Massachusetts estimated that about 17,000 sex offenders would be qualified to register.
[d] Also includes offenders who must register for certain violent offenses.

Source: U.S. Department of Justice, Bureau of Justice Statistics, *Summary of State Sex Offender Registries, 2001,* Fact Sheet NCJ 192265 (Washington, DC: U.S. Department of Justice, March 2002), p.6.

In the following chart, Thomas Blomberg shows the average length of imprisonment terms by state between 1844 and 1846 with the average being between four and seven years.

Table 6.4
Average Length of Imprisonment in U.S. Penitentiaries, 1844–1846

			Average Terms of Imprisonment		
State	*Year*	*Life Terms*	*Years*	*Months*	*Days*
Vermont	1844	2	4	2	15
	1845	2	4	0	21
Maine	1844	6	4	11	22
	1845	7	4	4	14
	1846	8	4	4	2
New Hampshire	1845	11	6	4	20
	1846	10	6	4	11
Michigan	1845	1	4	6	11
	1846	0	4	1	13
Ohio	1846	6	5	0	22
Rhode island	1844	3	5	11	10
Connecticut	1844	17	6	6	1
	1846	19	6	10	8
Massachusetts	1844	12	5	1	2
	1845	14	4	11	9
Virginia	1845	12	7	3	2
	1846	13	7	11	3
Maryland	1845	0	4	0	3

Source: Blombert, Thomas, and Karol Lucken. 2000. *American Penology: A History of Control.* New York: Aldine DeGruyter, p. 57.

The following figure illustrates the enormous growth of incarceration rates after 1980.

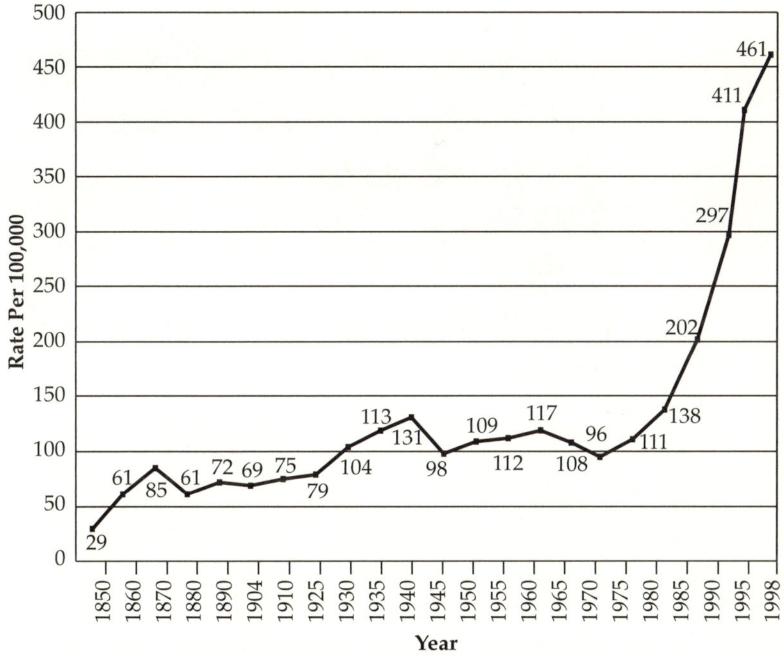

Figure 6.2 Federal and State Prison Incarceration Rates

Source: Blomberg, Thomas, and Karol Lucken. 2000. *American Penology: A History of Control.* New York: Aldine De Gruyter, p. 225.

The following figure clearly reveals the significant difference in the incarceration rates in the United States, Russia, and South Africa compared to other comparable nations.

Figure 6.3 International Incarceration Rates

Source: Mauer, Mace, and Meda Chesney–Lind. 2003. "Comparative International Rates of Incarceration: An Examination of Causes and Trends." Presented to the U.S. Commission on Civil Rights. Washington, DC: The Sentencing Project.

The next graph demonstrates the dramatic increase in incarceration rates since 1982.

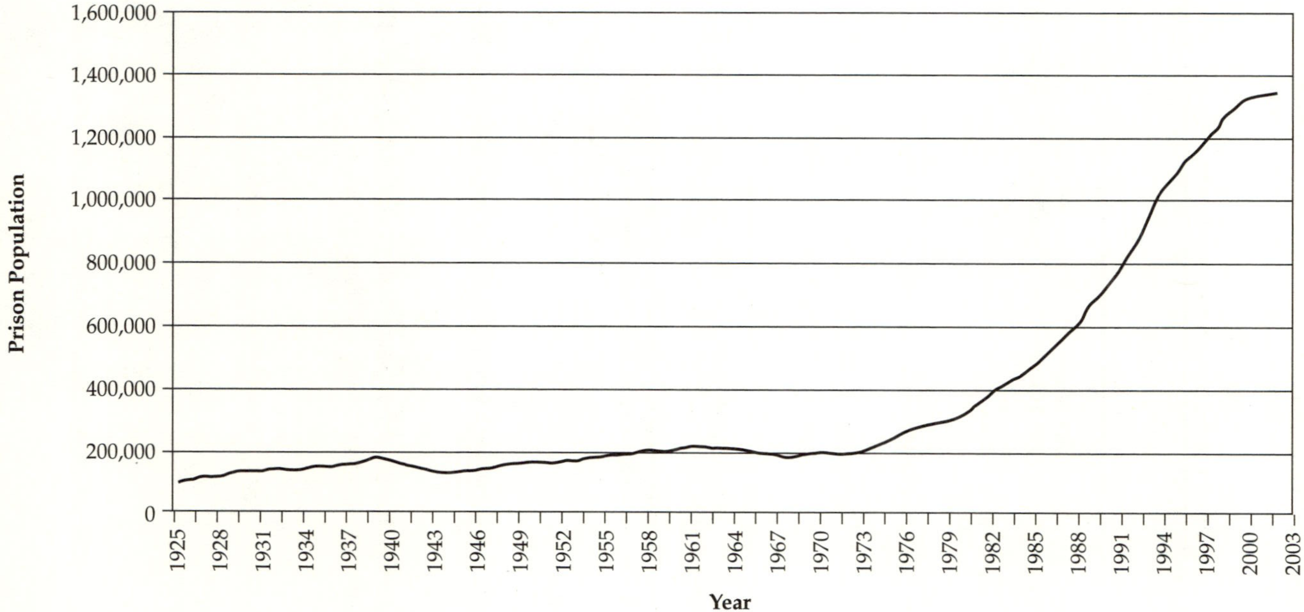

Figure 6.4 State and Federal Prisoners, 1925–2002

Source: Mauer, Mace, and Meda Chesney–Lind. 2003. "Comparative International Rates of Incarceration: An Examination of Causes and Trends." Presented to the U.S. Commission on Civil Rights. Washington, DC: The Sentencing Project.

The following chart reveals the increase in the number of persons under correctional supervision between 1995 and 2002.

Table 6.5
Persons under Adult Correctional Supervision, 1995–2002

Year	Total estimated correctional population[a]	Community supervision Probation	Parole	Incarceration Jail	Prison
1995	5,342,900	3,077,861	679,421	507,044	1,078,542
1996	5,490,700	3,164,996	679,733	518,492	1,127,526
1997[b]	5,734,900	3,296,513	694,787	567,079	1,176,564
1998[b]	6,134,200	3,670,441	696,385	592,462	1,224,469
1999[b]	6,340,800	3,779,922	714,457	605,943	1,287,172
2000	6,445,100	3,826,209	723,898	621,149	1,316,333
2001	8,581,700	3,931,731	732,333	631,240	1,330,007
2002	6,732,400	3,995,165	753,141	665,475	1,367,856
Percent change, 2001–02	2.3%	1.6%	2.8%	5.4%	2.8%
Average annual percent change, 1995–2002[c]	2.9%	3.1%	1.5%	4.0%	3.5%

Note: Counts are for December 31, except for jail counts, which are for June 30. Jail and prison counts include inmates held in private facilities. Totals in 1998 through 2002 exclude probationers held in jail or prison.

[a]Because some offenders may have multiple statuses, totals were rounded to the nearest 100.
[b]Coverage of probation agencies was expanded. For counts based on the same reporting agencies, use 3,266,837 in 1997 (to compare with 1996); 3,417,613 in 1998 (to compare with 1997); and 3,772,773 in 1999 (to compare with 1998).
[c]Percent change based on comparable reporting agencies, excluding 186,497 probationers in agencies added since 1995.

Source: Glaze, Lauren. 2003. "Probatim and Parole in the United States, 2002." *Bureau of Justice Statistics Bulletin,* NCJ 201135.

The following Bureau of Justice Statistics chart reveals the number executed by state between 1930 and 2003.

Table 6.6
Number of Persons Executed, by Jurisdiction, 1930–2003

	Number Executed	
	Since 1930	*Since 1977*
U.S. total	885	4,744
Texas	610	313
Georgia	400	34
New York	329	0
California	302	10
North Carolina	293	30
Florida	227	57
South Carolina	190	28
Virginia	181	89
Ohio	180	8
Alabama	163	28
Louisiana	160	27
Mississippi	160	6
Pennsylvania	155	3
Arkansas	143	25
Oklahoma	129	69
Missouri	123	61
Kentucky	105	2
Illinois	102	12
Tennessee	94	1
New Jersey	74	0
Maryland	71	3
Arizona	60	22
Indiana	52	11
Washington	51	4
Colorado	48	1
District of Columbia	40	0
West Virginia	40	0
Nevada	38	9
Federal system	36	3
Massachusetts	27	0
Delaware	25	13
Oregon	21	2
Connecticut	21	0
Utah	19	6
Iowa	18	0
Kansas	15	0
New Mexico	9	1
Montana	8	2
Wyoming	8	1
Nebraska	7	3
Idaho	4	1
Vermont	4	0
New Hampshire	1	0
South Dakota	1	0

Source: "Capital Punishment, 2003." Bureau of Justice Statistics Bulletin, NCJ 201848.

Methods of execution include lethal injection (most states), electrocution, lethal gas, hanging, and firing squad.

Table 6.7
Methods of Execution in States Authorizing the Death Penalty by State, 2002

Lethal injection				
Alabama[a]	Georgia	Mississippi	New York	South Dakota
Arizona[a,b]	Idaho[a]	Missouri[a]	North Carolina	Tennessee[a,i]
Arkansas[a,d]	Illinois	Montana	Ohio	Texas
California[a]	Indiana	Nevada	Oklahoma[a,f]	Utah[a]
Colorado	Kansas	New Hampshire[a,e]	Oregon	Virginia[a]
Connecticut	Kentucky[a,g]	New Jersey	Pennsylvania	Washington[a]
Delaware[a,c]	Louisiana	New Mexico	South Carolina[a]	Wyoming[a,h]
Florida	Maryland			

Electrocution	*Lethal gas*	*Hanging*	*Firing squad*
Alabama[a]	Arizona[a,b]	Delaware[a,c]	Idaho[a]
Arkansas[a,d]	California[a]	New Hampshire[a,e]	Oklahoma[a,f]
Florida[a]	Missouri[a]	Washington[a]	Utah[a]
Kentucky[a,g]	Wyoming[a,h]		
Nebraska			
Oklahoma[a,f]			
South Carolina[a]			
Tennessee[a,i]			
Virginia[a]			

Note: The method of execution of Federal prisoners is lethal injection, pursuant to 28 CFR, Part 26. For offenses under the Violent Crime Control and Law Enforcement Act of 1994, the method is that of the state in which the conviction took place, pursuant to 18 USC 3596.

a Authorizes more than one method of execution.
b Arizona authorizes lethal injection for persons whose capital sentence was received after Nov. 15, 1992; for those who were sentenced before that date, the condemned prisoner may select lethal injection or lethal gas.
c Delaware authorizes lethal injection for those whose capital offense occurred after June 13, 1986; for those whose offense occurred before that date, the condemned prisoner may select lethal injection or hanging.
d Arkansas authorizes lethal injection for those whose capital offense occurred on or after July 4, 1983; for those whose offense occurred before that date, the condemned prison may select lethal injection or electrocution.
e New Hampsire authorizes hanging only if lethal injection cannot be given.
f Oklahoma authorizes electrocution if lethal injection is ever held unconstitutional and firing squad if both lethal injection and electrocution are held unconstitutional.
g Kentucky authorizes lethal injection for persons whose capital sentence was received on or after Mar. 31, 1998; for those sentenced before that date, the condemned prisoner may select lethal injection or electrocution.
h Wyoming authorizes lethal gas if lethal injection is ever held unconstitutional.
i Tennessee authorizes lethal injection for those whose capital offense occurred after Dec. 31, 1998; for those whose offense occurred before that date, the condemned prisoner may select lethal injection or electrocution.

Source: Sourcebook of Criminal Justice Statistics Online. http://www.albany.edu/sourcebook/. Accessed December 2004.

The following chart shows the strength of public support for the death penalty.

Table 6.8
Attitudes toward the Death Penalty
United States, Selected Years 1965–2001

Question: "Do you believe in capital punishment, that is, the death penalty, or are you opposed to it?"

	Believe in it	*Opposed to it*	*Not sure/refused*
1965	38%	47%	15%
1969	48	38	14
1970	47	42	11
1973	59	31	10
1976	67	25	8
1983	68	27	5
1997	75	22	3
1999	71	21	8
2000	64	25	11
2001	67	26	7

Note: Sample sizes vary from year to year; the date for 2001 are based on telephone interviews with a randomly selected national sample of 1,022 adults, 18 years of age and older, conducted July 20–25, 2001.

Source: The Sourcebook of Criminal Justice Statistics 2002. Washington, DC: U.S. Department of Justice, Bureau of Justice Statistics, p. 143.

The following chart reveals the number of prisoners in private facilities by state.

Table 6.9
State and Federal Prisoners Housed in Private Facilities and Local Jails by Jurisdiction, on December 31, 2002 and 2003

	Private facilities			Local jails		
	Number		Percent of all prisoners	Number		Percent of all prisoners,
Jurusdiction	2002	2003	2003[a]	2002	2003	2003[a]
United States, total	93,912	95,522	6.5%	72,550	73,343	5.0%
Federal[b]	20,274	21,865	12.6	3,377	3,278	1.9
State	73,638	73,657	5.7	69,173	70,065	5.4
Northeast	3,146	3,201	1.8	2,234	1,911	1.1
Connecticut	0	0	X	(c)	(c)	(c)
Maine	8	30	1.5	0	0	X
Massachusetts	0	0	X	375	361	3.5
NewHampshire	0	0	X	11	7	0.3
New Jersey[d]	2,601	2,636	9.7	1,528	1,542	5.7
New York	0	0	X	320	1	X
Pennsylvania	537	535	1.3	0	0	X
Rhode Island[d]	0	0	X	(c)	(c)	(c)
Vermont[d]	0	0	X	(c)	(c)	(c)
Midwest	6,748	4,957	2.0	1,801	2,386	1.0
Illinois	0	0	X	0	0	X
Indiana	843	652	2.8	1,262	1,724	7.5
Iowa	0	0	X	0	0	X
Kansas	0	0	X	0	0	X
Michigan	460	480	1.0	30	42	0.1
Minnesota	0	0	X	221	283	3.6
Missouri	0	0	X	0	0	X
Nebraska	0	0	X	0	0	X
North Dakota	23	0	X	9	44	3.6
Ohio	1,927	1,901	4.2	0	0	X
South Dakota	32	25	0.8	12	29	1.0
Wisconsin	3,463	1,899	8.4	267	264	1.2
South	46,091	48,222	8.2	60,036	60,810	10.3
Alabama	0	1,698	5.8	2,449	1,340	4.6
Arkansas	0	0	X	1,172	1,016	7.8
Delaware	0	0	X	(c)	(c)	(c)
Florida	4,173	4,330	5.4	47	48	0.1
Georgia	4,573	4,589	9.7	4,975	4,949	10.5

(continues)

Table 6.9
State and Federal Prisoners Housed 2002 and 2003 *(continued)*

	Private facilities			Local jails		
	Number		Percent of all prisoners	Number		Percent of all prisoners,
Jurisdiction	*2002*	*2003*	*2003[a]*	*2002*	*2003*	*2003[a]*
Kentucky	1,635	1,640	9.9	3,657	3,969	23.9
Louisiana	2,929	2,918	8.1	16,022	16,549	45.9
Maryland	127	122	0.5	168	234	1.0
Mississippi	3,435	3,463	14.9	4,550	4,724	20.4
North Carolina	186	215	0.6	0	0	X
Oklahoma	6,470	6,022	26.4	1,497	1,869	8.2
South Carolina	21	44	0.2	415	424	1.8
Tennessee	4,200	5,049	19.9	6,717	6,283	24.7
Texas	16,773	16,570	9.9	12,375	13,331	8.0
Virginia	1,569	1,562	4.5	5,024	5,106	14.6
West Virginia	0	0	X	968	968	20.3
West	17,653	17,277	6.0	5,102	4,958	1.7
Alaska	1,360	1,386	30.6	(c)	(c)	(c)
Arizona	1,965	2,323	7.5	232	174	0.6
California	4,649	3,507	2.1	2,591	2,415	1.5
Colorado	2,452	3,013	15.3	160	221	1.1
Hawaii	1,347	1,478	25.4	(c)	(c)	(c)
Idaho	1,266	1,267	21.5	295	239	4.1
Montana	963	1,059	29.3	419	567	15.7
Nevada	434	0	X	177	190	1.8
New Mexico	2,690	2,751	44.2	0	0	X
Oregon	0	0	X	0	0	X
Utah	0	0	X	1,170	1,065	18.5
Washington[d]	0	0	X	0	0	X
Wyoming	527	493	26.3	58	87	4.6

[a] Based on the total number of inmates under State and Federal jurisdiction.
[b] Includes Federal inmates in non-secure privately operated facilities (6,598 in 2002 and 6,471 in 2003).
[c] Not applicable; prisons and jails form an integrated system.
[d] Inmates held in other state facilities include interstate compact cases.

Source: Sourcebook of Criminal Justice Statistics Online. http://www.albany.edu/sourcebook/. Accessed December 2004.

The following chart shows the type and number of state, federal, and private institutions.

Table 6.10
Census of State and Federal Correctional Facilities, 2000

Characteristic	*Federal*	*State*	*Private*
Number of facilities			
Total	84	1,320	264
Confinement	84	1,023	101
Community-based	0	297	163
Maximum security	11	317	94
Medium	29	428	65
Minimum	44	575	195
Under 250 average daily population	2	469	175
250–749	10	304	46
750–1,499	49	339	33
1,500 or more	23	208	10
Rated capacity	83,113	1,090,225	105,133
Percent occupied	134%	101%	89%
Staff			
All	32,700	372,976	24,357
Custody	12,376	243,352	14,589

Source: Stephan, James, and Jennifer Karberg. 2000. "Census of State and Federal Correctional Facilities, 2000." Washington, DC: U.S. Department of Justice, NCJ 198272.

The following figure shows the amount states spent on prisons between 1986 and 2001, revealing a steady increase in expenditure.

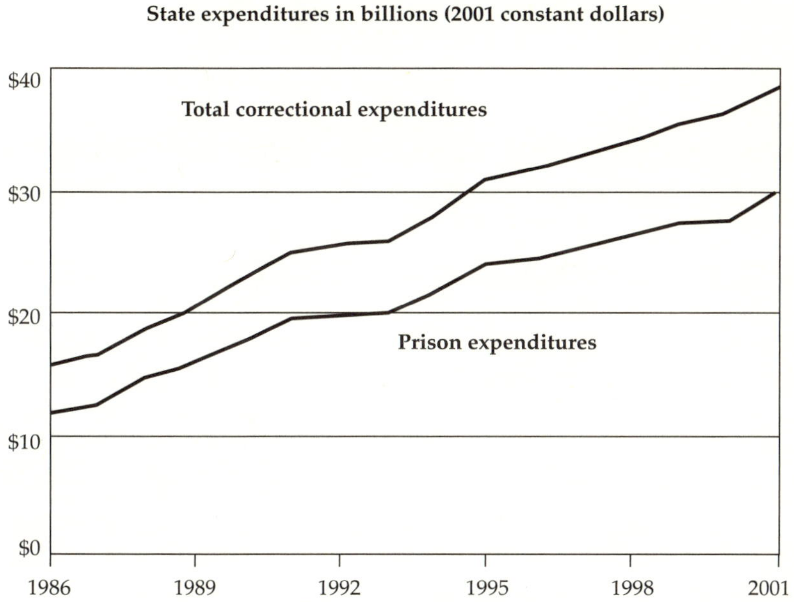

Figure 6.5 State Prison Expenditures, 2001

Note: Prison operations consumed about 77% of State correctional costs in FY 2001. The remaining 23% was spent on juvenile justice, probation and parole, community based corrections, and central office administration.

State prison costs per U.S. resident more than doubled between 1986 and 2001. State correctional expenditures increased 145% in 2001 constant dollars from $15.6 billion in FY 1986 to $38.2 billion in FY 2001; prisons expenditure increased 150% from $11.7 billion to $29.5 billion.

Excluding capital spending, the average cost of operation State prisons in FY 2001 was $100 per U.S. resident, up from $90 in FY 1996.

Outlays for new prison construction, renovations, equipment, and other capital account activities amounted to less than %4 of total prison expenditures in most states. Spending on medical care for State prisoners totaled $3.3 billion, or 12% of operating expenditures in 2001.

Source: "State Prison Expenditures, 2001." *Bureau of Justice Statistics Special Report.* Washington, DC: U.S. Department of Justice, NCJ 202949.

7

Agencies and Organizations

Information follows with respect to international, federal, state, and nongovernmental organizations related to punishment, penal reform, and penal issues generally.

American Civil Liberties Union National Prison Project
733 15th Street, NW
Suite 620
Washington, DC 20005
(202) 393–4930
http://www.aclu.org/issues/prisons

This ACLU project commenced in 1972, and its objectives include promoting constitutional conditions for confinement and strengthening prisoner rights through class-action litigation and public education. The project covers issues such as reducing prison overcrowding, improving medical care in prisons, and eliminating violence and maltreatment in prisons. The project publishes a quarterly journal and conducts public education through conferences. Among the publications of the project are a *Guide for Prisoners* and the 1998 *Aids in Prison Bibliography,* which catalogues resource material on AIDS in prisons.

Amnesty International, Program to Abolish the Death Penalty (PADP)
Amnesty International USA
322 Eighth Avenue
New York, NY 10001

(212) 627–1451
http://www.amnesty-usa.org

This program works toward the abolishment of the death penalty throughout the world. PADP also seeks clemency in individual cases and supports federal and state legislation that aims to limit use of the death penalty. There is also a focus on building coalitions with other abolitionist and social justice groups. Another program campaigns for the rights of women in prison. A 1998 report, "About Women in Custody—Sexual Misconduct and the Shackling of Pregnant Women," reveals how states have a poor record in providing female inmates with protection against sexual abuse and that many allow the shackling of women prisoners during pregnancy.

Bureau of Justice Statistics, Department of Justice
810 Seventh Street, NW
Washington, DC 20531
(202) 307–0765
http://www.ojp.usdoj.gov/bjs

An essential source of statistical and other information on the criminal justice system generally, including sentencing, sanctions, and prisons. Bureau reports can be downloaded, and it is possible to subscribe to an e-mail system for advance notification of publications.

California Coalition for Women Prisoners (CCWP)
100 McAllister Street
San Francisco, CA 94102
(415) 255–7036
http://www.womenprisoners.org

The CCWP fights for basic human rights and against the medical neglect of women prisoners in California. It aims to raise public awareness of the cruel and inhumane conditions under which women prisoners live and advocates for changes in those conditions. It promotes the leadership of, and giving voice to, women prisoners, including former prisoners and their families. The coalition visits women in prison, produces a newsletter, makes protests, and conducts advocacy, education, outreach, and support for former prisoners. The organization began in 1995 to support a lawsuit filed by women incarcerated at the Central

California Women's Facility and the California Institution for Women seeking adequate medical care.

Correctional Association of New York
135 East 15th Street
New York, NY 10003
(212) 254–5700
http://www.corrassoc.org

This association has a long history, having been founded in 1844. The Correctional Association of New York has long been concerned about conditions in prison and the lack of support services for former prisoners. In 1846 the association was granted the right by special law to inspect prisons and report its findings to policymakers and the public. The association maintains four working projects: the Public Policy Project, the Women in Prison Project, the Prison Visiting Project, and the Juvenile Justice Project. Using techniques like advocacy, public education, and the development of workable alternatives the Correctional Association of New York seeks to create a fairer and more humane criminal justice system and a safer and more just society.

The Corrections Connection
159 Burgin Parkway
Quincy, MA 02169
(617) 471–4445
http://www.corrections.com

The Corrections Connection terms itself "the official home of corrections" and provides a directory of information as well as links to many topics in corrections. It came online in 1996 as the first weekly news source committed to improving the lives of corrections professionals and their families. It is a useful source of information on corrections generally and, through its chat rooms and bulletin boards, provides insights into professional views, thoughts, and opinions in corrections.

The Drug Reform Coordination Network (DRCNet)
2000 P Street NW, 210
Washington, DC 20036
http://www.drcnet.org

DRCNet was established to stop the chaos and violence of the illegal drug trade and to put an end to the mass incarceration suffered by hundreds of thousands of nonviolent drug offenders. It supports the reform of drug laws and opposes the building of prisons that promote the continuance of the war on drugs. DRC-Net advocates dialogue on alternatives to current drug policies and the implementation of public health–based approaches rather than justice-based initiatives to reduce the suffering caused by the war on drugs.

Families against Mandatory Minimums Foundation (FAMM)
1612K Street, NW
Suite 1400
Washington, DC 20006
(202) 822–6700
http://www.famm.org

This organization was created in 1991 and aims to challenge the inflexible and excessive penalties required under mandatory sentencing laws. It advocates sentencing laws that allow judges to decide what punishment should be imposed after taking into account factors such as seriousness of the offense, potential for rehabilitation, and the role played by the defendant in committing the crime. FAMM provides education programs on the unjustness of mandatory minimum sentences and seeks to mobilize a reform movement through lobbying federal and state lawmakers, building coalitions, and promoting change at the grassroots level. FAMM argues that judges rather than lawmakers should fix the sentence for a crime. It calls for mandatory minimum penalties to be replaced by sentencing laws that contain flexible sentencing guidelines.

Federal Prison Policy Project
P.O. Box 742552
Riverdale, GA 30274
(770) 477–9814
http://www.fppp.org

This project seeks to return responsible justice to the judicial system by revising current laws to eliminate mandatory minimum penalties, by monitoring the work of the Bureau of Prisons and encouraging the rehabilitation of inmates. The project also challenges existing sentencing guidelines and promotes alternatives to incarceration. It publishes a newsletter and carries news announcements about sentencing and penal policies on its Web site and publishes an opinion column.

International Centre for Prison Studies
26–19 Drury Lane, 3rd Floor
London WC2B 5RL
United Kingdom
(44) 20–7848–1922
http://www.kcl.ac.uk/depsta/rel/icps

This centre is established at Kings College, London, and was founded in 1829. It provides assistance to governments and agencies in developing policies on prisons and the use of incarceration. It works on a project or consultancy basis for international agencies.

National Criminal Justice Reference Service, Department of Justice (NCJRS)
P.O. Box 6000
Rockville, MD 20849–6000
(800) 851–3420
http://www.ojp.usdoj.gov

NCJRS is a resource maintained by the Department of Justice that offers justice information to support research, policy, and program development worldwide. Its resources are available to all, and it offers extensive reference and referral services to deal with questions about crime and crime-related issues, including corrections. This information includes statistics, publications, and compiled information packages and assistance tailored to particular needs. By registering online with NCJRS, it is possible to receive a bimonthly newsletter and e-mail notifications about new publications and resources. Many reports are available through the NCJRS Web site, including reports on prison and jail inmates, mental health treatment in state prisons, and HIV in prison and jails.

National Institute of Corrections (NIC), U.S. Department of Justice
320 First Street, NW
Washington, DC 20534
(800) 995–6423
http://www.nicic.org

The NIC Information Center provides research assistance and document delivery for correctional policymakers, practitioners, elected officials, and members of the public interested in corrections issues. Its services are provided free of charge and cover a very wide range of policy and program issues concerning prisons and prisoners, and it produces a series of publications such as those concerned with jails, community corrections, and topics of general interest.

Penal Reform International (PRI)
1120 19th Street, NW, 8th Floor
Washington, DC 20036
(202) 721–5610
http://www.penalreform.org

PRI is an international, nongovernmental organization that was founded in the United Kingdom in 1989. PRI has members in five continents and in more than eighty countries and develops programs on a regional basis, assisting both nongovernmental organizations and individuals to establish projects in their own countries. It promotes the exchange of information and good practice among countries with related conditions. PRI's regional programs include sub-Saharan Africa, the Middle East, central and eastern Europe, and Central Asia, South Asia, Latin America, and the Caribbean.

Prison Activist Resource Center (PARC)
P.O. Box 339
Berkeley, CA 94701
(510) 893–4648
http://www.prisonactivist.org

PARC advertises itself as the source for progressive and reformist data on prisons and the criminal prosecution system. It provides news and support to activists and advocacy groups working on prison reform in the San Francisco Bay–area and nationally, and to groups to hold public forums, film showings, and demonstrations to build public awareness. The main goals of PARC are: to expose the myths that sustain widespread injustices in prisons; to inspire and motivate people to take positive action against the mass incarceration system and for prisoners, civil, and human rights; and to provide practical support to activists engaged in this advocacy. The PARC Web site contains many links to other organizations concerned with prison and prison reform, including those involved with women in prison.

Prison Reform Advocacy Center
617 Vine Street, Suite 1301
Cincinnati, OH 45202
(513) 421–1108
http://www.prisonreform.com

This organization is devoted to progressive prison reform and was founded in 1997 in Cincinnati to address the legal needs of Ohio. It was initially named the Prisoner Rights Advocacy Center. It provides regular information on prisoners and training on prisoners' rights issues and participates in reform activities throughout Ohio. It is committed to the fair treatment of all incarcerated persons.

United Nations Asia and Far East Institute for the Prevention of Crime and the Treatment of Offenders (UNAFEI)
1–26, Harumi-cho, Fuchu-shi
Tokyo 183–0057
Japan
81–42–333–7021
http://www.unafei.or.jp

UNAFEI is a United Nations regional institute established in 1962 by agreement between the United Nations and the government of Japan with the aim of promoting the development of criminal justice systems and cooperation in the Asia and Pacific regions. The activities of the institute include training courses and seminars for personnel in crime prevention and research studies of the treatment of offenders. UNAFEI also organizes two international training courses and one international seminar each year and publishes information on the criminal justice systems and treatment of offenders in the Asia and Pacific regions.

Vera Institute of Justice
233 Broadway, 12th Floor
New York, NY 10279
(212) 334–1300
http://www.vera.org

The Vera Institute's interests include sentencing and corrections and it gives information on its Web site concerning its current projects, which include diverting drug abusers from prison, the effect of state sentencing guidelines, and support for drug-abusing offenders and their families. Its research department has completed an evaluation of New York City's system of alternatives to incarceration for felons.

Western Prison Project
P.O. Box 40085
Portland, Oregon 97240
(503) 232–1922
http://www.westernprisonproject.org

This organization operates in the western states of Oregon, Washington, Idaho, Montana, Utah, Wyoming, and Nevada and aims to formulate a progressive response to the criminal justice system and to build a grassroots multiracial movement that reduces the overreliance on incarceration in these states. The project aims to achieve its goals through public education and outreach, community mobilization, and networking among grassroots groups.

Women Coping in Prison
Women Coping in Prison Study
University of Virginia—Institute for Law, Psychiatry, and Public Policy
P.O. Box 800660
1107 West Main Street
Charlottesville, VA 22908
http://curry.edschool.virginia.edu/prisonstudy/

Women Coping in Prison is a joint project of the University of Virginia and the Fluvanna Correctional Center for Women. The project explores the experience of women living in a prison environment both objectively and from the subjective experience of the women. The research takes into account patterns of victimization that existed prior to incarceration, the extent of violence occurring within a maximum-security prison for women, patterns of adjustment made by women as a result of incarceration, and family stress caused by confinement in prison. Inmates participate in this research through structured interviews and other studies.

8

Print and Nonprint Resources

This chapter includes books on punishment and penal issues and relevant chapters in books, journal articles, legal cases, government publications, important periodicals concerned with penal issues, and nonprint resources.

Print Resources

Books

Austin, James, and John Irwin. 2001. ***It's about Time: America's Imprisonment Binge,*** 3rd edition. Belmont, CA: Wadsworth.

As the title suggests, this book explores the reasons for the current focus on incarceration in the United States and provides an assessment of how this has happened and future developments.

Ayers, Edward L. 1984. ***Vengeance and Justice: Crime and Punishment in the 19th Century American South.*** New York: Oxford University Press.

The author reveals how punishment developed in the South during and after the Civil War. Lynching and vigilante violence are assessed and explained. This is a comprehensive and complex historical analysis of this period in the South.

Banks, Cyndi. 2004. ***Criminal Justice Ethics: Theory and Practice.*** Thousand Oaks, CA: Sage Publications.

A discussion of ethical issues in criminal justice with a chapter on the ethics of punishment. Useful for the philosophical arguments and for the wide-ranging nature of the issues covered.

Barnes, Harry. E. 1972. ***The Story of Punishment: A Record of Man's Inhumanity to Man.*** Mont Clair, NJ: Patterson Smith.

One of the first explorations of the history of punishment, this remains a standard work on the history of punishment, covering all aspects of the topic from the earliest beginnings.

Bean, Phillip. 1981. ***Punishment: A Philosophical and Criminological Inquiry.*** Oxford: Martin Robertson.

A philosopher takes a look at punishment, discussing the philosophical basis for punishment and its justifications.

Blomberg, Thomas, and Karol Lucken. 2000. ***American Penology: A History of Control.*** New York: Aldine De Gruyter.

An up-to-date and comprehensive study of the historical context of crime control that links the specific punishment policies and ideologies over time.

Brundage, W. Fitzhugh. 1993. ***Lynching in the New South: Georgia and Virginia, 1880–1930.*** Urbana: University of Illinois Press.

The author presents a historical study of why lynching developed in the South, its effect, and scope.

Carleton, Mark. 1971. ***Politics and Punishment: The History of the Louisiana State Penal System.*** Baton Rouge: Louisiana State University Press.

This is a history specific to the Louisiana penal system that provides valuable historical information on policy and issues of punishment in that state.

Christianson, Scott. 1998. ***With Liberty for Some: 500 Years of Imprisonment in America.*** Boston, MA: Northeastern University Press.

An exhaustive examination of the criminal justice system over

500 years, providing dramatic narratives of events including those occurring in the history of punishment.

Christie, Nils. 1993. ***Crime Control as Industry: Towards Gulags, Western Style?*** London: Routledge.

An important book that compares U.S. practice on incarceration with that of European states to demonstrate how mass imprisonment has become a feature of U.S. society.

Colvin, Mark. 1997. ***Penitentiaries, Reformatories, and Chain Gangs: Social Theory and the History of Punishment in Nineteenth-Century America.*** New York: St. Martin's Press.

An historical exploration through case studies that illustrate the shifts in the history of punishment in the United States. It includes excellent sections on women in prisons and reformatories as well as convict leasing and chain gangs in the South.

Dimsdale, Thomas. 1866. ***Vigilantes of Montana.*** Virginia City: Post Press, D. W. Tilton and Co.

A contemporary description of vigilantism in Montana.

Duff, Antony. 2001. ***Punishment, Communication, and Community.*** Oxford: Oxford University Press.

A philosophical exploration of the links between punishment and the community with a focus on the expressive side of punishment.

Duguid, Stephen. 2000. ***Can Prison Work? The Prisoner as Object and Subject in Modern Corrections.*** Toronto: University of Toronto Press.

The author reviews the philosophical and cultural contexts that produced the notion that criminals could be cured of their criminality through treatment and incarceration and presents two discussions of corrections, one sociological in nature and the other psychological.

Dumm, Thomas L. 1987. ***Democracy and Punishment: Disciplinary Origins of the United States.*** Madison: University of Wisconsin Press.

A study of the origins of discipline and punishment in the United States.

Dwyer, Daisy Hilse, ed. 1990. ***Law and Islam in the Middle East.*** New York: Bergin and Garvey Publishers.

A collection of articles on the interaction between law and Islam in this area of the world, covering both historical and present day aspects of the topic.

Elias, Norbert. 1994. ***The Civilizing Process.*** Oxford: Blackwell.

A classic work that seeks to explain how, over time, man became "civilized." The author shows through social history how the harshness of life was gradually blunted and how social practices became more refined.

Foucault, Michel. 1977. ***Discipline and Punish: The Birth of Prison.*** London: Penguin Books.

A major philosophical and historical work in the history and explanation of punishment. The author has revolutionized the study of punishment and discipline, heavily influencing all subsequent studies of penality. This is an immensely important work in understanding the notions of punishment and discipline.

Friedman, Lawrence. 1993. ***Crime and Punishment in American History.*** New York: Basic Books.

A history of the criminal justice system from colonial times set within the broader context of U.S. culture, covering the rise and decline of the penitentiary as well as extralegal methods of punishment.

Garland, David. 1985. ***Punishment and Welfare: A History of Penal Strategies.*** Aldershot: Gower Publishing.

Although based on English practice on welfare and punishment, this book offers an original historical and sociological perspective on penal change and the relationship between punishment and social structure.

———. 1990. ***Punishment and Modern Society.*** Oxford: Oxford University Press.

Garland's further contribution to the study of punishment breaks new ground and is the first attempt at a comprehensive account of punishment in modern society. The author surveys the major theoretical accounts of punishment and develops his own perspective from these accounts, pointing to the way in which punishment is determined by society and is itself a social institution.

Hirsch, Adam. 1992. ***The Rise of the Penitentiary: Prisons and Punishment in Early America.*** New Haven, CT: Yale University Press.

The author argues that the rise of the penitentiary in the United States has more to do with inherited English practice and that the United States cannot therefore claim to have originated the penitentiary.

Hudson, Barbara. 1996. ***Understanding Justice: An Introduction to Ideas, Perspectives and Controversies in Modern Penal Theory.*** Buckingham and Philadelphia: Open University Press.

A comprehensive and sophisticated account of ideas in modern penal theory, including the theoretical context.

Ignatieff, Michael. 1978. ***A Just Measure of Pain: The Penitentiary in the Industrial Revolution, 1750–1850.*** New York: Pantheon Books.

A classic study of the origin and rise and decline of the penitentiary in England, providing insights into its development in the United States.

Logan, Charles. 1990. ***Private Prisons: Cons and Pros.*** New York: Oxford University Press.

A study of private prisons, exploring their development, arguments for and against the continuance of private prisons, and the outlook for the future. A good source of information on this subject.

Marquart, James. W., Jonathan. R. Sorensen, and Sheldon Ekland-Olson. 1994. ***The Rope, the Chair, and the Needle: Capital Punishment in Texas, 1923–1990.*** Austin: University of Texas Press.

Explores the historical development of capital punishment in Texas with essential information and vivid accounts of those involved in the process, both offenders and victims.

Masur, Louis. 1989. ***Rites of Execution: Capital Punishment and the Transformation of American Culture, 1776–1865.*** New York: Oxford University Press.

A penetrating analysis of the cultural and social origins of capital punishment in the United States.

Melossi, Dario, and Massimo Pavarini. 1981. ***The Prison and the Factory: Origins of the Penitentiary System.*** Totowa, NJ: Barnes and Noble Books.

A Marxist-oriented account of the development of the prison that emphasizes the socioeconomic aspects and also draws on Foucault's arguments about the role of discipline in modern society.

Nozick, Robert. 1981. ***Philosophical Explanations.*** Cambridge, MA: Harvard University Press.

A leading philosopher offers his views on the philosophical underpinnings of punishment.

Nygaard, Richard. 2000. ***Sentencing As I See It.*** Incline Village, NV: Copperhouse Publishing Company.

A former judge offers his own views about sentencing offenders.

Pisciotta, Alexander. 1994. ***Benevolent Repression: Social Control and the American Reformatory Movement.*** New York: New York University Press.

The author's contention is that historical accounts of the success of the Elmira Reformatory ignore many issues and facts that show that the regime at the reformatory did not produce the advances in treatment and rehabilitation claimed for it and other reformatories for men.

Rothman, David. 1990. ***The Discovery of the Asylum: Social Order and Disorder in the New Republic,*** revised edition. Boston: Little, Brown and Company.

A classic study of the rise of the penitentiary that attributes its coming to a set of complex historical, cultural, and social factors that are explored in a comprehensive and insightful manner.

Rusche, Georg, and Otto Kirchheimer. 1939 (reprinted 1968). ***Punishment and Social Structure.*** New York: Russell and Russell.

This is a classic Marxist study that focuses on the relationship between the prison and the employment of the labor of the poorer classes.

Shichor, David. 1995. ***Punishment for Profit: Private Prisons/Public Concerns.*** Thousand Oaks, CA: Sage Publications.

The author assesses the case for and against the privatization of prisons.

Spohn, Cassia. 2002. ***How Do Judges Decide? The Search for Fairness and Justice in Punishment.*** Thousand Oaks, CA: Sage Publications.

A broad survey of the issues of justice and fairness in punishment with an emphasis on the actual operations of the criminal justice system.

Ten, C. L. 1987. ***Crime, Guilt, and Punishment: A Philosophical Introduction.*** Oxford: Clarendon Press.

A leading philosopher surveys theories of punishment.

Tucker, Judith. 1998. ***In the House of the Law: Gender and Islamic Law in Ottoman Syria and Palestine.*** London: University of California Press.

An interesting study revealing how in the past Islamic law operated to take account of gender concerns in both the court process and in terms of punishment.

Walker, Nigel. 1991. ***Why Punish?*** Oxford: Oxford University Press.

A classic discussion of the rationale for punishment, exploring the philosophical, social, and historical underpinnings.

Weiss, Robert P., and Nigel South. 1998. ***Comparing Prison Systems: Toward a Comparative and International Penology.*** Amsterdam: Gordon and Breach Publishers.

A collection of essays discussing and comparing prison systems worldwide. Contains significant information on various countries' systems and practices not easily located elsewhere.

Welch, Michael. 1999. ***Punishment in America: Social Control and the Ironies of Imprisonment.*** Thousand Oaks, CA: Sage Publications.

A collection of essays on various aspects of the criminal justice system and how social control is maintained through punishment. Particularly relevant to the policy and political considerations that influence decisions on punishment. The author argues that the criminal justice system ironically produces self-defeating measures and tramples on social equality.

Zimring, Franklin. 2003. ***The Contradictions of American Capital Punishment.*** Oxford: Oxford University Press.

A new study that attempts to answer the question, Why does the United States continue to maintain its belief in the death penalty in the face of almost universal opposition to this punishment? The author offers some fresh insights.

Zimring, Franklin E., and Gordon Hawkins. 1991. ***The Scale of Imprisonment.*** Chicago: University of Chicago Press.
A discussion of the extent of imprisonment in the United States in the modern day, highlighting the mass imprisonment that is now a feature of the penal landscape.

Book Chapters and Journal and Media Articles

Aja, Egbeke. 1997. "Crime and Punishment: An Indigenous African Experience." ***The Journal of Value Enquiry*** 31: 353–368.

The author investigates how one ethnic group in Nigeria attempts to harmonize indigenous and imported values to combat an alarming increase in crime.

Anderson, James. 2000. "Alabama Prison Chain Gangs: Reverting to Archaic Punishment to Reduce Crime and Discipline Offenders." ***The Western Journal of Black Studies*** 24 (1): 1–9.

An examination of the decision of the Alabama Department of Corrections to revive the use of chain gangs based on the argument that its use would reduce crime and address disciplinary problems in the department.

Ashworth, Andrew. 2001. "The Decline of English Sentencing and Other Stories." In ***Sentencing and Sanctions in Western Countries,*** edited by Michael Tonry and Richard Frase, 62–91. New York: Oxford University Press.

An analysis of the changes that have taken place in sentencing in England since the early 1970s, including how community penalties were revived, how the judiciary became increasingly involved in subverting legislative sentencing measures that it did not support, and the role of the mass media in promoting repressive sentencing.

Bessler, John. 1996. "The 'Midnight Assassination Law' and Minnesota's Anti-Death Penalty Movement, 1849–1911." ***William Mitchell Law Review*** 22: 577–730.

Although Minnesota no longer authorizes capital punishment, it once played a crucial role in shaping how other states conducted executions, because Minnesota's so called "midnight assassination law" is the only U.S. law requiring private, nighttime executions to come before the U.S. Supreme Court. Exploring the history of Minnesota and capital punishment reveals the sentiment that produced the decision that executions should be carried out in private and late at night.

Bonczar, Thomas. November 2003. "Capital Punishment, 2002." ***Bureau of Justice Statistics Bulletin.*** Washington, DC: U.S. Department of Justice.

A compendium of statistics on capital punishment from this authoritative source.

Brown, David. 1998. "Penality and Imprisonment in Australia." In ***Comparing Prison Systems: Toward a Comparative and International Penology,*** edited by Robert Weiss and Nigel South, 367–400. Amsterdam: Gordon and Breach Publishers.

The author explores the history and present structure and operation of the Australian prison system, comparing it to European and North American models.

Bureau of Justice Statistics. 2002. "Prevalence of Imprisonment in the U.S. Population, 1974–2001." ***Bureau of Justice Statistics Bulletin.*** Washington, DC: U.S. Department of Justice.

An authoritative set of statistics on the state of imprisonment in the United States.

Bush-Baskette, Stephanie. 1999. "The 'War on Drugs' A War against Women." In ***Harsh Punishment: International Experiences of Women's Imprisonment,*** edited by S. Cook and S. Davies, 211–229. Boston, MA: Northeastern University Press.

The author attempts to show how the war on drugs targeted and oppressed women in particular and how it has resulted in a substantial increase in the incarceration of women.

Cahn, Mark. 1989. "Punishment, Discretion, and the Codification of Prescribed Penalities in Colonial Massachusetts." ***American Journal of Legal History*** 33 (April): 107–135.

Analyzes the Laws and Liberties 1648 of colonial Massachusetts as a product of the movement to reduce the likelihood of arbitrary punishment and codify penalties.

Clear, Todd, and Anthony Braga. 1998. "Challenges for Corrections in the Community." In ***Community Corrections: Probation, Parole, and Intermediate Sanctions,*** edited by Joan Petersilia, 213–218. New York: Oxford University Press.

The authors explore the future challenges facing corrections in the community, arguing that unless existing programs are radically reshaped community corrections agencies will remain marginal in terms of the problem of prison overcrowding.

Cullen, Frank, Bonnie Fisher, and Branden Applegate. 2000. "Public Opinion about Punishment and Corrections." In ***Crime and Justice: A Review of Research,*** edited by M. Tonry, 1–79. Chicago: Chicago University Press.

A study of public opinion of various issues of crime, law and order, and punishment, including, especially, capital punishment.

Daly, Kathleen. 2002. "Restorative Justice: The Real Story." ***Punishment and Society*** 4(1): 55–79.

Examines the development and conceptual basis of restorative justice and raises a number of questions about its meaning and effect.

Davis, Philip W. 2000. "Get Tough Legislation as Represented Action: The Case of Caning, Paddling, and Flogging." ***Studies in Symbolic Interaction*** 23: 197–216.

Looks at proposals for legislation in some states promoting various forms of corporal punishment and suggests that policy makers represent these punishments as moderate and not extreme and argues the proposals incorporate and shape cultural images of crime and punishment.

Dean-Myrda, Mark C., and Francis Cullen. 1998. "The Panacea Pendulum: An Account of Community as a Response to Crime." ***In Community Corrections: Probation, Parole, and Intermediate Sanctions,*** edited by Joan Petersilia, 1–18. New York: Oxford University Press.

Dean-Myrda and Cullen argue that community corrections has suffered unpopularity, because there has been a failure on the part of practitioners to communicate about their programs, evaluate them for effectiveness, or educate the public about them. Amidst this vacuum of real information, the public, having relied on the media and politicians, has supported the politicians calls for tough-on-crime policies. When the pendulum swings back, the authors argue that administrators will be better prepared to proactively make a case for programs and policies that have been shown effective.

Dikotter, Frank. 2002. "The Promise of Repentance: Prison Reform in Modern China." ***British Journal of Criminology*** 42: 240–249.

A survey of prison reform in modern China tracing how incarceration developed and how it fits with traditional values.

Downes, David. 1998. "The Buckling of the Shields: Dutch Penal Policy 1985–1995." In ***Comparing Prison Systems: Toward a Comparative and International Penology,*** edited by Robert Weiss and Nigel Downes, 143–174. Amsterdam: Gordon and Breach Publishers.

A survey of changes in Dutch penal policy that changed Holland from the most liberal country in sentencing to one of the most severe.

Dubber, Markus Dirk. 1998. "The Right to Be Punished: Autonomy and Its Demise in Modern Penal Thought." ***Law and History Review*** 16 (1): 113–146.

Investigates the right to be punished during the period from 1750 to 1850, when the foundation of the modern system of punishment was laid in theory and practice.

Dutton, Michael, and Xu Zhangrun. 1998. "Facing Difference: Relations, Change and the Prison Sector in Contemporary China." In ***Comparing Prison Systems: Toward a Comparative and International Penology,*** edited by Robert Weiss and Nigel South, 289–336. Amsterdam: Gordon and Breach Publishers.

Looks at changes in the prison sector in modern China, noting the differences between the Chinese and other models of incarceration.

Emmanuel, Anne. 1996. "Essay: Lynching and the Law in Georgia Circa 1931: A Chapter in the Legal Career of Judge Elbert Tuttle." ***William and Mary Bill of Rights Journal*** 5 (1): 216–248.

Traces events in 1931 when Judge Tuttle, who later became the Chief Judge of the U.S. Court of Appeals for the Fifth Circuit, ensured that a fair trial was obtained for a black man accused by a white woman of rape.

Feest, Johannes, and Hartmut-Michael Weber. 1998. "Germany: Ups and Downs in the Resort to Imprisonment—Strategic or Unplanned Outcomes?" In ***Comparing Prison Systems: Toward a Comparative and International Penology,*** edited by Robert Weiss and Nigel South, 233–262. Amsterdam: Gordon and Breach Publishers.

The authors review the policy and planning associated with the use of imprisonment as a punishment in this country.

Feinberg, J. 1994. The Expressive Function of Punishment. In ***A Reader on Punishment,*** edited by A. Duff and D. Garland, 71–91. Oxford: Oxford University Press.

The author focuses on the expressive function of punishment, arguing that the meaning of punishment is just as important as its effect especially if punishment is viewed as expressing the community's condemnation of crime.

Finn, P. 1996. "No-Frills Prisons and Jails: A Movement in Flux." ***Federal Probation*** 60: 35–44.

The author looks at arguments that the prison experience should be more austere and severe and reviews the various policy changes that have occurred in this movement.

Foster, Burk. 2001. "Why Death Is Different: Capital Punishment in the Legal System." In ***Death Watch: A Death Penalty Anthology,*** edited by L. Nelson and B. Foster, 1–15. Upper Saddle River, NJ: Prentice-Hall.

The author focuses on different aspects of the death penalty using journalism and personal essays to convey the experience of being on death row as well as to explore many of the issues surrounding capital punishment in the United States.

Gaucher, Bob, and John Lowman. 1998. "Canadian Prisons." In ***Comparing Prison Systems: Toward a Comparative and International Penology,*** edited by Robert Weiss and Nigel South, 61–98. Amsterdam: Gordon and Breach Publishers.

Explores the features of the Canadian prison system.

Glaze, Lauren. 2003. "Probation and Parole in the United States, 2002." ***Bureau of Justice Statistics Bulletin.*** Washington, DC: U.S. Department of Justice. August 2003.

The authoritative source for statistical information on probation and parole in the United States.

Gorman, Tessa. 1997. "Back on the Chain Gang: Why the Eighth Amendment and the History of Slavery Proscribe the Resurgence of Chain Gangs." ***California Law Review*** 85: 441–478.

In 1995 the chain gang reappeared as a method of punishment in Alabama, thus, the author argues, resurrecting a powerful and shameful symbol of slavery and racial oppression. The author argues that chain gangs violate the Eighth Amendment prohibition on "cruel and unusual punishments."

Hagan, John. 1983. "Pride and Punishment: On the Social History of Criminal Sanctions." ***American Bar Foundation Research Journal*** (Winter): 203–210.

Reviews the work of four authors who have studied the social history of criminal punishments.

Harding, Richard. 1998. "Private Prisons." In ***The Handbook of Crime and Punishment***, edited by Michael Tonry, 626–655. New York: Oxford University Press.

A review of the origin and development of private prisons, looking at arguments for and against privatization of incarceration.

Harrison, Paige, and Allen Beck. July 2003. "Prisoners in 2002." ***Bureau of Justice Statistics Bulletin.*** Washington, DC: U.S. Department of Justice.

The Department of Justice statistical bulletin on numbers of persons incarcerated, with a wealth of associated and related information.

Holt, Norman. 1998. "The Current State of Parole in the United States." In ***Community Corrections: Probation, Parole, and Intermediate Sanctions***, edited by Joan Petersilia, 19–48. New York: Oxford University Press.

A review of developments in parole, including parole term-setting guidelines, the changing role of parole boards, parole conditions and parole supervision, and its problems.

Hunter, Donna. 2000. "Race, Law, and Innocence: Executing Black Men in the Eighteenth Century." ***Studies in Law Politics and Society*** 20: 71–97.

Examines the foundation upon which white representation of black subjects was built in colonial North America, investigates the legal status of Africans in seventeenth century New England, describes the execution sermon, and suggests what this genre has to say about the intersection of race and law.

Johnson, Elmer. 1998. "The Japanese Experience: Effects of Decreasing Resort to Imprisonment." In ***Comparing Prison Systems: Toward a Comparative and International Penology***, edited by Robert Weiss and Nigel South, 337–365. Amsterdam: Gordon and Breach Publishers.

Japan has a very low of rate of incarceration and the author explains why and the effect of this.

Kealey, Linda. 1986. "Patterns of Punishment: Massachusetts in the Eighteenth Century. ***American Journal of Legal History*** 33: 163–189.

An exploration of forms of punishment employed in Massachusetts in the eighteenth century, noting how many forms of punishment were inherited from England, but how they developed and changed as they began to reflect notions of proper punishment in a society experiencing social, economic, and political change.

Lenz, Nygel. 2002. "'Luxuries' in Prison: The Relationship between Amenity Funding and Public Support." ***Crime and Delinquency*** 48 (4): 499–525.

A study comparing the level of public opposition to prison amenities as a function of perceptions regarding who pays for such amenities. The study findings suggest that the issue of who pays for such amenities influences public willingness to support inmate access to them.

Levenson, L. 2003. "The War on Sex Abuse." ***National Law Journal*** 25 (37): 30–35.

Reviews recent legislation on sex abuse, including federal sentencing restrictions for sex offenders and new sex-offender registration requirements.

Lumer, Michael, and Nancy Tenney. 1995. "The Death Penalty in New York: An Historical Perspective." ***Journal of Law and Policy*** 4.

Reviews the evolution of New York's capital punishment statute, traces the history of the death penalty in New York from 1888, and reviews executions looking at categories of race, gender, age, and location by county.

Madow, Michael. 1995. "Forbidden Spectacle: Executions, the Public and the Press in Nineteenth Century New York." ***Buffalo Law Review*** 43: 461–562.

The author seeks to show how the privatization of capital punishment in the United States was a complex exercise; hanging moved from being a public spectacle to a private rite. The study focuses mainly on developments in nineteenth-century New York.

Maier-Katkin, D., and R. Ogle. 1997. "Policy and Disparity: The Punishment of Infanticide in Britain and America." ***International Journal of Comparative and Applied Criminal Justice*** 21 (2): 305–316.

A study of the crime of infanticide in the United States and England that illuminates the different approaches taken to this crime by the criminal law in these countries. In the United States this crime is given no special status, but in England, it carries a special status under the Infanticide Act that provides an absolute defense to the accused in certain circumstances.

Martinson, Robert. 1974. "What Works? Questions and Answers about Prison Reform." ***The Public Interest*** 35: 22–54.

A notorious article that promoted the notion that "nothing works" in penal policy and that was instrumental in shaping the movement away from rehabilitation and toward just deserts and retribution.

———. 1979. "New Findings, New Views: A Note of Caution Regarding Sentencing Reform." ***Hofstra Law Review*** 7: 242–258.

The author retracts his earlier opinion, but he is too late to change the course of the movement toward retribution as the justification for punishment.

Mauer, Marc. 2003 "Comparative International Rates of Incarceration: An Examination of Causes and Trends." Washington, DC: The Sentencing Project.

The author looks at levels of incarceration worldwide while asking why rates in the United States are so much higher than in most countries.

Meranze, Michael. 2000. "A Criminal Is Beaten: The Politics of Punishment and the History of the Body." In ***Possible Pasts:***

Becoming Colonial in Early America, edited by Robert Blair St. George, 302–323. Ithaca, NY: Cornell University Press.

The author looks at the social history of punishment, asking why punishment developed and changed in the ways that it did.

Meyers, Jack, Kevin Wisniewski, Jonathan Wells, and Maggie Mulvihill. "Special Report: Tracking Sex Offenders; Losing Track; Florida's Sex Offenders Flock to Mass., Then Disappear." ***The Boston Herald.*** 6 November 2003.

Reports about how tracking sex offenders is no easy task especially when they move from state to state.

Millender, Michael. 1998. "The Road to Eastern State: Liberalism, the Public Sphere, and the Origins of the American Penitentiary." ***Yale Journal of Law and the Humanities*** 10: 163–189.

A review of Michael Meranze's book above.

Mohsen, Safia. 1990. "Women and Criminal Justice in Egypt." In ***Law and Islam in the Middle East,*** edited by Daisy Dwyer, 15–34. New York: Bergin and Garvey Publishers.

An account of women and the criminal law in Egypt, showing attitudes toward crimes committed by and against women by agencies within the criminal justice system.

Nelson, Lane. 2001. "The Great Writ—Re: The Condemned." In ***Death Watch: A Death Penalty Anthology,*** edited by L. Nelson and B. Foster, 120–127. Upper Saddle River, NJ: Prentice-Hall.

Discusses the restrictions on appeals in death penalty cases introduced by the Anti-Terrorism and Effective Death Penalty Act of 1996.

Olivero, J. Michael. 1998. "The Crisis in Mexican Prisons: The Impact of the United States." In ***Comparing Prison Systems,*** edited by Robert Weiss and Nigel South, 99–114. Amsterdam: Gordon and Breach Publishers.

An account of the conditions inside Mexican prisons that shows how many offenders are imprisoned because of offenses connected to the United States.

Paton, Diana. 2001. "The Penalties of Freedom: Punishment in Postemancipation Jamaica." In ***Crime and Punishment in Latin America,*** edited by Ricardo Salvatore, Carlos Aguirre, and Gilbert Joseph, 275–307. Durham, NC: Duke University Press.

Examines how the abolition of slavery in Jamaica in 1838 resulted in a changed prison system, because prior to abolition, prisons were used mainly to supplement the disciplinary systems employed on the plantations.

Petersilia, Joan. 1998. "Community Corrections for Drug-Abusing Offenders." In ***Community Corrections: Probation, Parole, and Intermediate Sanctions,*** edited by Joan Petersilia, 111–113. New York: Oxford University Press.

In an introduction, considers how community responses to drug offenders have worked to prevent drug addicts from committing further crimes.

———. 1998a. "The Current State of Probation, Parole, and Intermediate Sanctions." In ***Community Corrections: Probation, Parole, and Intermediate Sanctions,*** edited by Joan Petersilia, 19–20. New York: Oxford University Press.

An introduction to a series of articles on these subjects that notes how little attention is paid to these topics and to community sanctions generally despite the fact that studies do show a measure of success for community correctional programs.

———. 1998b. "Experience with Intermediate Sanctions: Rationale and Program Effectiveness." In ***Community Corrections: Probation, Parole, and Intermediate Sanctions,*** edited by Joan Petersilia, 68–70. New York: Oxford University Press.

An introduction to articles on this topic that describes the purpose of intermediate sanctions and reviews their usefulness as forms of punishment.

Petersilia, Joan, and Elizabeth Piper Deschenes. 1998. "What Punishes? Inmates Rank the Severity of Prison Versus Intermediate Sanctions." In ***Community Corrections: Probation, Parole, and Intermediate Sanctions,*** edited by Joan Petersilia, 149–159. New York: Oxford University Press.

Results of a Minnesota study on perceptions by inmates about the relative severity of imprisonment as compared to intermediate sanctions. Among other findings, inmates ranked five years of intensive probation supervision as harsher than one year in prison but less harsh than three years in prison.

Petrunik, Michael. 2002. "Managing Unacceptable Risk: Sex Offenders, Community Response, and Social Policy in the United States and Canada." ***International Journal of Offender Therapy and Comparative Criminology*** 46 (4): 483–511.

A detailed survey of legislation and punishment of sex offenders in these countries, revealing how the new community protection risk management model applied to these offenders reflects the new penology of retribution. Innovative Canadian approaches involving support circles of volunteers for released sex offenders are also discussed.

Pope, Amy. 2002. "A Feminist Look at the Death Penalty." ***Law and Contemporary Problems*** 65 (1): 257–282.

Considers various aspects of the death penalty through a feminist lens, noting among other aspects how the system of capital punishment has affected women's lives, asking whether it reflects women's voices and why so few women are sentenced to death.

Pratt, John. 2001. "Beyond Gulags Western Style? A Reconsideration of Nils Christie's Crime Control as Industry." ***Theoretical Criminology*** 5 (3): 283–314.

The author argues that the model of the former Soviet gulag, suggested as being representative of the current state of imprisonment in the United States, may not in fact be severe enough to absorb the punitive sentiments now at work in modern society.

Prendergast, Michael, M. Douglas Anglin, and Jean Wellisch. 1998. "Treatment for Drug-Abusing Offenders under Community Supervision." In ***Community Corrections: Probation, Parole, and Intermediate Sanctions,*** edited by Joan Petersilia, 113–124. New York: Oxford University Press.

Discusses the various treatment programs for drug offenders, including community sanctions for drug offenses and results from evaluations of these programs.

Preyer, Kathryn. 1982. "Penal Measures in the American Colonies: An Overview." ***American Journal of Legal History*** 26: 326–353.

Compares the development of penal policies and measures in the American colonies with the problems and solutions employed in England and the continent of Europe. Covers the period from 1607 to 1733 with particular reference to various forms of punishment employed in the then colonies.

Ptateck, Monika. 1998. "Penal Practice and Social Theory in Poland before and after the Events of 1989." In ***Comparing Prison Systems: Toward a Comparative and International Penology,*** edited by Robert Weiss and Nigel South, 263–288. Amsterdam: Gordon and Breach Publishers.

The author traces the development of the penal system in Poland after liberation from the former Soviet Union.

Radelet, Michael, and Marian Borg. 2000. "The Changing Nature of Death Penalty Debates." ***Annual Review of Sociology*** 26: 43–61.

Focusing on the last twenty-five years, the authors examine the changing nature of the death penalty debate in six specific areas including deterrence, incapacitation, and innocence. The authors review recent changes in public opinion and suggest that social-science research is changing the way Americans debate the death penalty.

Ramirez, Chris. "Parole Monitoring Goes Global." ***Albuquerque Journal.*** 29 July 2003.

A report that parole monitoring will now employ satellite-position fixing to keep track of parolees.

Ruggiero, Vincenzo. 1998. "The Country of Cesare Beccaria: The Myth of Rehabilitation in Italy." In ***Comparing Prison Systems: Toward a Comparative and International Penology,*** edited by

Robert Weiss and Nigel South, 207–232. Amsterdam: Gordon and Breach Publishers.

A detailed discussion of the Italian prison system with particular reference to legal provisions that mandate rehabilitation of prisoners but, which the author argues, are negated in actual prison practice, especially for prisoners falling into the category of organized crime.

Ryan, Mick, and Joe Sim. 1998. "Power, Punishment and Prisons in England and Wales 1975–1996." In ***Comparing Prison Systems: Toward a Comparative and International Penology,*** edited by Robert Weiss and Nigel South, 175–205. Amsterdam: Gordon and Breach Publishers.

A review of developments in the prison system in England and Wales, showing how there has been a move toward greater use of this sanction and away from alternative sanctions such as punishment in the community.

Simon, Jonathan. 2000. "Symposium Introduction: Law, Democracy, and Society: Megan's Law: Crime and Democracy in Late Modern America." ***Law and Social Inquiry*** 25: 1111–1150.

Looks at sex offende–registration policy and the legal processes that affect such offenders after their release from prison and raises issues about the purpose and nature of how we punish sex offenders.

Souryal, Sam, Dennis Potts, and Abdullah Alobied. 1994. "The Penalty of Hand Amputation for Theft in Islamic Justice." ***Journal of Criminal Justice*** 22 (3): 249–265.

A detailed explanation of this form of punishment, emphasizing the social and religious context in which it occurs.

Stern, Vivian. 1999. "Alternatives to Prison in Developing Countries." ***Punishment and Society*** 1 (2): 231–241.

Looks at developments in Africa where, in contrast to the situation in many western countries, there has been a move toward using customary and informal sanctions for offenses and a reluctance to expand the use of imprisonment for offenders.

Tak, Peter. 2001. "Sentencing and Punishments in the Netherlands." In ***Sentencing and Sanctions in Western Countries,*** edited by Michael Tonry and Richard Frase, 151–187. Oxford: Oxford University Press.

Reviews sentencing practices in Holland.

Tkachuk, Brian. 2002. ***Criminal Justice Reform: Lessons Learned: Community Involvement and Restorative Justice.*** Heuni Paper No. 17. Helsinki: The European Institute for Crime Prevention and Control, Affiliated with the United Nations.

A review of community involvement and restorative justice in European states.

Tkachuk, Brian, and Roy Walmsley. 2001. "World Prison Population: Facts, Trends and Solutions." Heuni Paper No. 15. Helsinki: The European Institute for Crime Prevention and Control, Affiliated with the United Nations.

A review of worldwide trends in incarceration, showing a general increase in its employment worldwide.

Tonry, Michael. 1999a. "Parochialism in U.S. Sentencing Policy." ***Crime and Delinquency*** 45 (1) 48–65.

The author looks at forms of punishment not found in the United States and suggests that some European models might be effective in the United States, cautioning, however, that the get-tough-on-crime policies of the United States tend to preclude any penalties other than imprisonment from active consideration.

———. 1999b. "Community Penalties in the United States." ***European Journal on Criminal Policy and Research*** 7: 5–22.

The author reviews community sanctions such as probation and intermediate penalties in the United States.

Trevaskes, Susan. 2003. "Public Sentencing Rallies in China: The Symbolizing of Punishment and Justice in a Socialist State." ***Crime, Law and Social Change*** 39: 359–382.

An illuminating discussion of how the Chinese treat serious offenders through a shaming process before they are executed as a lesson to others who might be tempted to offend.

Van Zyl Smit, Dirk. 1998. "Change and Continuity in South African Prisons." In ***Comparing Prison Systems: Toward a Comparative and International Penology,*** edited by Robert Weiss and Nigel South, 401–426. Amsterdam: Gordon and Breach Publishers.

A review of developments in the prison system of this country.

Von Hirsch, Andrew. 1994. "Censure and Proportionality." In ***A Reader on Punishment,*** edited by A. Duff and D. Garland, 112–132. Oxford: Oxford University Press.

The author raises questions about censure as a justification for punishment and argues that the severity of the punishment must be proportionate to the seriousness of the offense.

Von Hirsh, Andrew. 1998. "The Ethics of Community-Based Sanctions." In ***Community Corrections: Probation, Parole, and Intermediate Sanctions,*** edited by Joan Petersilia, 189–198. New York: Oxford University Press.

Discusses ethical issues in community-based sanctions, including the need for these punishments to be proportionate to offenses and for persons to be able to undergo such punishments with dignity.

Walmsley, Roy. 1995. ***Developments in the Prison Systems of Central and Eastern Europe.*** Heuni Paper No. 4. Helsinki: The European Institute for Crime Prevention and Control, Affiliated with the United Nations.

A review of developments in the prison systems in these parts of the world.

———. 2001. "World Prison Population: Facts, Trends and Solutions." In ***World Prison Population: Facts, Trends and Solutions.*** Heuni Paper No. 15, edited by Brian Tkachuk and Roy Walmsley, 14–24. Helsinki: The European Institute for Crime Prevention and Control, Affiliated with the United Nations.

Data on prison populations worldwide is presented and analyzed.

Cases Cited

Brown v. Mississippi 297 U.S 278 (1936)

The court ruled that the Fifth Amendment protected individuals from being forced to confess. An African American was physically tortured with the aim of eliciting a confession from him, and the court ruled that a state cannot secure a conviction through a trial that is a pretense, using perjured testimony and in violation of the right to liberty, life, and due process.

Connecticut Department of Public Safety v. Doe 123 S. Ct. 1160 (2003)

In 1994, Congress legislated to require the registration of sex offenders in all fifty states. In 1996 Megan's Law added a mandatory community notification provision that requires each state government to make private and personal information on such convicted sex offenders available to the public. Pursuant to Megan's Law, many states now post sex-offender registry information on the World Wide Web. In this case an offender argued that the due-process clause of the Fourteenth Amendment prevented Connecticut from listing him in a publicly disseminated sex offender registry without first affording him an individualized hearing on his current dangerousness. The Supreme Court ruled that he was not entitled to a hearing to determine the fact that he was not dangerous, this not being a requirement of the statute.

Furman v. Georgia 408 U.S. 238 (1972)

The Supreme Court held that the death penalty as it had been inflicted up to that time violated the prohibition against cruel and unusual punishment contained in the Eighth Amendment. The Supreme Court cited factors such as racial discrimination, the poor quality of court-appointed lawyers, arbitrariness, and the risk of executing an innocent person as reasons for the violation of the Eight Amendment. New death statutes were passed almost immediately by several states.

Gregg v. Georgia 428 U.S. 153 (1976)

The Supreme Court reinstated the death penaty in 1976 through this decision by recognising new death penalty statutes in Florida, Georgia, and Texas. In effect, it declared that all the issues raised in Furman could now be resolved through the implementation of the new procedures contained in these new state statutes that established "guided discretion" for death sentences.

Kansas v. Hendricks 521 US 346, 117 S. Ct. 2072, 138 L.Ed. 2d 501 (1997)

Kansas' Sexually Violent Predator Act establishes procedures for the civil commitment of persons who, due to a "mental abnormality" or a "personality disorder," are likely to engage in "predatory acts of sexual violence." Kansas filed a petition under the Act to commit Hendricks, who had a long history of sexually molesting children and was scheduled for release from prison. Hendricks challenged the Act's constitutionality on due process grounds, but the Supreme Court ruled that the Act satisfied substantive due process requirements.

In re Kemmler 136 U.S. 436 (1890)

The Supreme Court applied the Eighth Amendment in death penalty cases by comparing challenged methods of execution to inhuman techniques of punishment. In this case, challenging the use of electrocution as cruel and unusual, the Court upheld this form of execution and declared that punishments are cruel when they involve torture or a lingering death.

Louisiana ex rel. Francis v. Resweber 329 U.S. 459, 464 (1947)

The petitioner was convicted in a state court of murder and sentenced to be electrocuted. A warrant for his execution was duly issued. He was prepared for electrocution, placed in the electric chair, and subjected to a shock that was intended to cause his death; but it failed to do so, presumably because of some mechanical difficulty. He was removed from the chair and returned to prison; but another warrant for his execution at a later date was issued. It was determined that the proposed execution would not violate the double jeopardy clause of the Fifth Amendment nor would it violate the cruel and unusual punishment clause of the Eighth Amendment.

Michael Austin et al. v. Fob James Jr. Governor of Alabama and Ron Jones, Commissioner of ADC Case No. 95-T-637-N (1996)

In 1995 Alabama enacted legislation reviving chain gangs and this was challenged as being a violation of the prohibition on cruel and unusual punishment. Without any necessity for a court order, the state entered into a settlement with the Southern Poverty Law Center to cease the punishment.

Powell v. Alabama 287 U.S. 45 (1932)

Nine black youths were arrested and charged with the rape of a white woman in Scottsboro, Alabama. Upon the day of the trial, the attorney appointed to represent Powell refused to represent him; when the judge ordered any attorney present in the courtroom to serve as his counsel, they all refused. Once counsel willing to represent him was found, the attorney had no time to review the case and only a half hour to meet with his client before the hearing. As a result of this inadequate defense, Powell was sentenced to die along with his eight friends. The Supreme Court reversed the verdict asserting that indigents facing the death penalty must be provided with counsel.

Robinson v. California 370 U.S. 660 (1962)

A California law imprisoning those with the "illness" of drug addiction was a cruel and unusual punishment in violation of the Eighth Amendment. The law punished people because of their "status" of addiction and was not aimed at the purchase, sale, or possession of illegal drugs.

Smith v. Doe 123 S. Ct. 1140 (2003)

This case concerned public notification of the particulars of a convicted sex offender by placing information on the web. Was the notification an impermissible punishment because it punishes for past conduct in the guise of preventing future conduct? Assuming that the public notification is constitutional, is the defendant entitled to a hearing at which he may attack the basis for the notification and demonstrate factors that mitigate against punishment? The court found that the purpose of the statute was prospective and preventive, not retrospective and penal. Rejecting the defendant's arguments that being labeled a sex offender would have dire punitive consequences, the court ruled that public notification was not penal, because the state clearly articulated a preventive purpose. Since this was a prospective measure intended to protect the community, any harm it did to the defendant's reputation was outweighed by the potential benefit to the community.

Trop v. Dulles 356 U.S. 86, 101 (1958)

The Supreme Court ruled that depriving an army deserter of citizenship was cruel and unusual punishment. Although not a death penalty case, in this case the Court decided that the interpretation of the Eighth Amendment contained an "evolving standard of decency that marked the progress of a maturing society."

Weems v. United States 217 U.S. 349 (1910)

The Bill of Rights of the Philippines prohibited cruel and unusual punishment. The U.S. Supreme Court held that this safeguard was violated when an officer of the government who had been convicted of making false entries in the public records was subjected to a heavy fine, sentenced to imprisonment for fifteen years, and condemned to carry a chain attached at the ankle and hanging from the wrist.

Wilkerson v. Utah 99 U.S. 130 (1878)

The U.S. Supreme Court ruled that the firing squad was a constitutional method of execution.

Core Periodicals

Corrections Today
American Correctional Association Publications
4380 Forbes Boulevard
Lanham, MD 20706

This is the magazine of the American Correctional Association and provides current information about the correctional scene with a focus on those employed in the correctional system.

Federal Prisons Journal
U.S. Department of Justice, Federal Bureau of Prisons
320 First Street, NW, Room 738
Washington, DC 20534

This journal includes articles on management and policy issues concerned with the federal prison system.

International Journal of Offender Therapy and Comparative Criminology
Sage Publications, Inc.
2455 Teller Road
Thousand Oaks, CA 91320–2218

Covering both treatment issues for prisoners and alternatives to imprisonment, this journal provides a broad forum for research and discussion on offenders and incarceration and it also has a comparative focus.

Journal of Offender Rehabilitation
Haworth Press
10 Alice Street
Binghamton, NY 13904

This journal provides a forum for the publication of research studies and discussion concerned with the rehabilitation of offenders.

National Prison Project Journal
National Prison Project
ACLU Foundation
1875 Connecticut Avenue, NW, #410
Washington, DC 20009

This is published by the American Civil Liberties Union and is a valuable resource for current information on litigation affecting prisoners' rights.

The Prison Journal
Sage Publications, Inc.
Thousand Oaks, CA 91320–2218

This journal presents material on imprisonment in the form of research studies and discussions of penal policy, incarceration, and alternatives to imprisonment. It contains comparative material and is a leading periodical in its field.

Punishment and Society: The International Journal of Penology
Sage Publications, Inc.
Thousand Oaks, CA 91320–2218

The leading journal in the field of punishment, this periodical covers penal institutions as well as penal theory, punishment, and comparative penology.

Nonprint Resources

Videos

Boot Camps in Corrections
Type: VHS format
Date: 1995
Source: American Correctional Association

An informative presentation about boot camps—What are they? Who goes to them? And what are their goals? The methods used are discussed with staff cadets and graduates.

The Capital Punishment Industry
Type: VHS format
Date: 1993
Length: 28 minutes
Source: Films for the Humanities and Sciences Association

A specially adapted Phil Donahue show provides a look at the business of putting people to death—what does it feel like to execute someone and how does it feel to be on death row?

Condemned
Type: VHS format
Date: 1999
Length: 50 minutes
Source: A & E Films

An ex-convict turned warden discusses what really goes on in prison in the United States.

Convicts on the Street: One Year on Parole
Type: VHS format
Date: 1990
Length: 60 minutes
Source: Ambrose Video

Follows a parole officer and his fifty charges. He makes surprise visits to the homes of those he suspects of violating their paroles.

Crimes and Punishments: A History
Type: VHS format
Date: 1993
Length: 30 minutes
Source: Films for the Humanities & Sciences Association

Traces the often-brutal history of criminal punishment from medieval times through to the present. Prison officials discuss the problems of running a large prison and prisoners and staff provide insights into daily prison life.

Cruel and Unusual?
Type: VHS format
Date: 1996
Length: 45 minutes
Source: Films for the Humanities & Sciences Association

This program covers California's three strikes law, and a Memphis judge takes on alternative sentencing that allows burglary victims to commit reverse theft.

The Death Penalty
Type: VHS format
Date: 1987
Length: 26 minutes
Source: Films for the Humanities & Sciences Association

Examines the cases of two men who committed almost identical murders and were tried in the same court only two weeks apart. Discussions with prosecutors, lawyers, jurors, and victims center on whether the death penalty works and how it is applied.

Drugs and Punishment: Are America's Drug Policies Fair?
Type: VHS format
Date: 1996
Length: 51 minutes
Source: Films for the Humanities & Sciences Association

Traces the development of drug use in the country from marijuana in the 1960s to the use of hard drugs in the 1980s and 1990s. Looks at the new Reagan administration drug laws. Former drug czar William Bennett defends mandatory sentencing for drug possession, which many say unfairly penalizes minor offenders and minorities.

The Farm: Life Inside Angola Prison
Type: VHS format
Date: 1998
Length: 100 minutes
Source: American Correctional Association

The story of six inmates at this infamous prison in Louisiana.

History of American Corrections
Type: VHS format
Date: 2001
Length: 30 minutes
Source: American Correctional Association

Follows the development of corrections from ttheir earliest beginnings to the present day, including the ideologies that have shaped prisons.

Life or Death: A Battle over Capital Punishment
Type: VHS format
Date: 2000
Length: 50 minutes
Source: A & E Films

Examines the controversy surrounding the death penalty in the United States.

Parole Board: Montana
Type: VHS format
Date: 1991
Length: 50 minutes
Source: A & E Films

Follows three inmates through the process of facing the parole board.

Prisons
Type: VHS format
Date: 2000
Length: 50 minutes
Source: A & E Films

A comprehensive look at the development of the prison from ancient lockups to Alcatraz and the federal supermax prison of Marion.

Reclaiming Offender Accountability: Intermediate Sanctions
Type: VHS format
Date: 1993
Source: American Correctional Association

A comprehensive look at intermediate sanctions and their application to probation and parole. Examines the application of these sanctions at state, federal, and local levels and makes recommendations for the future.

Solitary Confinement
Type: VHS format
Date: 2000
Length: 50 minutes
Source: A & E Films

A comprehensive examination of what life is like for those who serve their sentences in isolation.

Supermax Prisons: Beyond the Rock
Type: VHS format
Date: 2003
Source: American Correctional Association

Looks at the evolution of the supermax prisons and at their actual operation, including aspects such as planning such prisons, their mission and goals, and use of force.

Women in Prison
Type: VHS format
Date: 1993
Length: 50 minutes
Source: A & E Films

Looks at this subject, revealing the abject failure of the prison system when it comes to female prisoners, many of whom are trapped in a lifelong cycle of pain and suffering.

Internet Sites

Amnesty International USA
http://www.amnestyusa.org/

Drug War Facts
http://www.drugwarfacts.org/

Faces from the Human Rights and Drug War Exhibit
http://www.hr95.org/hr95faces.html

Families against Mandatory Minimums
http://www.famm.org/index2.htm

Justice Policy Institute: The Education vs. Incarceration Clearinghouse
http://www.cjcj.org/jpi/clearinghouse.html

Prison Activist Resource Center: Women
http://www.prisonactivist.org/women/

The Sentencing Project
http://www.sentencingproject.org/

Glossary

assize In the late medieval period in England, the king used the procedure known as an inquisition during which he sought to establish his rights, especially to land. In time the inquisition came to be employed by the king to secure a statement from a group of leading citizens about the taxable wealth of their community or the state of peace and good order, especially in relation to offenses against the king's peace. When the Normans conquered England in 1066, they took this process with them and after awhile the royal form of inquisition came to be called an assize.

Auburn system A system of confinement and discipline within a penitentiary, comprising congregate work during the day and separation at night, accompanied at all times by enforced total silence on the part of inmates.

benefit of clergy During medieval times, the church in England protected its own clergy through doctrines like benefit of clergy, which granted clergy immunity from the ordinary civil courts. This doctrine was not confined to clergy, because the benefit came to be extended to all who could read or recite a verse from the Bible.

blood feuds Early forms of punishment involved acts of private vengeance, and during the pre-700 A.D. period, disputes among tribal societies were usually settled through processes such as blood feuds.

boot camps A term applied to court ordered programs of punishment, usually for minor offenses, where the offender spends time in a camp setting that maintains a military-style disciplinary regime, something like recruit camps for those entering the armed forces.

capital punishment The ultimate punishment of death, also known as a death sentence, carried out by state-sponsored execution, usually by lethal injection.

cat-o'-nine-tails The name is derived from the construction of a whipping instrument that is shaped in the form of nine knotted cords or thongs of rawhide attached to a handle. In its heyday flogging with the cat was executed with great vigor and brutality, and the backs of criminals were cut to ribbons, with salt often being rubbed into the wounds to increase the level of pain.

censure Relates to blameworthiness and holding someone accountable for his or her act as well as giving a message that society does not approve of that wrongful act. Another aspect of censure is how punishment can communicate or express the condemnation or disapproval of society. Some argue that punishment for a crime should communicate or express to offenders the censure they deserve to receive for their crime and should attempt to make those who have offended repent their crimes, reform themselves, and reconcile with those they have injured or wronged in some way. In this way punishment is seen as having a symbolic significance, that is, it is seen to represent society's condemnation of a wrongful act.

chain gangs A form of punishment involving shackling prisoners with ankle chains and then chaining a dozen or more men together, even when in their beds at night, thus severely limiting their freedom of movement. It is largely associated with the southern states.

community service The notion that the punishment for what are regarded as minor offenses could include some work or activity by the offender in his or her community as a means of atoning for the offense.

compurgation In this ancient remedy, an accused person collected together a group of relatives or neighbors known as compurgators. The accused would swear his innocence to the group of compurgators and they would then themselves take an oath attesting to their belief that the accused was telling the truth in making his declaration of innocence. Usually there were twelve compurgators reflecting the religious significance of this number in the Christian gospels. In this procedure it did not matter that the relatives or neighbors knew the accused to be guilty, and the oath-giving really constituted only a formal process not to be equated with the giving of testimony under oath as is found in modern-day trials. The decision as to guilt rested on the conclusiveness of the oaths, and if no decision could be reached, trial by battle or an ordeal compurgation would decide the issue or a demand for compensation would be made. Over time, compurgation was transformed into a form of testimony concerning the good character of an accused. Compurgation was usually reserved for the elite or higher-class members of a society.

conjugal visits Visit by a husband or wife to his or her spouse in prison, during which they are allowed to be alone and enjoy private time together.

convict leasing A practice that developed mainly in the South following the Civil War and continued for about twenty years, involving prisoners being leased out to private companies by the state to perform private labor. The system came about when southern state governments suddenly found themselves responsible for millions of blacks who had previously, in the antebellum period, been divorced from the state and state control. They had been housed on plantations and placed totally under the control of slave owners. The southern planters, faced with no large and free pool of labor because of the end of slavery, needed to secure a substitute, dependent labor force over which they had total control. Many states turned to leasing as a temporary expedient as convict populations increased and no funds existed to refurbish the crumbling penitentiaries.

day fine Established early in the century in Scandinavia. The basic notion is that the court can reflect an offense's severity through a monetary penalty by ordering payment of a larger or smaller number of day fines according to the seriousness of the crime. Also, the fine can be further adjusted to take account of the actual income and assets of an offender. Day fines are most appropriate for minor offenses and can replace short terms of imprisonment, relieving the stress on prison capacity. In the United States, a pilot day-fine project was introduced in New York and the findings were positive with some qualifications, including the lack of an intention to use day fines as a substitute for short prison sentences. This led to the project being extended to four other states; however, in one of them, Arizona, day fines came to be used as a substitute for probation.

day-reporting centers These locations, dating from the mid-1980s, are where an offender spends the day under supervision and surveillance, taking part in treatment programs. Many are run by correctional departments into which are placed those released early from jail or prison for treatment, and others are true sentencing options with programs ranging from forty days to nine months.

deterrence utilitarians People who argue that we punish citizens, because we seek to deter crime and offenses; therefore, punishment is justified because it is thought to have beneficial effects or consequences. Thus, a utilitarian will argue that the right punishment is one that will produce the most beneficial effect on the general welfare of all those affected by the criminal act. Generally, studies have shown that there is no evidence that deterrence actually works to prevent crime occurring.

ducking stool A stool employed for minor crimes, especially for village scolds and gossips. The individual, seated on a stool or chair fixed to the end of a long pole, would be submerged in water while being jeered at by onlookers.

Elmira Reformatory system The notion that a reformatory type of prison discipline ought to be instituted to replace an oppressive system was only realized, and then only in imperfect form, in the Elmira Reformatory system introduced into New York State in 1876. Elmira housed first-time felons between the ages of sixteen and thirty who had received indeterminate sentences.

eugenics movement The early part of the twentieth century saw the birth of the eugenics movement and associated genetic theories of crime. The movement can be seen as part of the battle against immorality and vice. It was linked to fears about the effects of large-scale immigration into the United States seen by some as threatening the values of those already established in the country and polluting the nation with inferior peoples. The proponents of eugenics believed that "defectives" and "degenerates" would engulf "true Americans" and their values, and the only solution was to sterilize them. The rationale was that this would prevent them from breeding and thus overwhelming the nation.

flogging A form of corporal punishment employed to punish a crime or as a disciplinary measure in prison. This punishment consisted of beating or whipping the criminal with a rod, cane, whip, or **cat-o'-nine-tails**.

gaol delivery An event in Massachusetts after independence when a jail was effectively emptied of most of its inmates by the local court, leaving only debtors and political and religious offenders there.

house arrest and electronic monitoring Ordered on its own or as part of a sentence of **probation** or **parole**. In practice, most sentenced to house arrest are permitted to leave their homes for employment and to take part in treatment programs. Sometimes, but not always, house arrest is accompanied by electronic monitoring using bracelets. Originally, programs were used primarily for driving-while-intoxicated cases and for minor property offenders, and programs are now quite large in some states.

incapacitation The idea that punishment can, by confining offenders, make it impossible for them to act in the same way again. Some claim that incapacitating offenders in a selective way will ensure that so-called career criminals will be unable to reoffend, and society will be spared their actions, thus assisting in the prevention of crime.

infanticide The crime of killing an infant.

intensive supervision Known as ISP and used for probationers and parolees. ISP was adopted by most states in the 1980s and 1990s. During this period penal conservatives wanted a way to demonstrate a tough stance on crime, which would also avoid any more prison overcrowding and thus increase prison expenditure while at the same time preserving the policy of punishment in the community. Essentially, ISP provides a higher level of supervision and control of probationers and parolees.

intermediate sanctions Penalties lying somewhere between **parole** and **probation** that emphasize intensive supervision and compliance with conditions and that involve a higher level of supervision and control of probationers and parolees.

iron maiden A form of torture composed of a shallow statue constructed from iron or wood with iron strips and long spikes. When the accused was placed inside and the entrance closed, the spikes would pierce his body.

jurata A group of leading citizens in England who, in the late medieval period, informed the king during an inquisition about the taxable wealth of their community or the state of peace and good order, especially in relation to offenses against the king's peace. Their report to the king was termed a *veredictum*.

just deserts Associated with the notion that punishment is justified as retribution. That is, once a set of legal rules have been agreed upon by a society those rules must be adhered to, and when they are violated, the outcome should be an act of **retribution**. **Retribution** also advocates proportionality; that is, the punishment imposed should be proportionate to the wrongdoing that has taken place. Thus a retributionist would ask how to calculate the just deserts of an offender.

lex talionis The notion that punishment be inflicted using the same method as was employed in the original injury. Thus, under the *lex talionis* punishment demanded "an eye for an eye, a tooth for a tooth."

lockdown A condition associated with various forms of imprisonment during which prisoners are confined to their cells for lengthy periods of time. For example, in **supermax prisons** during lockdown all inmates are confined to their cells for twenty-three hours each day.

lockstep A special method of marching, developed in the **penitentiary,** that required the prisoners to become interlocked in a human chain, which kept them in a strict formation and prevented any communication among them. It was derived from military practice and emphasized the wardens' discipline and control over the convicts.

ordeal An early form of trial and punishment incorporating the notion that the gods would favor the innocent party, and this would be made manifest by undergoing torture or some similar feat and surviving. Modes of ordeal included carrying a piece of hot iron, walking through fire, plunging an arm into boiling water, and running the gauntlet. Ordeals waned following their condemnation by the Lateran Council in 1215, and gradually the emergence of trial by jury appeared in England at the end of the first quarter of the thirteenth century.

Panopticon The title of a book by Jeremy Bentham published in 1787 in England. In his work, Bentham designed a **penitentiary** that he called the *Panopticon,* modeled on a factory his brother had constructed in Russia. The structure was circular and allowed guards at the center to constantly view all the prisoners located in cells around the circumference of the building. Bentham reasoned that constant observation of conduct would instill a habit of obedience, good industry, and conformity.

parole Release from prison, usually by a parole board, and placement under the supervision and control of a parole officer. Parole developed in association with the indeterminate sentence. Parole helped support the indeterminate sentence, because release decisions could be made knowing that an offender would remain under supervision by a parole agent.

peine forte et dure Used in medieval times. A form of torture employed during the final stage of the process of torture where the accused was stretched so thoroughly on the rack that death resulted as the body gave way under the strain.

penitentiary A place of incarceration developed in the United States around 1820. The word was first used in 1779 in the English Penitentiary Act. The term is associated with the **Auburn system** and the **Pennsylvania system** of incarceration.

Pennsylvania system Under this system, those convicted of the most serious crimes were kept in separate cells in solitary confinement, and by 1829 the system became finally established in its entirety, with **solitary confinement** in hard labor.

privatization of the prison system The practice in some states of contracting with private companies to operate and maintain prisons. Privatization has prompted debate concerning the ethics of handing over punishment of offenders to private entities.

probation An alternative to incarceration involving placing the offender under the supervision of a probation officer under a probation order usually containing conditions with which the probationer must comply or be returned to prison.

prosecutorial fine An option for the prosecutor in Germany. In 1970 legislation was passed discouraging the courts from imposing prison sentences of less than six months unless there were exceptional circumstances. Since 1975 German prosecutors have had the option to invite the accused to pay a sum of money to the victim, to the state, or to a charity in exchange for the dismissal of the charge. The accused does not have to enter a guilty plea but must pay a fine equivalent to that which would have been ordered on a conviction.

public sentencing rally A form of public vilification of offenders in China involving the parading and denunciation of large groups of offenders before the public in staged forums.

the rack A form of corporal punishment typically used in the later stages of torture. The offender is strapped to a table and his or her arms and legs are pulled in opposite directions. Sometimes, the torture would go so far as ***peine forte et dure,*** where the body of the accused was stretched so far on the rack that death resulted.

rehabilitation Connotes a concern not only for the offense committed but also for the offender and his or her social and economic background. Those who support rehabilitation as an objective of punishment argue that punishment should fit the offender and that individual circumstances do matter in the task of reforming or rehabilitating an offender so that they will not reoffend. Essentially, rehabilitationists see crime as the symptom of a social disease and the aim of rehabilitation is to produce a cure through a course of treatment.

restorative justice Generally includes a variety of practices at different stages of the court process that take the form of diversion away from court action. They are also actions taken at any stage of the court action, such as meetings between the offender and victim. Generally, the common elements of what is termed restorative justice are an emphasis on the victim in criminal cases, a process that involves all the relevant parties associated with the crime in discussing its effect and what should be done to repair the harm caused by the offense, and decision making by both the court and lay persons.

retribution The notion that punishment is justified because it is deserved. Retributionists argue that society should punish the guilty or that justice demands punishment. This perspective does not pay any attention to the consequences of punishment; it is only concerned with responsibility and accountability. Retribution represents an often intuitive response to criminals, that is, that the guilty deserve to suffer.

scavenger's daughter In this form of torture, the accused's knees were pulled up against the chest and the feet held against the hips by iron bars. This position caused heavy bleeding from the nose and mouth. The ribs and breastbone were often crushed.

the schnure In this form of torture, a rope was tied around the wrists and then drawn back and forth with a sawing motion, gradually cutting through the flesh to the bone.

solitary confinement A correctional, disciplinary method where the prisoner is removed from the general population and is allowed no contact with other people. Although no harm typically comes to the body in this form of punishment, the negative psychological effects of isolation are extensive.

supermax prison A prison holding prisoners in conditions of maximum security, often under **lockdown,** which is said to be necessary for the most dangerous prisoners.

tariff sentencing The wide discretion of parole boards as well as the wide sentencing powers of judges that led to many states passing legislation requiring that sentences be calculated by reference to a set of legal guidelines. A set amount of punishment for each offense is calculated, similar to a tariff, according to the nature of that offense. An example is the Minnesota Sentencing Guidelines.

vengeance An early punishment of offenders where private retribution was sought for wrong doings.

wheelbarrow men Prisoners who, in the late 1780s in Philadelphia, were sentenced to supervised hard labor in public work gangs. They were often harassed and abused by the public; however, sometimes people provided them with alcohol, tobacco, and food. The men fought their guards and conspired to escape.

white-collar crime There is no consensus on exactly how to define the concept of white-collar crime. Many continue to use criminologist Edwin Sutherland's working definition established in 1949 as those offenses "committed by a person of respectability and high social status in the course of his occupation." Generally, white-collar crime includes several categories of crime: elite deviance, occupational deviance, and organizational or corporate offending.

workhouse A forerunner of the prison workhouses or houses of correction began to appear about the middle of the sixteenth century in Europe; they were used to confine vagrants and paupers but not to house convicted felons. The colonial-American model followed this example, combining the functions of the poorhouse with the jail.

Index

About the Author

Cyndi Banks is an associate professor of criminal justice at Northern Arizona University, Flagstaff, Arizona. Her published works include *Developing Cultural Criminology: Theory and Practice in Papua New Guinea,* (2000) ABC-CLIO's *Women in Prison: A Reference Handbook,* (2003) and *Criminal Justice Ethics: Theory and Practice,* (2004). Additionally, she works with juvenile justice and legal rights as the juvenile justice specialist on a legal reform project in Bangladesh.